STORIES OF LIFE IN THE WORKPLACE

Addressing both renowned theories and standard applications, *Stories of Life in the Workplace* explains how stories affect human practices and organizational life. Authors Larry Browning and G. H. Morris explore how we experience, interpret, and personalize narrative stories in our everyday lives, and how these communicative acts impact our social aims and interactions. In pushing the boundaries of how we perceive narrative and organization, the authors include stories that are broadly applicable across all concepts and experiences.

With a perception of narrative and its organizational application, chapters focus on areas such as pedagogy, therapy, project management, strategic planning, public communication, and organizational culture. Readers will learn to:

- differentiate and gain an in-depth understanding of perspectives from varying narrators;
- recognize how stories are constructed and used in organizations, and modify the stories they tell;
- view stories as a means to promote an open exchange of creativity.

By integrating a range of theories and practices, Browning and Morris write for an audience of narrative novices and scholars alike.

With a distinctive approach and original insight, *Stories of Life in the Workplace* shows how individuality, developing culture, and the psychology of the self are constructed with language—and how the acceptance of one's self is accomplished by reaffirming and rearranging one's story.

Larry Browning is a Professor at the College of Communication, University of Texas at Austin and adjunct Professor of Management, Bodø Graduate School of Business at the University of Nordland, Norway. His studies include structures in organizations as evidenced by lists and stories, information-communication technology and narratives, cooperation and competition in organizations, and grounded theory as a research strategy.

G. H. Morris is a Professor at California State University San Marcos. He is a conversation analyst and communication theorist interested in how people align with each other in everyday talk, organizational discourse, and psychotherapy.

Praise for *Stories of Life in the Workplace*

"Browning and Morris have crafted a timely and captivating book that integrates narrative theory with naturalistic organizational studies. Peppered with rich and evocative stories, the authors embrace multiple perspectives for exploring the key features, premises, and functions of workplace narratives. The book makes its mark in situating communication and rhetorical processes as pivotal to the ways we experience and interpret organizational stories."

—**Linda L. Putnam**, Professor and Chair,
Department of Communication, University of California,
Santa Barbara

"In a penetrating and systematic analysis of the uses of narrative, Browning and Morris make clear that not only is a life without stories not worth living, but that scholars can understand the critical components of effective narrative in a way that allows us to appreciate, study, and teach about effective storytelling. This book is an important contribution to our understanding of narrative in organizational life."

—**Sim Sitkin**, Professor of Management, Faculty Director,
Center on Leadership and Ethics, Duke University:
The Fuqua School of Business

"Storytelling replaced corporate culture as the fashionable management tool, and is by many considered the main mode of communication in contemporary societies, as it has been in pre-modern ones. There are a great many books about storytelling but this book is unique, as it offers insights to both critics and apologists of this phenomenon. Management practitioners will learn how to construct such stories well, their subordinates will learn how to evaluate the stories coming to them, and management researchers will be helped to understand which stories work, and why."

—**Barbara Czarniawska**, Professor of Management Studies,
University of Gothenburg, Sweden

"For the past 30 years, organizational scholars have shown that storytelling and narrativity constitute essential features of organizational life. In their wonderful book, Larry Browning and G. H. Morris go one step further by helping us develop a deeper appreciation of the narratives that pervade organizations. Analyzing multiple stories they recorded over the years, they encourage us to adopt an eclectic approach to narrativity, borrowing from the work of key scholars like Algirdas Julien Greimas, Paul Ricœur, and William Labov. It is a must-read for anyone interested in learning how people organize their world by narrating it."

—**François Cooren**, Director, Department of
Communication, University of Montreal, Canada

Routledge Communication Series
Jennings Bryant/Dolf Zillmann, Series Editors

For additional information on these and other Routledge titles, visit www.routledge.com

STORIES OF LIFE IN THE WORKPLACE

An Open Architecture for Organizational Narratology

Larry Browning and G. H. Morris

Routledge
Taylor & Francis Group

NEW YORK AND LONDON

First published 2012
by Routledge
711 Third Avenue, New York, NY 10017

Simultaneously published in the UK
by Routledge
2 Park Square, Milton Park, Abingdon, Oxon OX14 4RN

Routledge is an imprint of the Taylor & Francis Group, an informa business

Library of Congress Cataloging in Publication Data
Browning, Larry D.
Stories of life in the workplace : an open architecture for organizational
narratology / Larry Browning, G.H. Morris.
p. cm.
1. Discourse analysis, Narrative. 2. Storytelling--Social aspects. 3. Narration
(Rhetoric)--Social aspects. I. Morris, G. H. II. Title.
P302.7.B76 2012
401'.41--dc23
2011035935

ISBN13 978-0-8058-5890-7 (hbk)
ISBN13 978-0-415-53999-9 (pbk)
ISBN13 978-0-203-14763-4 (ebk)

Typeset in Bembo
by Taylor & Francis Books

Printed and bound in the United States of America by
Walsworth Publishing Company, Marceline, MO.

CONTENTS

PREFACE

Stories of Life in the Workplace: An Open Architecture for Organizational Narratology

It is irresistible to begin this book on what we call *organizational narratology* with a story: the artist, Robert Irwin, was invited in 1980 to create an art installation in a building that had housed his studio many years before. Believing we take our environment for granted as truth and being quite a trickster, he found a way, by altering just a single element of a scene, to call attention to how we perceive, recognize, and navigate through space. According to his biographer:

> He cleaned out the large rectangular room, adjusted the skylights, painted the walls an even white, and then knocked out the wall facing the street, replacing it with a sheer, semi-transparent white [fabric] scrim. The room seemed to change its aspect with the passing day: people came and sat on the opposite curb, watching, sometimes for hours at a time. The piece was up for two weeks in one of the more derelict beachfront neighborhoods of Los Angeles: no one so much as laid a hand on it.
>
> *(Weschler 1982, cover notes)*

In essence, Irwin caused passersby to do a double take and perhaps be perplexed, when they realized that a solid wall was not really solid at all, but was actually fragile, permeable, transparent, and almost not there. Because the scrim was backlit by the skylights, people who saw it during the day could literally see through the wall at a constantly changing interior. Years later, the same artist designed the equally captivating central garden at the Getty Museum in Los Angeles, California.

When we learn of a story like that, it fills us with something like the curiosity Irwin's audience found and also with wonder. We want to know more about how he did it, and why. What would it have been like to stumble upon this scene, just like the passersby, with no warning it was an art installation? What was he trying to teach his audience? Would it have worked as well elsewhere than Venice, California in 1980? What does his art installation say about him and the arc of his artistic career? Why was it memorable? Was it beautiful? How would a different narrator than biographer Weschler have told it? Was he true to what really happened, and is our version faithful to his?

The book you are about to read encourages you to ask those same questions, and many more, about the stories you see, hear, and tell in organizations. The hoped-for result is that you will obtain a deeper appreciation of the narratives that are every-where around you and that you will be better able to recognize and perhaps modify the stories you tell, especially the stories you tell about your own organizational lives.

Robert Irwin is supposed to have referred to his design for the Getty's central garden as "a sculpture in the form of a garden aspiring to be art." Although our book is no work of art and we are not so notable as Robert Irwin, it might be useful to see our project as similar to his. We are "sculpting" the existing body of work on nar-ratology into a "garden" that offers a number of viewpoints on narrative scholarship, an area to which we aspire to contribute. We refer to the viewpoints as "angles," and we selected them because they afford a good chance for readers to better appreciate narratives. We are marking off a territory, giving it the name "organizational narratology," and calling readers' attention to what is within it. What is there is diverse and remarkable.

We imagine that most people share our love of stories and that people working in many academic disciplines will benefit from a deeper appreciation of what nar-ratologists have said about how stories are constructed and used in organizations. Storytelling is wonderful entertainment, but that is not all; stories can teach moral lessons, but there is much more they can do. With Ricœur, we believe narratives are ways of knowing and achieving personal meaning. Following Polster, we believe humans who know how to locate themselves as characters in a story *and how to rework the story* are at an advantage. We subscribe to Bruner's conception that we experience and know most things through narrative, and that our actual cognitions apprehend possible combinations of worlds. We agree with writers on narrative research methods that stories have the advantage of the focus on experience. When we do research on narratives, we claim we are reflecting some person's life experience. We are drawn to the believability of narrative because we readily cast our own experiences in terms of narrative. We judge a story more favorably and believe it more when it reflects our own experience.

In this book, we argue strenuously for an "open architecture" for organizational narratology. We pass through a number of the different camps in which narratologists place themselves, but we refrain from throwing in our lot with any of them. We think there is plenty of room in this territory for authors to define narratives differently, draw distinctions among narratives, and dispute how they work. Nevertheless, readers will find some strong commitments in our views.

To rehearse just a few of the issues we will touch upon: we advocate a con-ception of narrative broad enough to spark lively exchange and open enough to promote creativity. We insist that stories of all kinds deserve to be listened to. Sometimes the best stories are incomplete, because the incompleteness is the hook that draws the listener in. We view stories as communicative acts, which means that they are told and can be co-told by people in social interaction, for identifiable purposes, in various ways, with various results. We understand stories to be rhetorical because they cannot help being seductive. We think stories are devices people are drawn into and which make up their understandings of reality. For organizational actors' sensemaking purposes, the process of connecting the sequence of events into a plot intersection, including several possible and interacting influences, and capturing the meanings, especially for things that have already happened, is vital. But, because everyone can have stories, it is wrong to claim privilege about stories—that mine counts more than yours.

Also in keeping with the theme of open architecture, not only do we accept a broad spectrum of what counts as a *narrative* in this book, we are equally as open about what counts as *organizational*. In one story, we relate the autobiographical tale of a young woman with a summer job at a day camp who comes to work and without warning is tossed the responsibility for keeping an entire group of grade school age children entertained for an entire day. She not only makes it through the day, she realizes that she has managing talent that she did not know she had. In all the stories in this book, there is a structure lurking in the background or one operating directly in the person's existence. We push out the boundaries of what counts as organizational such that the stories are broadly applicable across experience. Thus, open architecture refers to both what counts as organization and what counts as a narrative.

One of the effects of our appreciation of narratives and our eclectic, open architecture for understanding them is to lament the paucity of stories in the literature in proportion to their worldly importance. We incorporate dozens of stories we encountered during the time we were writing this book and we are constantly in search of more. We hope readers are encouraged to accumulate and revere corresponding stories of their own.

And then there is the story of how this book came into being and all the people who helped. In May, 2009, we took a road trip from San Diego, California to Austin, Texas, and then on to Crestone, Colorado. Larry's plans and drafts of the book were revised as we drove along, through Palm Springs, Globe, Geronimo, Lordsburg, Las Cruces, El Paso, Ft. Stockton, Junction, San Antonio, and many more places on the way to the mountains. Our conversations were digitally recorded, reviewed, and many were transcribed. They became the grist for three summers of work in Colorado and a stint in San Diego, during which the book took its current state. One author told the other, or co-told to each other, on that trip, many of the stories in these pages.

Many people helped us commence and complete this project. We are most indebted to Larry's wife, Victoria, and Bud's wife, Pat, who were so generous in letting us have the time in Colorado and San Diego to think and write. Bud, in particular, has always dreamed of working in a remote writer's cabin, so theirs is a fabulous gift. Both also helped us to get the manuscript in shape. Linda Putnam made important suggestions after reading our proposal and was an encouraging voice for us with the publisher. George Cheney and two anonymous reviewers gave us careful and eye-opening comments on drafts of the manuscript. Ellen Morris alerted us to some pertinent literature on memory we had overlooked, and also transcribed some of the stories for us. Chris Morris helped us deepen our understanding of locale through his descriptions of scenic and architectural design. Thierry Bodes and Judy Shetler contributed to the early-stage development of the book and made significant contributions for what we think about stories. Our students at the University of Texas at Austin and California State University San Marcos contributed stories and lively discussion of them. Two of Larry's graduate assistants, Kate Blackburn and Naddy Sandlin, were helpful in showing how to make the material more accessible to students. Kerk Kee assisted us by gathering and sorting our collection of stories with accuracy and care. Dana LeBarr and John Trimble helped us sharpen and edit the manuscript.

We wish to thank Linda Bathgate, our editor at Taylor and Francis, and her editorial assistant, Katherine Ghezzi, for keeping us on track in the process of production.

Larry's Norwegian braintrust, including Jan Sornes, Frank Lindburg, and their graduate students, helped us by reminding us there was other work to be done and helped set our sights on subsequent projects.

Others who are anonymous helped us without even knowing it. We encountered interesting people all across the western United States whose names and stories we wish we knew. For instance, between Johnson City and Ozona, Texas we shared the highway with a woman whose entire apartment-worth of belongings, including her dog, was stuffed inside her convertible Mustang. She embodied the American dream of escape to the West. What was her story? We encountered a group of Missourians who appeared to step out of the nineteenth century with a horse and mule train, out hunting for elk antlers in the Sangre de Cristo Mountains. We ate alongside and were silently welcomed by a Mexican-American family in Globe, Arizona, an otherwise forlorn-looking old mining town.

1

NARRATIVE APPRECIATION

So natural is the impulse to narrate, so inevitable is the form of narrative for any report of the way things really happened, that narrativity could appear problematic only in a culture in which it was absent.

—Hayden White

This book encourages appreciation of stories in and about workplaces. It is a guide for more fully grasping the power of stories to enrich organization members' lives, affect activities, and enable better sensemaking. It will teach readers how better to evaluate the stories they hear and how to construct such stories themselves. We draw attention to everything from fully developed, dramatic narratives, such as biographies of famous leaders or histories of organizations, to smaller-scale stories told around the coffee pot common in daily work interaction, and much in between.

In line with Hayden White's (1987, p. 1) statement above, we argue that coming to know organizations and what goes on in them without focusing on narratives would be unproductive. Further, efforts to treat narratives in organizations as trivial or peripheral would be misguided. Stories abound in workplaces, and our lives would be strange and bland without them. As we tune into the stories people tell, read about workplaces and the lives that go on in and around them, take stories from the media with us to work and tell co-workers about our experiences, we equip ourselves to understand what is going on and, sometimes, to make better responses to the circumstances we face at work and in our lives beyond. Although few people, such as comedians, make their living entirely with stories well told, others, such as ministers, salespersons, and teachers, tell stories as a regular feature of their workdays. We all listen to and tell stories. Sales presentations, briefings, reports, recruitment interviews, press releases, consultations, carpools, team meetings, hallway conversations, lunch breaks, and retirement ceremonies are all common sites for workplace storytelling.

Narrative Appreciation

Readers might have heard of music appreciation, but never thought about narrative appreciation. In the former, people learn to apply music theory about such concepts as melody, rhythm, chord progressions, and harmony, plus knowledge of musical genres and styles, to performances in which they participate through listening or performing. Some people who learn to better appreciate music do so for professional reasons; others, to deepen their enjoyment. Narrative appreciation is analogous to music appreciation in that it brings theoretical concepts from narratology to bear on how people experience and assess stories. Readers will be introduced to quite a large number of such concepts in this book, such as action, sequence, irony, plot, and complication. If readers are able to understand and use such concepts, we hope they will benefit both professionally and personally. They will be equipped to understand more about workplaces and the lives of their occupants, to get a better grasp of challenges and opportunities at work, to connect with fellow employees or others in the same profession, to exercise leadership, or to interact more effectively with customers. It is also possible simply to appreciate workplace narratives because they are everywhere around us, highly varied and sometimes even beautiful.

The Ubiquity of Workplace Narratives

Our examination of workplace stories began with a collection of stories published in articles in academic journals, management books, case studies, and similar literature. Of the 150 stories we acquired from such sources,[1] nearly all are worthwhile and credible items to examine and many are instructive, but few have the fully worked-up, dramatic character of Joseph Campbell's (2008) heroic tales. Few are so well-told that they transport the reader or listener to the scene of action. Our experience with the stories in our original story collection seems to mirror Gabriel's (2004), whose interview-based collection of stories from organizations also had few fully developed narratives. However, rather than lamenting the infrequency of such "stories with a capital S," our attention has been drawn toward the "small s" stories that pervade work in sports, business, politics, warfare, health care, education, and various kinds of at-home work. As we started to be less restrictive about what counts as an organizational narrative, we were treated to a fascinating array of stories and we were led to explore more and more narratological concepts in order to make sense of them. The approach we take to narrative appreciation in this book is aimed at giving readers a similar experience.

Conversational Narratives

Many workplace stories start out as anecdotes shared in conversations with coworkers. Individuals tell about experiences they have had, events they have observed, and media stories that captured their attention. Often, the stories told by one person spark a related story from another, resulting in what Boje (1991) calls "story rounds."

For instance, the authors began their workday recently when one related Gabriel's (2004) ambiguous story about the lorry driver who may have killed two cats accidentally. The story goes that an unfortunate woman watched a driver kill her pet cat as it was sleeping by the side of the road. After she complained to police, they caught the driver and asked him what had happened. He explained that he had hit the cat with his van, and since it would have been cruel to leave the wounded cat in misery, he finished it off by bashing it over the head. But was it a case of mistaken identity? When police examined his lorry, they found another dead cat beneath the wheel well.

Relating Gabriel's story touched off another about a kid in Oklahoma accidentally hitting a dog during his first trial of driving a tractor on public roads and being unjustly accused of doing so on purpose. The elements of pets being run over by vehicles and attributing the responsibility of death to a person made these stories a pair. Such a chaining of stories in a series of topics is common (Bormann, 1972).

Stories in Songs and the Media

Another way in which meaning is chained out is when melody and rhythm are tied to story. Our mentioning songs in connection with workplace stories may seem a bit unusual, but it is completely in keeping with narrative appreciation. Authors have noted the importance of song at work, such as the use of rock music by soldiers during the Vietnam War (Grossberg, 1988) and, more recently, the Iraq War, where American troops used heavy metal and rap music in their Humvees, in part to amp up their aggressiveness as they entered battle (Pieslak, 2009). The contemporary workplace is far more music-filled than ever. People at work are now listening through earphones to songs and podcasts.

Much of the content of workplace talk is the importation of mass media stories into personal conversations. For example, as we were working on this book in the spring of 2009, a sassy, midde-aged auditioner on *Britain's Got Talent*, Susan Boyle, knocked the whole world's socks off with her performance of "I Dream a Dream" from *Les Miserables*. Judges and the show's live audience changed instantly from smug disbelief to wholehearted approval as she began to sing. When she walked on stage, appearing almost preposterously frumpy and, oddly, both self-confident and diffident, the judges were seen rolling their eyes. But once she struck her first notes, the entire audience, judges included, openly marveled at the power of her singing and her sensitive delivery. She did an amazing job by any standard. Many of the 26 million viewings of Susan Boyle on YouTube as of that time, especially for the first two weeks after her audition, were shared by people at work. She became a story as people analyzed her popularity, marveled at her ability, sought out details on her authenticity, noticed her costume makeover the next week, and guessed that she was likely to continue to win. Part of the power of her story, of course, was its liminality, the uncertainty of what would come next (Turner, 1987). Polster refers to this as directionality in stories (1987). People at parties and over the cafeteria table made guesses as to why she had become a cultural icon. Maybe, they concluded, it's because we like to see a person move from singing in the shower to singing on the grand stage, someone who rises above it all, who surprises us, who teaches us a moral and cultural lesson: don't judge a book by its cover.

The picture of a New York street scene from the June 2009 cover of *The New Yorker* was composed entirely on the artist's iPhone. He commented in that same issue that drawing in this way allowed him to turn an observed scene into a story immediately and portably. *The New Yorker*'s website even contains a video (Colombo, 2009) of the cover being drawn on the iPhone application. This suggests that producers of such media are conscious of capturing and sustaining people's attention with the kinds of stories they tell, the tools they draw upon, and the process used to tell the story.

Rather than seeing organizations as story-free zones, a better characterization is that they are about as full of stories in routine conversation as they ever were, and *on top of that* there has been a tremendous increase in the availability of stories in song and other media. We view organizations as story-rich zones. Events occurring outside organizations, such as in the home, the community, or society at large, are fodder for workplace conversations in which stories are exchanged. People on the way to work, at work, and on the way home are taking with them smartphones, tablet computers, and digital music players to look at and listen to all kinds of content that includes stories. They are checking blogs, checking news-aggregating sites, looking at newspaper sites and cable news sites, talking to each other, and listening to music and podcasts. They are going on YouTube and seeing videos of everything from *The Daily Show* to Ali G pretending to interview Andy Rooney, to someone being interviewed on *Inside the Actor's Studio*, to narrations of John Prine about the origins of his song "Chain of Sorrow," to a podcast of a culture innovator giving a 20-minute lecture at TED or a radio broadcast of *This American Life*. All of these sources and sites and thousands more are purveyors of stories that individuals share with each other in the workplace.

Because there are so many independent producers of content, professional media products are not the only ones that get people's attention. Instead, people can put songs up on their websites. It is easy to put a podcast up on iTunes. There is great availability of independently produced material, and many people shun corporate media content in favor of listening to "indy" media. Younger and middle-aged people now seldom go anywhere without their phones and earphones, and it is hard to keep them from listening, even when we would prefer their attention was concentrated elsewhere.

Both when face-to-face and when communicating via media, stories are often about what people have heard lately. We can't throw a party for people from work anymore in which several don't get out their smartphones to show what they heard, or saw, or were able to do in the last week. People really love doing this. Sharing of song lists would be a perfect example. The ability to show things on computer screens is driving technology design so that people can comfortably display for others what is on their computer screen. Not long ago, to share stories via media, we would gather around computer screens as though they were one-sided campfires. We didn't anticipate that the laptop and the tablet computer, without the tether of a power cord, would so easily facilitate moving the computer from lap to lap. The smartphone allows people to show each other things from YouTube or Hulu or other video sites, and people are frequently playing tunes for each other. We defy anyone to say media are not entering workplaces. This is not just "banana time" (Roy, 1959). This is fully integrated with how people work today.

In sum, there is just more now to appreciate, since the artistry exhibited in these mass media and independent productions means the sheer volume of workplace narratives is greater than ever before. Our access to wonderful stories, and, of course, our exposure to stories that meet few people's critical standards, has never been greater.

Criteria for Narrative Appreciation

With the greater availability of stories comes a greater opportunity for narrative appreciation. In our view, people who have learned to recognize and prize stories are more likely than others to engage in the following:

1. They notice the stories around them and attend not just to the content, but to the telling itself. Style and culture are evidenced in stories; you have no story without them.
2. They actively search for compelling stories as they listen to conversations, read, and view media. In Weick's (1995) terms they are continually sensemaking their environments. They interpret the world through stories, and each story begins with a sequence. What to make of this event? How did this start? What are its causes?
3. They cultivate a memory for stories, much like wannabe comedians remember jokes they hear. A sage uses narratives to interpret a culture and cannot offer an interpretation without them.
4. They check out the stories for verisimilitude, rather than necessarily taking them at face value. We not only listen to stories; we assess them for their ability to represent some version of reality accurately.
5. They become more sensitive to nuances of stories. For example, given the character of the actors, they might attend to whether and how characters are changing and why. They make more fully formed and complex interpretations by including as many forces that contribute to the plot as they can imagine.
6. They relay stories they have run across to others who like stories. Stories spread virally as people pass them on from one storyteller to another. Stories are like peanuts: having one invites another.
7. They are more willing to narrativize their own lives and see them as grand, developing stories (Polster, 1987). They are willing to tell or write stories of their own rather than missing out on storytelling opportunities.

8. They utilize stories as a vehicle in their communication with others. The practical knowledge of stories, how they can be used in the workplace, has a robust history. One can sell a product with a story, promote an image with a story, tell a story to make life interesting, and learn through a story.
9. Through practice, they get better at telling stories, listening receptively to others' stories and, consequently, at communicating. They become willing participants in story rounds.

Six Stories

In the following, we provide six abbreviated examples of workplace stories to illustrate the wide range of story types and content we will be considering throughout this book. The first two of them were conversational narratives exchanged between the authors. The third and fourth were told in oral history interviews and are part of the American Folk Life Collection in the Smithsonian. The fifth is a story song, by American folk singer/songwriter Woody Guthrie, about an important battle in American labor history that occurred in 1914. The sixth and final is a selection from the memoir *The Liars' Club* by Mary Karr. We make no particular claims about these narratives except that they all pertain to people working, encountering organizations, and telling about their experiences, and they are typical of the stories we examined as we were writing this book.

1. Told by one author of this book to another on a road trip:
   Have you ever seen the TV show The Office? *One of my favorite episodes is when Ryan, who's taking business courses, asks Michael, his delusional manager, to speak to one of those classes as a visiting expert. And of course Michael agrees, sure that he's just the expert that's needed but not knowing that students who persuade their bosses to speak are given extra credit. So Michael comes to class and, fancying himself like the inspirational teacher in* Dead Poets Society, *he insists that the students tear out the Table of Contents of their expensive business textbook. He's thinking he'll teach them that life experience always trumps book learning. What makes the scene particularly hilarious is that it relies on our having seen the movie and knowing that the* Dead Poets *teacher, played by Robin Williams, wasn't trying to make that point at all. He was simply trying to teach his students to resist wholesale categories and to think independently, which is why he insists that they shred the Table of Contents of their literature textbook. Anyway, at the end, Michael walks away complacently saying, "They're inspired now," when, in fact, the students have simply been left dumbfounded.*
2. From a conversation between two of the authors on a road trip:
   Larry: *I once told [consultant and former University of Texas Communication professor] Ron Bassett a story of one of the most horrifying experiences I ever had. As an eighth grader, I was taller than the other kids and I was sure I'd make the school basketball team. When it came time to reveal who had actually made it, the coach stood in the middle of all ten of us would-be's holding just nine jerseys—eight beautiful black-satin ones, plus one*

dingy orange one. If you were among the chosen, he'd toss you a jersey and you'd know you had made the team. So I'm wondering which of the black jerseys is mine. Well, he tosses out the first one, then the second, then the third. I'm still waiting for mine. But now, instead of wondering when I'm getting my fancy jersey, I'm down to wondering, "Am I going to get a black one? Jeez, I hope I don't get that old dingy orange one. That one's obviously for the weakest of the weak."

Bud: And then someone wouldn't get anything at all?

Larry: Right. There were ten of us and just nine jerseys. Well—and I'm remembering it like it was yesterday—it got down to just two black jerseys and one orange one. So then my hope changes to, "Omigod, I hope I at least get the orange jersey." And, wouldn't you know, he tosses that final dingy jersey to somebody else. So, a team that I thought I was going to be a star on, the coach says, "No, not really, Larry. You're not on the team." But at least I had the satisfaction later that same school year of making a speech that got me to the state championships.

Ron, an old friend, hears all this and says, much to my surprise, "Larry, you're like that. If someone closes you off from one avenue, you will go find another one."

I had never made the connection. Never. And he saw it instantly. After that, I knew it was true. In that sense he made a therapeutic intervention, saying, "Look what you did!" And both things—the failure and the achievement—have always meant a lot more to me. I had moved from pain to learning. I had been in horrifying pain. I found myself asking, "How did I let that happen to me? How could I be so foolish to be so out of it?" I was probably sort of impossible then, and I think the coach was, in fact, trying to teach me a lesson. I was acting like I knew I had the team made, and I wasn't trying. Hell, I was already six feet tall, and everyone else was way shorter, and they were putting more effort into it in some ways than I was. I thought, "Shit, I'm big. Why do anything?" Coach was probably right, for all I know.

3. From StoryCorps Oral History Project, The Chaplain's Story (Isay, 2007, pp. 98–99):

In the basement of the hospital, in a windowless room, they pack the surgical instruments before surgery. Each surgery has a list of all of the instruments they need, and at the top of the list is the patient's name. The technician is given this list and it is up to her or to him to pack these instruments and take them up to the OR for a particular surgery. One of the women told me that as she packed these instruments and she knew the patient's name, she would pray for that patient, and that she had been doing that for 40 years. And I thought, "No one knows that she is doing this, but here she is, a person who has been working at that hospital for longer than most of us, who is doing this incredibly important job that has to be done precisely and carefully, and as she's doing this, she's praying for the patients she will never meet and the patients she'll never see, she'll never know the outcome but she knows that she's helping to make their surgery possible." Then, I found out that most of them [the other instrument packers] did it.

You know, people work really hard and are so essential, but often not seen by patients and families. They just assume these people are doing their work, and they don't realize how rich their lives are and how rich their stories are.

4. From the StoryCorps Oral History Project (Isay, 2007, pp. 89–90):

We had this man, Old Man Pete, who lived across the street. He had a defect in his spine and never could stand up straight. He was always bent over as if he was picking up a quarter off the sidewalk. He always did odd jobs … There was a truck that would deliver coal. It would back up into the driveway, and we had a window that went to the cellar. It would take me two or three days to shovel five tons of coal into the cellar. One day I asked Old Man Pete would he want to shovel in five tons of coal? He said, "Sure, I'll do it." So the next load that came—it was wintertime—I went across the street to where he lived, and I said, "How much would you want?" He said, "A dollar a ton." He made five dollars.

About thirty minutes later the doorbell rings, and Old Man Pete's at the door. I said, "You all done?" He said, "Oh, yeah, I'm done. You got the five dollars?" I gave him the five dollars, and I said, "How did you get that coal in there so quickly?" He said, "I'll tell you how it's done. You take the shovel, you fill it up with coal in one big scoop, and then you put it in the window. Keep doing it in a motion that's constant and don't look up to see what you have left. The trick is to not look up to how much more you have to do but just to keep doing it. If your body goes into a motion of shoveling and tossing it, shoveling and tossing it in, all of a sudden you have no more to shovel." That's when I learned when you have a job to do, don't keep looking up to see how much left there is to do. If you keep working at your job, it'll be done. That's one piece of advice that I've lived by.

5. Lyrics from "Ludlow Massacre" by Woody Guthrie. Used by permission:[2]

It was early springtime and the strike was on,
They moved us miners out of doors,
Out from the houses that the company owned,
We moved into tents at old Ludlow.

I was worried bad about my children,
Soldiers guarding the railroad bridge,
Every once in a while a bullet would fly,
Kick up gravel under my feet.

We were so afraid they would kill our children,
We dug us a cave that was seven foot deep,
Carried our young ones and pregnant women,
Down inside the cave to sleep.

That very night you soldiers waited,
Until us miners were asleep,
You snuck around our little tent town,
Soaked our tents with your kerosene.

You struck a match and the blaze it started,
You pulled the triggers of your gatling guns,
I made a run for the children but the firewall stopped me,
Thirteen children died from your guns.

I carried my blanket to a wire fence corner,
Watched the fire till the blaze died down,
I helped some people drag their belongings,
While your bullets killed us all around.

I will never forget the looks on the faces,
Of the men and women that awful day,
When we stood around to preach their funerals,
And lay the corpses of the dead away.

We told the Colorado Governor to call the President,
Tell him to call off his National Guard,
But the National Guard belong to the governor,
So he didn't try so very hard.

Our women from Trinidad they hauled some potatoes,
Up to Walsenburg in a little cart,
They sold their potatoes and brought some guns back,
And they put a gun in every hand.

The state soldiers jumped us in a wire fence corners,
They did not know that we had these guns,
And the Red Neck Miners mowed down them troopers,
You should have seen those poor boys run.

We took some cement and walled that cave up,
Where you killed those thirteen children inside,
I said, "God bless the Mine Workers' Union,"
And then I hung my head and cried.

6. From the memoir *The Liars' Club*, by Mary Karr (1995, pp. 57–58):[3]

The men of the Liar's Club arrived with their pickups and toolboxes to turn our garage into an extra bedroom for my parents who had been sleeping on a pull-out sofa in the living room during Grandma's visit. I guess they wanted to make her a nicer place in which to die. That didn't register in me at the time. I had nearly blocked all glimmer of her very existence—alive or dead, sick or well—from my waking thoughts. Each morning, about the time Lecia and I reached the bottom of our soggy Cheerios, somebody's work boots would stamp up the porch steps, and the screen would bang open, and Daddy would start getting down clean coffeemugs.

The men arrived early and worked steadily through the hotter part of every day. They had all taken their vacations then in order to help out. They worked for nothing but free coffee and beer. By mid-morning they had stripped off their shirts. They had broad backs and ropy arms. They suffered the fiercest sunburns that summer I ever remember seeing. Ben Bederman had a round hairless beer belly that pooched over his carpenter apron, and his back burned and peeled off in sheets, then burned again until it finally darkened to the *color of cane syrup. The men pulled Lone Star beers all afternoon from the ice in two red Coleman coolers that Daddy packed to the brim every morning.*

A few times a day, somebody's wife would show up with food. Say what you like about the misery of hard labor—I once had a summer job painting college dorms that I thought would kill me—but it can jack up the appetite to the point where eating takes on a kind of holiness. Whether there were white bags of barbecued crabs from Sabine Pass or tamales in corn husks from a roadside stand, the men would set down their tools and grin at the sheer good fortune of it. They always took time to admire the food before they started to eat—a form of modesty, I guess, or appreciation, as if wanting to be sure the meal wouldn't vanish like some mirage. Daddy would stop to soak his red bandana in a cooler's slush and study whatever was steaming out of the torn-open sack while he mopped himself off. "Lord God, look at that," he'd say, and he'd wink at whoever had brought it.

Ben's wife, Ruby, pulled in once with a washtub of sandy unshucked oysters that … took two of the men to heave out of the truck bed. She spent the better part of a morning opening them with a stubby knife. When she was done, there were two huge pickle jars of cleaned oysters sitting in the washtub's cold water. We ate them with hot sauce and black pepper and lemon. (Lecia says I would eat them only in pairs, so none would feel lonely in my stomach.) The oysters had a way of seeming to wince when you squeezed the lemon on them. They started off cold in your mouth, but warmed right up and went down fast and left you that musty aftertaste of the sea. You washed that back with a sip of cold beer you'd salted a little. (Even at seven I had a taste for liquor.) And you followed that with a soda cracker.

Before that summer, I had many times heard long-winded Baptist preachers take ten minutes to pray over card tables of potato salad and fried chicken at church picnics, but the way those sweating, red-faced men sat around on stacked pallets of lumber gulping oysters taught me most of what I know about simple gladness. They were glad to get fed for their labor, glad they had the force to pound nails and draw breath. Of course, they bitched loudly about their aches and mocked each other's bitching. But unless I've completely idealized that fellowship, there was something redeeming that moved between these men. Even the roofing part of the job, which involved a vat of boiling tar and whole days on top of the new garage beyond the shade of our chinaberry, didn't wipe it out. At evening, they would pull off their work boots, then peel off their double layers of cotton socks and lay them to dry across the warm bricks. Daddy had a habit of tipping the beer coolers out right where they stood in the grass, so cool water rushed over their sweaty feet. At that time of day, with night coming in fast, and the men taking a minute to pass a pint of Tennessee whiskey between them or to light their smokes, there was a glamor between them that I sensed somehow was about to disappear. When they climbed into the cabs of their trucks, I sometimes had a terrible urge to rush after them and call them back.

Six Angles for Narrative Appreciation

The six clusters of ideas that we introduce here and explain fully in subsequent chapters represent interpretative viewpoints for understanding and appreciating narratives. We refer to them as "angles" instead of story components or elements because we want to make it clear that they are interpreters' resources, not intrinsic features of the narratives. We arrived at them first by categorizing narratives from the workplace using such categories as action, character, motivation, and complexity. We discovered that we could make capable interpretations of the collected narratives using such categories, but that our interpretations were deeper when we utilized several of the categories. In fact, our failure to use multiple categories left us with interpretations that were hardly more than restatements of the narratives themselves. For instance, although it is possible to talk about action, motivation, and moral outcome but not talk about the character/actor who is doing the action, it doesn't make for as illuminating an interpretation as when both angles, and others as well, are all drawn upon to interpret a story.

The six angles seem to accommodate most of what narrative scholars have written over the years and, at the same time, seem to find ready application to workplace narratives. Each particular angle overlaps with, and is supported by, the others. Each will be addressed in a separate chapter below.

Action, motivation, and moral outcome. These three concepts encompass what is done in a narrative, why it is done, and its assessment as right or wrong. They cluster together because they all are involved whenever questions of responsibility and accountability arise, and these are key topics for understanding organizations (Douglas & Wildavsky, 1983). To put it most bluntly, there is no story without action; there is no action without motivation; and there is no motivation without moral assessment—or in Stanley Fish's (2010) words, learning. We find motivations especially interesting when there are mixed motivations—when there are multiple reasons for actions, and when moral assessments are difficult to calculate. The moral of the story is the result of action—the difference between an assessment at time one, when the story starts, and time two, when the story ends (Czarniawska, 1998).

Sequence and locale. Stories have spatio-temporal dimensions that are inseparable (Hawes, 1973, 1974). Stories make more sense and are more interesting when the action is located in a specific time and place. The place may be on an island, it may be in the center of a city, it may be in outer space, but the context of the place helps the listener calibrate and make sense of what is going on in the story. Sequence refers to the temporal unfolding of events over time. In a story it's important to know what preceded the current circumstance so as to know what put the actors in the present position. Sequence is especially important as the events of the story develop across time in a way that leads to their coming together in a moment of truth. All the past makes sense in relation to the climax of the story.

Character and identity. Character and identity are paired because they work together to make up an assessment of who a person is in the story and how you know who they are. "Characterization is the presentation of the nature of the people in a story" (Bal, 1997, p. 59). Character tends to be an external evaluation, an assessment of the person from the outside by a community, or by someone in a hierarchy whose assessment matters. In the person's favor is identity construction, his or her way of saying, "This is who I am." Actors tend to draw on nationalities, organizational identities, gender, size, looks, age, and anything else that constructs an identity that will leave the impression they want on the observer. Note that identities are not automatically directed toward putting one's best foot forward. Some may want to leave the impression they are "the bad boy" or the "screw-off" because they want attention, or because such an impression gives them latitude in behavior, or because it causes onlookers to be amazed that anything good came of them.

Interest and memory. Stories are more interesting than mere facts because cognitive processes that draw causal relations among important elements of the story give the listener work to do. The result of the interpretations the listener makes causes the story to be interesting and memorable. Some stories are fascinating since they produce such intense interest as to be spellbinding for the listener (Green & Brock, 2000). Memory also comes into play when the storyteller draws on her or his memory to select what to put into the story. This selection of materials is no innocent act. Telling one story, utilizing one set of facts, not only tells that story but also masks other interpretations of what went on (Lyotard, 1984; Fisher, 1987).

Aesthetics. Aesthetics has to do with the beauty of a story. We can understand aesthetics by looking at its polar opposite, anesthetics, which is a medical term for shutting down the senses. Aesthetics is a sensory response to stories, epitomized by ones that make the hair stand up on the back of our neck. Aesthetics is difficult to classify because it comes in many forms, some elegant, others natural, or coarse. Style is connected with aesthetics because it is a kind of personal expression of beauty, represented by how a person presents her- or himself through actions and decisions (Brummett, 2008).

Complexity and control. Complexity and control operate together because complexity refers to conditions that cannot be predicted, that are beyond control. Something, or maybe a host of things, is in play that cannot be corralled and managed in a predictable way. The axiom that "truth is the first casualty of war" is applicable. Once the fighting starts, things fall apart in a hurry, not only because interpretation becomes confusing; also, coalitions frame and interpret happenings and evidence for their own purposes. In narratives, against the likelihood of things falling apart, or not going as predicted, is the desire to control—to affect outcomes, to hold things together. In Bakhtin's famous terminology, these are called the centripetal and centrifugal forces—the things that hold the structure (relationship, family, organization, culture) together, and the things that tear it apart (Bakhtin, 1981). The integration of complexity is achieved by drawing inferential conclusions from ambiguous data by "connecting the dots."

Applications for Narrative Understanding

The knowledge of the six angles we will be explaining might be utilized whenever anyone seeks to present or interpret a story. But knowledge of the angles can be applied more particularly to successfully negotiate various kinds of recurrent organizational activities. We refer to these more particular contexts of narrative use as "applications." All are forms of communicative action that can be pursued narratively and which are relatively common forms of organizational activity. We conceive of an application as a verb such as to transport, celebrate, or elevate that can be enacted and elaborated with major points that could be practiced, as in an exercise on the topic in a classroom, or from observation in the world of work. By transferring concept to application, we intend to show what people can do with stories when the topics of these chapters are invoked or made use of for a particular purpose in a particular setting. We caution, however, that the six applications we develop in this book are by no means the only applications. Our fondest hope is that readers will be able to use what they find here and make novel applications. We will have more to say about this in the next chapter, in which we unveil what we call an "open architecture" for organizational narratology that promotes broad and creative uses of the narrative concepts we develop.

We draw attention to six applications. Below, each is explained briefly.

Explanation. The essential activity goes from a partial understanding of a set of events toward a fuller interpretation that reveals more precisely what happened and why. The organizational actor seeks and finds evidence that a particular sequence of actions captures what happened and that a particular set of causal relationships, whether physical or motivational or metaphysical, plausibly explains why it happened. Explanation requires selection from alternative ways of describing events and alternative motives for them.

Explaining a scientific finding by relating a story is an example of the use of explanation. In the history of organizational studies, one can see the importance of and possibility for explanation by starting with particular studies, such as the Stanley Milgram authority experiments (1963) that caused experimental subjects to think they were giving electric shocks to strangers. The finding represents the story's punch line: people were willing to punish and injure others merely because they were ordered to do so. Over the years since the study was conducted, its ethics, both for Milgram and for what his results show about the morality of his findings, have been a controversial topic. Stories about the experiments, such as what it was like to participate in them, can give a deeper understanding of the meaning of the events to the actors and, therefore, a more nuanced view of why they acted as they did. To bring these experimental findings to life, nothing explains it quite like a story (Polkinghorne, 1988). In short, many experimental findings tell a simplified version of a larger concept. The sensemaker can build on the main nugget of the story to communicate a stronger grasp of the concept.

Imagination. Imagination is central to the creation of an image in a narrative; it is about being able to see other times and places through indirect experience. Imagination is placing a set of circumstances and people in a different space and time continuum via a story and hypothesizing about them to construct an idea of what might have been, or what will be. The concept is about liberating the mind to fantasize about something that is not presently real, but is capable of generating an emotional involvement from playing out the implications of those circumstances (Snowden, 2003).

The imagination application is about mining stories about other times, other people, and other situations for their personal significance. This has to do with re-applying narrative from something about someone else to something that pertains to one's own life and circumstances; thus imagination both reaches out and draws in. Applying their knowledge of narratives, though, means that people are able to imagine how their own situation would be different if the events narrated in a story happened to them (Browning & Boudes, 2005). Imagination involves telling a story that appears to end at one time and place but that, more interestingly, and in fact, ends at another time and place. Such stories take a grand perspective or vista about a circumstance. They stretch time across an extended period (weeks, years, decades) to tie what happened at one moment to a distant past or future. The essence here is to apply the transformational power of stories we encounter to improve our own lives and careers. The essential movement is from personal stasis or decline to change based on a renewed understanding of what is possible (Browning, 1991).

Celebration. At the root of the celebration of character and identity is the modulation from a restricted or unappreciated identity toward a more complex viewpoint involving more dimensionality and a capacity for change. The celebrated character is not one who does only what was expected, only what was in keeping with an initial set of conditions and opportunities, but rather someone who transcends the limits of initial conditions, resources, and personal qualities to turn into some-one better (McAdams, 1996). Thus, in memorializing someone, we narrate what it might have been plausible for them to become had it not been for their sterling character, then we praise them for rising above normal expectations.

Celebration calls attention to the qualities possessed by the actor and to the pos-sibility of reauthoring the self by characterizing them in favorable ways. Perhaps the most powerful application is to use stories for the redefinition of the self. This begins by being able to place an actor in a historical context and entails seeing characteristics that had previously been left out or understanding and building upon strengths that were overlooked in previous interpretations.

Transportation. The transportation application addresses how a story moves, or transports, a listener or reader by its sheer power. The gist of the idea is telling a story that so moves listeners that they lose awareness of their current setting, are shocked when they "come out of it," and are affected by their moment of trance by the story to such an extent that they are changed by it (Green & Brock, 2000). This is one of those applications that is better known in everyday parlance by its opposite. What we say when a story flops is, "I guess you had to be there." The potential to be transported was there, but the particular telling was unsuccessful. So the real objective for this application is to take people somewhere, to move them out of their cubicle into a drama.

Of course, the power to move people is not universal; what moves one listener might not affect another. For instance, the chaplain's story about people in the basement of the hospital blessing surgical instruments they were assembling was transportative for the authors. We were moved by the employees' faith or hope that their distant caring could make a difference, perhaps saving the patient's life. We were also moved by the chaplain's insight that there are people throughout organizations who are aligning their routine tasks with larger, more elevated goals, even though their activities are not celebrated.

Circumspection. We use the term "circumspection" to mean reflecting upon what happened in the past, altering understandings about the circumstances of action, and prudently anticipating future events. Circumspection "is the ability to understand how to stage an optimal performance and to anticipate any difficulties that may arise. It also entails the ability to select the kind of audience that will be most receptive to one's performance" (Quinn, 2005, p. 344). The ability to anticipate events, to foresee what a different narrative future might be like, is operationalized in the writing and interventions of David Snowden (2000). His work emphasizes the capacity of stories to carry an ambiguous array of events and then interpret meaning from these events as though they were informative. Many examples of circumspection occur in educational settings where participants are asked to reflect on what happened, what might have happened, and what can be learned from it. Circumspection as we use it here has a dual meaning: it invites philosophical reflection, but is also "grounded in the pragmatic orientation of getting around, coping, 'doing a life'" (Scult, 2004).

Events like those that must be planned for by High Reliability Organizations (HROs) are complex and unpredictable, yet structures for managing them need to be created, utilized, and adapted. Circumspection is the process through which a collection of people can design these new structures. Moreover, people managing the unexpected prepare themselves in certain ways to be able to be resilient, to learn from mistakes, to not exhibit hubris, to be open to diverse ideas, to be ready to improvise, and so forth. Preparation largely means coming up with an integratively complex response to complex-chaotic-unpredictable circumstances. Improvisation means continuously adapting activities as matters progress. The chief movement is from what have been termed "terrible simplifications" (Watzlawick, Weakland, & Fisch, 1974) toward more complicated understanding of states of affairs, along with a movement from a fixed or rigid response to one that is more provisional, flexible, and fitting.

Stories about saving for a rainy day, developing slack resources, enlarging personal competencies, learning from experience, taking timely action, not jumping the gun, building high-quality connections before they are needed—all of these put this kind of circumspection on display.

Elevation. We use the term "elevation" in one sense to mean creating heightened sensory awareness. The epitome of aesthetic response to a story is to have the hair stand up on the back of one's neck. The ghost story told by the campfire is a good example. The problem with that is that with a horror story, usually violence is involved or implied. One of the reasons that violence is so prominent in popular culture is that the easiest way to create hair-raising, to arouse the audience, is to depict blood and sex—as if to say, "Okay, if that's aesthetics, and aesthetics is arousal, vitality, and aliveness, then the easiest thing to do is blood and sex," which is why people take effortless means in popular culture to create responses. The more blood the better.

With this as a standard, there is real timidity in the workplace stories we collected, with very few having anything to do with violence or desire. In fact, the only stories are about efforts to avoid creating desire and cautionary tales about people caught with their pants down (Boje, 2001). We do not suggest upping the violence and portrayal of desire as means of application. Rather, the challenge is greater.

The second sense of the term "elevation" is to raise the audience's horizons about what is possible, as in "raising the level of play" or "elevating one's game." We know that people can arouse audiences through stories of sex and violence, but how else? Can other themes of human capability, striving, coordination, accomplishment, and revelation be drawn upon to transport listeners? The elevation application shifts the audience from a dulled to a thrilled attentiveness and from a base to an elevated horizon of possibilities. Consider hearing powerful harmony created by a duet or choir. For example, one of the authors was rehearsing for a wedding with a woman he had never sung with before. In the Guy Clark song, "I Don't Love You Much, Do I?" the harmony became so rich that 16 years later it remains a spine-tingling experience.

Conclusion

In this chapter we have called attention to the presence and variety of narratives in the workplace and argued for the centrality of narratives for understanding workplaces and the lives of people who comprise them. To make this point, we have shown how ubiquitous narratives are in the contemporary organization and we have tried to suggest the vast variety of stories available to people at work today.

We have not contented ourselves to write about stories in the abstract, but have also revealed six stories that made an impression on us. The stories that were provided are examples of those to which we have attended as we sought to explore and develop the concepts of narrative appreciation this book unveils.

Six angles on narrative appreciation have been introduced. Each of these is a concept or combination of concepts that helps to refine and illuminate knowledge of what is happening when people tell and consume stories. Our purpose in identifying these angles on narrative is to isolate a few ways of examining narratives that can significantly enhance how they can be understood and appreciated. Each of these angles will be elaborated upon in a subsequent chapter.

The distinctiveness in our presentation will become more evident in Chapter Two, where we address an expanse of previous literature on narratives and position our own work within that tradition. In that chapter, we argue for what we call an "open architecture" for organizational narratology. We develop the open architecture by explaining several important narratological principles that form a platform upon which subsequent narratology can be created and expanded. After showing our indebtedness to previous scholarship and highlighting a few of the divergences between its perspectives and our own, we devote one chapter each to the six angles on narrative appreciation. In each case, we highlight an application to show how the particular angle can empower action and understanding of that application. Our book concludes with a chapter that addresses complications of our approach and implications of our work for narrative research in organizations.

We conclude with a few directions for subsequent writing and thinking about the place of narratives at work.

2

AN OPEN ARCHITECTURE FOR ORGANIZATIONAL NARRATOLOGY

Introduction

This book cultivates appreciation for—and celebrates the beauty, power, and usefulness of—stories in organizational life. To set the stage for the discussions of the six angles for narrative appreciation contained in the following chapters, in this chapter we propose what we term an "open architecture" for the analysis of organizational narratives. Our approach is analogous to open architecture of computer operating systems, like Linux, in comparison with proprietary systems, such as Apple's OS X or Microsoft's Windows. One advantage of open architecture is that there is a common platform users must employ, but wide latitude beyond that for them to augment and refine the system. The system thus has the potential to get better, faster. The other key advantage is the democratic nature of open architecture; anyone with the requisite knowledge and skill can add to it, so its future capabilities are less restricted. Applications that the original designers could not anticipate can be incorporated into the system by the universe of designers seeking to augment it.

In this case, our idea of open architecture is composed of eight premises about the nature of organizational narratives with which existing narrative research is consistent, along with six angles for deepening narrative appreciation. We are essentially recommending that narratologists examine the goodness of fit between their favored approaches to narrative and the eight premises we identify, then use one or more of the six angles to deepen their understanding of and appreciation for a particular narrative and narratives in general.

Since we are proposing an open architecture for subsequent narrative analysis and research, our approach invites augmentation and refinement. We explain our position by offering and expounding upon eight premises about the nature of organizational narratives. As we discuss each of these premises, we call attention to a few of the prominent scholars of narrative whose work is aligned with or diverges significantly from our approach. Where there are major points of divergence between ours and others' approaches, we will point them out without dwelling upon them.

In the conclusion of this chapter, we amplify on what our open architecture for narratology affords for organizational actors and researchers.

1. Narratives are Communicative Acts

In this book, we situate ourselves as cognizant of not only the "linguistic turn" (a focus on the philosophy of language, as in the work of Wittgenstein) but also of how it applies to the interpretive approach to organizations (Putnam & Pacanowsky, 1983) and various approaches to the analysis of talk and writing as discourse (Fairhurst & Putnam, 2004). This positioning will enable us to mesh what we understand about narrative discourse with what we take to be some of the best theorizing about organizations. Often this centers on the issue of how people engage in interpretation in the workplace (Cohen, March, & Olsen, 1972). As a result, we set up a strong emphasis on stories as sensemaking (Weick, 1995).

For this reason we, like Czarniawska (2004), emphasize the distinction between action that is interpreted versus mere behavior that is measured. "Behavior" is the preferred term of industrial psychologists because it is a limited term—the number of swings of a hammer or the number of keystrokes in a day are "behaviors" because they are measurable and ordinal, and because they are either happening or not. In their 1972 treatise *The Explanation of Social Behavior*, Harré and Secord showcase "the act–action" sequence, which refers to behavior (an act) that is interpreted (an action). Czarniawska (1998), extending that notion, argues that conduct can be treated as action when it can be accounted for in narrative terms that are acceptable in a given social setting. In that positioning, her work accords with constructionism. For her, the response an audience makes to a narrator's claim will determine the actual effect of the speaker's words.

Taylor and Van Every's (2000) work on narrative has come to define the Montreal school of organizational communication. They place communication at the center of the organizing process and construe an organization as "a form of life" that operates within the conversational practices of its members. As a result, it operates as a "social and cultural world to produce an environment whose forms both express social life and create the context for it to survive" (p. 324). Following Bruner (1986, 1990), they conceptualize narrative as a causal, problem-laden structure that requires resolution.

Part of Taylor and Van Every's (2000) contribution has been to help English-speaking narratologists understand the abstruse conception of narrative developed by the French semiotician Algirdas Greimas. For Greimas, most narratives involve two stories at once, each on an intersecting path, between a "sender" (protagonist) who initiates the action and a "receiver" (antagonist) who must respond to that action, and with an outcome (usually in a conflict narrative) that is euphoric for the protagonist and dysphoric for the antagonist—there is always good news and bad news in stories. The moral of any story depends on the point of view taken, both by the writer and by the reader. The protagonist's and antagonist's story paths have in common an issue that intersects and explains the motivation of the actors. But Taylor and Van Every observe that Greimas' idea extends beyond the specific story being told to represent grander cultural themes, Good vs. Bad, Individualism vs. Community, and so on. In Greimas' terms, each narrative will have "an abstract deep level and a more concrete surface level" (Greimas & Ricœur, 1989, p. 554). Complex oppositions often display these contrasts between cultural themes. For instance, a narrative might focus on a character who is standing up for good but also has his or her moral limitations. Thus there are ambiguous oppositions between grand meanings and local specifics. Such ironies keep us attentive in stories.

Greimas' use of the term "receiver" opens the door to linking narratology to traditional communication theory that identifies the basic SMCR model of communication, made up of a *Sender, Message, Channel,* and *Receiver.* He says the "narrative ... posits relations between ... the sender and receiver" (Greimas & Ricœur, 1989, p. 554). Despite all the attention given to the senders' art of crafting a message or initiating an action, receivers are important because in their own kind of ambiguity, receivers tend to apprehend a narrative differently; hence the use of the term "polyvocality." What a receiver wants within a story often changes over time, including preferences that can shift at any given moment.

2. Narratives Occur in Conversations as Well as Monologues

Traditionally, narratives are understood as monologues offered by a single storyteller—for example, Winston Churchill's famous speech to the House of Commons about the forthcoming Battle of Britain. But people also tell stories in conversations (Czarniawska, 1998; Tracy, 2002) and in story rounds (Boje, 2011). In Tracy's (2002) view, narratives are told for all sorts of reasons, including to entertain, persuade, instruct, explain, warn, threaten, and praise, to name just a few. When, during a conversation, we elect to use a story to accomplish one or more of these acts, we need to make way for that story in the ongoing stream of interaction. Often we'll do some initial work to find out what our intended listeners, or "recipients," may already know about the event in order to best tailor our telling of it to them (Nofsinger, 1991). In the view of conversation analysts, we need to arrange for listeners to grant us an extended turn at talk within which to tell the story (Goodwin, 1984), since most stories are involved enough to require our listeners' forbearance. A story preface, such as "Did I tell you about what Sarah Palin did now?" creates this opportunity. Conversationalists play out interacting roles as they offer explanations, request reasons, and provide other opportunities for the storyteller to continue with his or her story.

After the story is launched, others present play important roles that determine how the story comes out (Mandelbaum, 1989, 2003). Recipients of stories can and do ask questions about the action which can actually "drive" stories in a new direction and therefore can influence how a story ends up getting told. For example, a listener could ask, "So, what was so-and-so doing while that was going on?" which would introduce another actor into the story. Or the hearer might ask the primary teller how s/he was feeling about the action, or what s/he thought the action meant, or what might be done about it. By such maneuvers, hearers modify the story in its telling as opposed to being passive recipients of story set-pieces.

It is very commonplace for stories to be co-authored as opposed to being told by just one person. The idea of co-authorship of stories (Mandelbaum, 1989) is that people assist each other in their telling of them. Although co-authors might not contribute components of the story, they nevertheless participate through what they say as they listen, offering acknowledgment tokens, assessments, and continuers to align with the telling (Nofsinger, 1991; Bavelas, Coates, & Johnson, 2000). In other words, even when one party is the primary teller, others show their appreciation, acknowledgment, humorous uptake, and confusion, to name just a few of the possible contributions.

3. Narratives Engage Listeners Through Incompleteness

Listeners are drawn into narratives. On some occasions their engagement involves merely experiencing a story as entertainment, as when they might exclaim, "That book proved a really fast read." In other instances, when listeners become unaware of where they are—become lost in the narrative—they are in effect "transported" by the story (Green & Brock, 2000). In these instances, narratives have the power to increase the effort and involvement by the listener in making sense of the story.

Stories are engaging for what they leave out as well as for their specifics or other aspects of their production, such as the language used. Because good stories tend to omit material, they are not at their best when they are completely comprehensive. Instead, people are drawn into stories when the listener imagines and fills in story details with missing information that requires inferences. The listener is required to fill in the blanks for the story to make sense (Weick & Browning, 1986). The main narrative literature that supports this position is Reader Response Theory (Lang, 1980; Tompkins, 1980), which assumes that the story is nothing until and unless the respondent, the listener, makes sense of it. Such a position affirms the basic communication model, which posits that the feedback stage of any message is the moment when the influence of that message is affirmed or denied by the recipient.

The other literature that is friendly to the conception of narrative as incomplete is rhetorical theory, especially as represented in the concept of the enthymeme. In classical rhetorical theory (Aristotle, 1991), an enthymeme is a truncated syllogism— a set of premises and a conclusion used in formal logic—with a missing premise. The audience participates by supplying the missing premise based on cultural identification with the story (Weick & Browning, 1986).

Literally, the word enthymeme means "something in the mind" (Aristotle, 1991, p. 33). When narrators share a story that matches a cultural identity, they can "communicate without making every assumption explicit." In its simplest form, the enthymeme is an inside joke between narrator and listener. In its most powerful conceptualization, it is the basis for persuasion. Enthymemes are a prevailing tool of persuasion because they allow audience members to draw on beliefs that they already have—beliefs that are integral to the institutional order (Hartelius & Browning, 2008).

Part of the incompleteness of narratives is the moral implications that listeners might draw from them. The moral component of narratives is part of the reason people can find them engaging. We enlist narrative in our daily communication by marking off a piece of time, saying what went on within it, painting a picture of characters that listeners will find convincing, and drawing some kind of conclusion from what is said that has an evaluative, moral component (Ricœur, 1974; Polster, 1987).

4. Narrative Meanings are Negotiable

Organizational narratives often require some kind of uptake from listeners. People who listen actively to others' stories often summarize what they took it to mean. In conversation analysis, this is termed "formulating" the gist or upshot of the story (Heritage & Watson, 1979). An example would be, "So you are saying you can't deliver until the damaged part is repaired?" Such a formulation reveals what the interpreter thought the story meant, something that can be negotiated subsequently. In couples therapy, therapists respond to the stories husbands and wives tell them by coming up with a formulation, essentially supplying the couple with a new way to understand what their stories mean (Weick & Browning, 1991; Buttny, 2004). Buttny (2004) has shown that therapists negotiate these problem formulations when clients do not initially concur.

If stories were told as set pieces, and if listeners passively absorbed them without making their own contributions to the telling, then there would be limited chances to respond to and interpret stories. But even viewers of media narratives, such as narratives of health and illness portrayed on television, are far from passive. Rather, according to Davin (2003, p. 674) they actively construct responses to media narratives as they:

> produce complex, multi-layered, sometimes contradictory and/or unexpected interpretations. They read and use broadcasts according to their mood and wants at a particular moment. They generate meanings in their encounters with flexible texts, meanings which cannot be predicted by content analysis of broadcasts alone … By empathizing with characters, by assessing the disadvantages of different courses of action, by discussing storylines with relatives and friends, by filling in the blanks, by creating narratives, by playing games with the stories, etc., … viewers engage with, and learn from broadcasts.

In the case of conversational stories, due to the interactional nature of storytelling, virtually any moment within a telling can alter the progress of the story and what it is taken to mean. A key for the negotiation of meaning in a story is the point of view of the teller, the protagonist, and the listener. The most important element of point of view is the vested interest of these three positions and the closeness of the teller to the action he or she narrates. As Bruner says, "The Self as narrator not only recounts but justifies" (1990, p. 121).

As people tell stories, they may also try to influence the significance others will attach to them. For instance, they may offer disclaimers (Hewitt & Stokes, 1975) in the midst of stories, such as by saying "I don't mean to be judgmental, but ... " before going on to say something judgmental. Another aligning action (Stokes & Hewitt, 1976) is to qualify what one is saying, such as by acknowledging that a piece of research is at an early stage and the conclusions drawn are just tentative. Accounts (Scott & Lyman, 1968) may also be given to explain why the narrator acted in ways others might think are questionable. Stories launched on one trajectory often change as tellers and listeners negotiate what really happened and what it really means (Mandelbaum, 1989).

5. Narratives Invite Sensemaking

Weick (1995) views narrative as the basic tool for achieving what he calls "sensemaking"—the cognitive process for rendering varied and uncertain information into plausible causal explanations. The fused term "sensemaking" is Weick's own neologism. He devised it to convey the idea that sensemaking, as he defines it, is so all-encompassing in organizations that it deserves being distinguished as a new usage about a new concept (Browning & Boudes, 2005). Sensemaking is always retrospective. People within any organization are constantly trying to create order and to make retrospective sense of what has occurred (Weick, 1995). Accordingly, organizations become interpretation systems of participants who, through the back and forth of their own understandings, provide meanings for each other via their everyday interactions. For Weick, actors know who they are by what they say to others and how others respond to them (Browning & Boudes, 2005). Weick (1995, p. 8) observes, "People verbalize their interpretations and the processes they use to generate them." A distinctive feature of sensemaking is the way action (what people say) and organization (the formal system that those people are in) collaborate to make up the structure. For example, say an author and her editor collaborate with an agreed-upon contract to improve the author's book manuscript. That contract, which might include, among other things, the technology they'll use, the hourly rate, the authority of the editor, and the work site of their collaboration, is their organizational structure. Their discussions that hammer out an agreement on the best wording and meaning make up their interactions. Weick would have us see those discussions as a type of action because generating discourse is an act of performance and production. Sensemaking is about composing and delivering a message as well as interpreting one—in his words, "authoring as well as reading" (Weick, 1995, p. 7). For Weick, sensemaking is placing an interpretative structure on some incident or environment—that is to say, offering a plausible understanding of it that is based on assessing various pertinent factors, which might include historical precedents, the social context of the decision-makers, the knowledge of people "on the ground" as opposed to what is understood by management sometimes far removed from the scene, and so on. Additionally, Weick views sensemaking as best done in small pieces, or what he calls "chunks," to avoid premature, wholesale conclusions. One's specific understanding of those chunks enables one to combine the causal inferences that can be interpreted narratively. Stories "gather strands of experience into a plot" or a "good narrative" that provides a "plausible frame for sensemaking" and a way of mapping formal coherence on "what is otherwise a flowing soup" (Weick, 1995, p. 128). Narrative is the container, if you will, for the interpretation process that is involved in making sense out of an uncertain and sometimes deceptive world.

Of course, others besides Weick have understood narratives as central to interpretation processes in organizations. Boje (1991), Czarniawska (1997) and Polkinghorne (1988) also view narratives as the grist for sensemaking. As stated by Starkey and Crane (2003, p. 221):

> At a time when the past monopoly of the sciences on rationality has been weakened, narrative can endow our experience with meaning and generate stories that allow or motivate us to see new connections between events. Narrative can draw our attention to blind spots and help us see what we could not see before: that key concepts do not so much constitute a theory with predictive validity as provide a guide for interpretation.

Robichaud (2001, p. 619) asserts that "the role of narration in organizational communication and sensemaking is now widely accepted" and credits the contributions of Czarniawska, Cooren, Fisher, Boje, and Bruner, among others, for this newly prominent role.

Fundamental to the understanding of a narrative is the causal interpretation. One statement of causal development in narrative is Roland Barthes' (1996) interpretation of the row of telephones from an early scene of the James Bond movie *Goldfinger*. That there are two phones in that scene only makes a difference if at some future point in the narrative their presence becomes causal by driving the story in a particular direction. Any force that causes the story to pivot (to turn dramatically), whether it be a telephone or a hero, carries what Barthes labels a "cardinal" function. Narratives are causal whether they are multi-causal with several explanations for what happened or whether the cause is singular and a clear point of the story.

6. Narratives are Culturally Styled

To transport a reader or listener to a different culture, a story needs to provide adequate detail about the setting, good continuity, and incidents that are plausible to its place and time (Aristotle, 1981). The good narrative, then, is essentially a good imitation (Aristotle, 1981). Narratives are culturally styled in the sense that they are authentic in terms of what members do, say, and think about their actions. For example, Clifford Geertz (1973) considered the cockfight to be characteristic of an aspect of Balinese culture, a "text" that could be interpreted to better understand Balinese life. Narratives arising in and from a culture are similarly revealing. About the Balinese cockfight text, Geertz (1973, pp. 449–50) concluded:

> Every people, the proverb has it, loves its own form of violence. The cockfight is the Balinese reflection on theirs: on its uses, its force, its fascination. Drawing on almost every level of Balinese experience, it brings together themes—animal savagery, male narcissism, opponent gambling, status rivalry, mass excitement, blood sacrifice—whose main connection is their involvement with rage and the fear of rage, and binding them into a set of rules which at once contains them and allows them play, builds a symbolic structure in which, over and over again, the reality of their inner affiliation can be intelligibly felt.

Karen Tracy (2002) summarizes three ways culture influences narrative activity. First, listeners from a culture different than the teller's may assess the character of the narrator or other actors in unanticipated ways because they are likely to make different moral assessments of the actors. Second, topics for narratives will often vary from culture to culture. Third, narrative style varies by cultural group. Some prefer a linear style; others may skip from topic to topic. To sensitize you to such differences, we invite readers to reflect upon the kinds of research stories that are privileged in their ways of doing social science. Since opinion varies as to what constitutes convincing evidence, some of us would never imagine conducting an experiment or administering a questionnaire as part of our research method, while others would not consider research that did not involve one or the other of these procedures. Another quick way to grasp the cultural styling of narratives is to imagine the difference between a telling in which the narrator mimics the dialect of the actors, versus the narrator who fails to do so, either through indifference or ineptitude.

According to Bittner (1982), style is one feature that accounts for the distinctive way things are done in organizations. For example, the U.S. Army has uniforms with brass buttons that require polishing prior to inspection whereas the Air Force, having wanted to establish itself as unique from the Army, has tarnished silver that goes unpolished. Or take the Modern Language Association and the American Psychological Association. Though both are huge multidisciplinary academic entities existing side by side, each has developed its own very elaborate style manual for properly formatting research documents, and woe to any doctoral student who fails to follow the prescribed form. Such cultural styling of narratives is nicely illustrated in Russell and Porter's (2003) study of single older men's narratives of household experiences. They observed that these narratives were framed by the importance of money in these men's everyday lives. Money was seen to be an index for these men in that their stories often told how much they could do in their bygone workdays.

One indicator of a culture's style is its proportion of lists to stories (Browning, 1992). For example, a technical culture, such as one focusing on accounting or engineering, would almost certainly be list-driven, whereas a religious organization is more likely to base its direction on what it considers holy stories. The former illustrates what Fisher (1984) would call technical rationality, while the latter illustrates what he would term narrative rationality. Both have important communicative roles. All of us would support technical rationality because we want our engineers and architects to build structures rationally, and all of us want our pilots, before takeoff, to be consulting a flight checklist rather than simply depending on what they learned from a narrative. By the same token, though, but for the Ten Commandments and similar codes, monotheistic religions are built around stories because they are faith-based and because our belief in them arises from historical narrative documents. We conclude that most cultures evidence a mix of lists and stories, for people have both procedural parts of their jobs and lives but will also often interpret those procedures with stories (Browning, 1992).

7. Narratives Come in Many Forms

We side with those, such as Roland Barthes (1996), Barbara Czarniawska (1998, 2004), and Walter Fisher (1987) who propose a broad, rather than a restricted, idea of what counts as narrative. Our view permits an almost limitless variety of forms. Barthes (1996, p. 45) declares:

> There are countless forms of narrative in the world. First of all, there is a prodigious variety of genres, each of which branches out into a variety of media, as if all substances could be relied upon to accommodate man's stories. Among the vehicles of narrative are articulated language, whether oral or written, pictures, still or moving, gestures, and an ordered mixture of these substances; narrative is present in myth, legend, fables, tales, short stories, epics, history, tragedy drame (suspense drama), comedy, pantomime, paintings (in Santa Ursula by Carpaccio, for instance), stained-glass windows, movies, local news, conversation. Moreover, in this infinite variety of forms, it is present at all times, in all places, in all societies, indeed narrative starts with the very history of mankind; there is not, there has never been anywhere, any people without narrative.

Likewise, Riessman (2008) recognizes a wide variety of forms of narrative. She includes the memoir (personal account), biography (story of the other), auto-biography (story of the self), diaries (daily musings of details), archival documents (official record of activity), social service and health records (professional proof of action and accountability), other organizational documents (hard copies that affirm a history), scientific theories (explanations of probabilities), folk ballads (musical representations of culture), photographs (visual records of scenes), and other works of art. Riessman's (2008) criterion for what counts as narrative is that it comprises a consequential linking of events that are otherwise disconnected; all the above forms meet this criterion. Taylor and Van Every argue that narrative is not limited to merely telling a story, but instead is a "basic trait of all forms of cognitive processing of social information" (2000, p. 41). Cognitive processing is the causal connections we make to create understandings, and these connections, say Taylor and Van Every, are invariably perceived in narrative form.

Considering the full array of forms, many of which differ from the literary works of art which were the original objects of narratology, we join those who make no distinction between a narrative and a story, including Czarniawska (1988), Reissman (2008), and Polkinghorne (1988), and we will use both terms interchangeably. The range of stories we consider includes the *petit récit* (Lyotard, 1984), the monomyth (Campbell, 2008), and everything in between, including the personal story (Bochner, 1994). However, just because something is *petit* doesn't mean it is necessarily underdeveloped. There are a few essential elements to stories/narratives as we view them, and we would not confuse a story preface or story fragment with a story. In our view, it is not sufficient that a person attaches meaning to a set of events or that an interpretation remains implicit to an individual (Lazaroff & Snowden, 2006); a narrative is a communicative act and, as such, it is both produced and interpreted.

Rather than relegating the term "story" to the basement of narratology, our approach equates stories with narratives. However, we concur with those authors, such as Gabriel (2004) and Boje (2001), who recognize that many contemporary organizational texts are too partial and/or fragmented to be considered narratives. We think Boje's term "antenarrative" (2001), applies fairly straightforwardly to an attempt to engage in narrative that doesn't get fully launched. Either because others' stories are told instead, or one can't get the conversational opportunity to give a narrative, it is certainly possible for tellings to be "anted" (or offered up) without being developed fully enough to count as narratives or stories.

We acknowledge Gabriel's (2004) concern that the popular interest in organizational stories has fragmented and diminished conceptualizations of narrative. For him, a narrative must contain a plot, a sequence, and verbs denoting what happened. This conceptualization roughly matches our own, yet our position is less exclusionary. We agree with him that a mere report is not a story. However, we disagree that calling something a story rather than a narrative is a useful distinction. One reason narratology has grown as an intellectual force is the breadth and applicability of what counts as a narrative. By joining Barthes (1996), Czarniawska (1998, 2004), Polkinghorne (1988), Fisher (1987), Reissman (2008), and Taylor and Van Every (2000), we can propound an approach to narrative that is fairly broad but still makes a few key distinctions. Even though we exclude antenarratives and narrative fragments, the domain of organizational narrative is very expansive. And it is growing. Recently, Pentland and Feldman proposed the idea of a narrative network that "expresses the set of stories (performances) that have been, or could be, generated by combining and recombining fragments of technology in use" (2007, p. 781). As such, combinations of technologies, in relation to a person, can elicit a particular story, such as a story about how a new application proved useful or a new ICT was more trouble than it was worth.

8. Narratives Fulfill Many Different Purposes

Many popular books aimed at managers and political candidates highlight the usefulness of narratives for rhetorical purposes (Hartelius & Browning, 2008). One of the advantages of consciously mimicking narrative themes is their effectiveness even when the strategy is transparent. As Joseph Campbell made clear in a PBS series entitled *The Power of Myth* (Moyers & Campbell, 1988), a particularly powerful form of the hero narrative is a personal sacrifice on the part of the actor. The ultimate hero, Campbell said, is one who sacrifices. It is not uncommon for candidates for political office to attempt to capitalize on the hero myth by making their war experiences salient in their campaigns.

But narratives fulfill many different purposes. Prominent communication narratologists understand this versatility and apply narratives in a host of distinctive ways, all of which seem compatible with the open architecture we are considering. Bochner (1994), for example, emphasizes the usefulness of narrative for capturing the drama and meaning of personal relationships in an individual's life. Boje (2001), meanwhile, articulates a complete theory of the antenarrative concerning what leads to a narrative and how it remains essentially incomplete as a story. At the very least, his work exhaustively describes the conditions from which narratives might arise. Bruner (1986, 2002) emphasizes the way narratives are used for meaning in every phase of life, from the self-concept to the legal system. Zechmeister and Romero (2002) concentrate on how victims utilize narratives as accounts for what happened to them as well as narratives of forgiveness. A related approach focusing on narratives as accounts is that by Walzer and Oles (2003), who observed face saving in the accounts of people undergoing divorce. Eisenberg and his colleagues (Eisenberg, Pynes, & Baglia, 2003) show how narratives are important in a hospital's emergency room as a comprehensive shorthand for complex, but vitally important, medical communication. For the ER, people must decide whether the mix of information, including tests, the patient's self-report, and the doctor's assessment, adds up to a "good story"—that is, one that makes sense and that can thus be acted on confidently. Fisher (1987) celebrates the value of narrative and Aristotle's *Poetics* with his claim that all human events start with a story and that humans may thus be properly defined as *homo narrans* (human the narrator); also, that the story is itself a kind of persuasive communication, making the *Poetics* a perfect complement to Aristotle's *Rhetoric*. Green and Brock (2000) extend the case for poetics as a replacement for rhetoric in their development of their concept of the transportation narrative. They begin their article with this statement: "The scientific study of persuasion has reflected an unfortunate displacement of poetics by rhetoric" (p. 701), and they offer an extended list of examples of how stories have greater influence than specific attempts at persuasion. They proclaim, "Novels, films, soap operas, music lyrics, stories in newspapers, magazines, TV, and radio command far more waking attention than do advertisements, sermons, editorials, billboards, and so forth" (p. 701).

Although many of the purposes of narrative turn out to be persuasive or ideological in character, Robichaud (2001) reminds us that narratives need not be carrying a social agenda. Remarking about memoires by Frank McCourt and Mary Karr, she commented: "Beautifully written and exquisitely told, these are stories about the resilience of the human spirit, not the flaws of our social system" (p. 719).

Proliferating Genres of Organizational Narratology

The growing legitimacy of narrative approaches has led to an enormous expansion of narrative genres in recent years. Researchers recast what was previously understood as a particular concept, such as retirement or organizational turnaround, as a category of narrative. For example, entrepreneurial narratives (Martens, Jennings, & Jennings, 2007) show how start-up business promoters propose their idea in story form to elicit support. The organization man narrative (Hanson & O'Donohue, 2010) demonstrates the lasting effect of the conception of the organization member as the rule-bound and cardboard character. The reform narrative (Skoldberg, 1994) captures types of organizational change in bureaucracies. The green narrative (Starkey & Crane, 2003) demonstrates how disparate items and facts about the natural environment can be made meaningful to human identity via the story. The forgiveness narrative (Zechmeister & Romero, 2002) shows how forgiveness occurs (or fails to occur) in natural settings for the person doing the forgiving. The sexual jealousy narrative (Workman, 2004) elaborates how a jealous person is constrained by telling a story even though s/he doesn't know the actual point of beginning. The psychopathological narrative (Lysaker, Lancaster, & Lysaker, 2003; Salvatore, Dimaggio, & Semerari, 2004) shows how clinicians use narrative to help clients organize their past experiences into a meaningful whole. The brand product narrative (Ramzy, 1992) shows how product commercials enact a narrative in which the product/brand has a central role. The community narrative (Roos & Lombard, 2003) is a story that is constructed and shared by a group of people. Uncoupling/divorce narratives (Walzer & Oles, 2003) show how people who are separating explain their experiences. Retirement narratives (Randall & McKim, 2008) show how people adjust to aging by addressing the dramatic challenges that later life can bring.

Some of the new genres focus on communication, such as communication theory narratives (Galbo, 2004) that contrast the limited effects model and the hypodermic needle theory where messages are injected into the listener; nature narratives (Bryson, 2003) that show how science writers use narrative strategies to explain natural and scientific concepts and advance an ethical view of nature and a suspicion of a blind faith in technological progress; and television medical narratives (Davin, 2003) that portray television viewers as sophisticated receivers of stories who make complex and media-literate interpretations. Relatively unrestricted uses of the narrative idea have enabled new narrative genres to spring up in environments that would previously have been hostile. And that, in our opinion, is all to the good.

However, the proliferation of narrative genres seems to have been proceeding with minimal attention to what the various approaches have in common and what makes them distinctive. What Almén (2003, 2008) observes about musical narrative also applies to the other new narrative genres and to organizational narratology more generally:

> Assuming one could put musical narrative on a firmer footing, there is nevertheless no universally agreed upon definition of what it might actually be: that is, what its preconditions, sources, and most significant properties are. Consensus about the characteristics, strengths, and limitations of musical narratives might lead to a better sense of direction with respect to research and analysis.
>
> *(2003, p. 1)*

Although we have no interest in establishing restrictive limits on such definitional matters, we recognize the value in identifying a few key features of narrative and common terms for narrative analysis. This is analogous to the arguments for the development of general systems theory, which used terms such as system, environment, input, and output to facilitate communication among scientists working in different physical, biological, chemical, and, eventually, social science disciplines. An open architecture for organizational narratology, to which we now turn, has similar potential to increase the likelihood of novel stories that cross generic narrative boundaries and to integrate previously unrelated narrative approaches to both advance theoretical development and facilitate novel applications.

Open Architecture

We invoke the open architecture idea because it is in keeping with the uniqueness of the individual; thus it would be shameful to leave any character's story out of consideration. Randall and McKim (2008) cite Oliver Sacks: "Biologically, physiologically, we are not that different from each other; historically, as narratives—we are each of us unique" (p. 22). That every person's story counts is in keeping with the interest in identity. Open architecture is in keeping with the celebration of the unique individual because any story can be formed to include the four features we will identify.

The various positions on narrative drawn from students of literature, science, management, and communication all have somewhat different views on what counts as a narrative and what most deserves emphasis. Scholars of written literature—say, a poem or short story—are more likely to focus on a key phrase to represent what is important in a given work. Communication scholars tend to emphasize narrative as a kind of persuasive communication often found in a speech or conversation. Managerial narratologists usually link the narrative with the institution of the leader telling the story. In organizations, narrative is considered a tool for influencing organizational action (Hartelius & Browning, 2008).

Even though these perspectives take different tacks, all operate from positions that overlap minimally and independently of a coalition of theorists that decides what qualifies as a narrative. Our aim here is to consolidate what the disparate approaches to narrative have in common, using the commonalities as a platform for understanding, examining, and generating stories. Since our open approach is not exclusive, we anticipate that many will recognize at least parts of their preferred approaches and will be able to make interesting use of points of divergence. Beyond that, in subsequent chapters we explain six angles on narrative appreciation that invite deepening and extension of this basic platform.

We consider narratives to have four key features. All of them do the following:

1. *Foreshadow a problem.* A situation develops that is somehow challenging or threatening for the actors. The development casts a shadow over their routine or ongoing activities and becomes something that requires their attention.
2. *Provide a sequential rendering of actions in the face of complications leading toward resolution.* The narrator selectively describes a series of actions aimed at facing up to the problem and surmounting it (Franklin, 1986). Difficulties are encountered along the way that need to be recognized and handled. The actions taken progress toward a resolution of the problem. It is the hope of resolution that pulls the story forward while the threat of the problem and complications push it from behind.
3. *Achieve closure.* Matters reach an end, though this end may not resolve the problem and it might foreshadow new problems to follow.
4. *Invite or pronounce moral implications.* Either the narrator supplies the story's moral significance or it is drawn by the reader/listener; King (1999, p. 30) calls this the "moral experience" of the story. Ideally, this significance is nonobvious and debatable. It invites subsequent (re)interpretation.

But while all narratives, we believe, have the four elements just listed, we also recognize, like Reissman, Barthes, Fisher, and Polkinghorne, among others, that they can be combined in an almost limitless variety of forms—for example, memoirs, biographies, autobiographies, folk ballads, pictures, gestures, myths, short stories, paintings, and so on. So for the deeper appreciation of narrative and how it can be applied, we recommend, and will apply here, the concept of "open architecture," using that term analogously to how Wikipedia defines it: "a type of computer architecture or software architecture that allows adding, upgrading and swapping components" (http://en.wikipedia.org/wiki/Open_architecture).

Our own ideas in this book reflect such adding and swapping. Our goal is to increase narrative flexibility and application across settings (Wright, 1995). We suggest using open architecture in a way that applies across examples and is to some extent standardized (Várady, Benyó, & Benyó, 2002). In Fisher's terms, "Narratives enable us to understand the actions of others 'because we all live out narratives in our lives and because we understand our own lives in terms of narratives'" (1987, p. 66).

Meyrowitz's (2008) article on narratives of media influence helps to bolster the open architecture concept. He analyzes three narratives of human experience that undergird three ways of examining media influence: critical/cultural studies, uses and gratifications research, and communication medium theory. He uses a short cut for meaning of these three theoretical approaches by calling them the power and resistance narrative, the purposes and pleasure narrative, and the structures and patterns narrative. His goal is to take the three disparate approaches and to identify the underlying foundational narrative that ties them together. Meyrowitz says:

> each of these root narratives tells a relatively simple story. Each story incorporates assumptions about human nature and emphasizes particular dimensions of human experience. Each narrative provides a different way of answering the question, "What do media do to us or for us?" Most significantly, each story—at least its broad dimensions—is obviously true, and yet obviously incomplete.
>
> *(2008, p. 644)*

He claims that each of the three positions can marginalize or critique the other two for what it does that the others fail to do, but that it is more fruitful to examine what the other stories add that one's own story fails to accomplish. Our open architecture in this book resembles Meyrowitz's expanded approach to media narratives and, similarly, affords opportunities for novelty.

Our idea of open architecture includes a wide but definitive sweep of what counts as a story and a set of six angles that are *topoi* for narrative appreciation. The advantage of the wide latitude of acceptance we offer in this book is that it provides a platform for narratologists to weigh in with a story and to critique each other's stories. Another advantage of our ecumenical approach to narratives is an understanding and acceptance of the very permeable boundary between people's lives outside organizations and their lives inside the workplace. Managing and maintaining those boundaries is a recurrent human problem. The way people show up as actors in organizations is partly determined by the things they do outside their organization, including, for instance, the media representations of work that they consume.

It is important to recognize that a few story-like texts don't meet our definition. The most apparent of these is the chronicle, which is a temporal listing of events without causal inferences about their development. A chronicle also lacks foreshadowing of a problem, action leading to a resolution, closure, and moral implications. That it does not contain or invite moral implications can be an especially important distinction. One of the advantages of relying on the chronicle rather than a narrative is that there is less disagreement about its correctness by self-interested readers. When Judy Shetler and Larry Browning wrote a chronology for the major events affecting the development of SEMATECH (the chip testing and development consortium) as part of writing a book about it (Browning & Shetler, 2000), they had no struggles with participants over the order and type of events that were important for that chronology. But interpreting the causes for success of the efforts that produced those events was vigorously contested both by people who wanted the story of the success to focus on them and for those who wanted others not to get credit. Some of the actors threatened our writing contract if we did not interpret the causes the same way they did. That is why who tells the story, who chooses its causal functions, is paramount.

The definitive qualities of narratives we identify are consistent with a view of narratives as social constructions. That narratives are socially constructed means that the interpretations created and held by readers are the ultimate in any theoretical analysis. The value of an analysis is answered by the question: does the analysis cause the reader to be drawn into the topic? If so, narratology functions like a story itself: the ideas are like a fast car on a well-paved surface—they have takeoff power and they have traction.

Conclusion

The distinctive contribution we make in this book is that we integrate a variety of materials on narrative in organizations and synthesize elements in a novel way. This is consistent with contemporary viewpoints on the nature of communication in organizations that are the impetus for organizational narratology. Organizations are mixes of communication systems, including behaviors, technology, economic forces, interesting characters, and bureaucratic structures, all of which are grist for members' stories that make sense of organizational life.

3
ACTION, MOTIVATION, AND MORAL OUTCOME

Picture an island and imagine how your perspective of it changes as you move from point to point along the shore. Each new angle of view enables you to see some things and obscures others. In this book, we use the metaphor of angles to establish different interpretative viewpoints on narratives. We establish six such viewpoints, which are part of what in the last chapter we termed an "open architecture" for organizational narratology. In this chapter we explore the angle of action, motivation, and moral outcome. These seem a natural starting place since they are so integral to an understanding of narratives, and also because all three are invoked whenever issues of responsibility and accountability arise in organizations, which is to say, nearly all the time. We begin with action because action is continuous and multi-faceted. If the story is not advancing (through the introduction of new action) it is withering (Randall & McKim, 2008). At any moment, anything can become a Barthesian (1996) cardinal function and drive the story in a new direction. When anything can account for direction in a story, observers of narratives look for details and watch the story unfold.

As we develop each of the angles we will be concerned with in this book, we tell stories that illuminate important points along the way. To avoid a routine protocol, stories are offered at different places in chapters and will differ in length and style. In this chapter we relate a story about the rocky beginning and endings of a United States senator's service on a presidential commission during the 1960s. After telling it, we lay out a series of analytic features of action, motivation, and moral outcome that both help to explain the story and illuminate action concepts related to narrative. After telling and analyzing the Fred Harris–Lyndon Johnson story, we turn to a broader review of the concepts of action, motivation, and moral outcome in narratology as they affect people in day-to-day circumstances. Our chapter ends with a story that shows how the concepts of action, motivation, and moral outcome are fused in making an explanation. The tie between the angle of action, motivation, and moral outcome and the application of explanation is that explanation always occurs after action has been taken and generally involves citing reasons for what people did (i.e., motivation). Explanations are usually called for when the moral status of actions is questionable. The explanation in this case is about the inconceivably high cost of medical care in a Texas city, and the heroic research efforts of an outsider who brought it to light.

The Fred Harris–Lyndon Johnson Story

President Lyndon Johnson formed a commission in 1967 to investigate the causes of urban violence in Black America in the 1965–67 time period. Named after its chair, Governor Otto Kerner of Illinois, the Kerner Commission conducted hearings, consulted expert research, and ultimately published a report identifying the causes of urban violence and making policy recommendations. Fred Harris, a senator from the state of Oklahoma, was one of the Commissioners. Many years later, on November 17, 2008, in the Lady Bird Johnson Room of the School of Communication at the University of Texas, with a statue of Walter Cronkite placed on a stand nearby, Senator Harris gave a presentation about his participation in the Commission at which the senior author of this book was present. Our telling of the story is based on how Senator Harris told it that day.

In that presentation on the occasion of the fortieth anniversary of the Kerner Commission, Harris recalled that he and his family were at their DC home when the call from the president of the United States, Lyndon B. Johnson, came in, asking Harris to serve on the Commission. The phone was in the kitchen, attached to the wall. Senator Harris' daughter answered, then said "Daddy, it's the president on the phone." One can just imagine Harris walking over to the phone, summoning his composure, as anyone would under that circumstance. If you have memories of President Johnson, it wouldn't be difficult also to imagine his hulking, intimidating frame and the sound of his voice on the other end of the line. After the president asked him to serve on the Commission, he continued, saying, "Now, you are a Johnson man, right? 'Cause if you aren't, I'll take my pocket knife and cut your BLANK off!"[1] So, coupled with Senator Harris' enrollment in the work of the Commission came a direct and blatant threat about what would happen if he deviated from his loyalty to the president.

Harris later learned that Lyndon Johnson had already formed the conclusion that the Commission was supposed to come to, which was that one riot was caused by militant Black agitators. Rather than reaching this conclusion, however, the Commission placed the cause in the squalid, unsafe, and segregated conditions of life in the inner city for African Americans in the United States, and to capture this theme offered the following phrase in their report: "Our nation is moving toward two societies, one black, one white—separate and unequal."[2] The phrase "separate and unequal" is not innocent. By using it, the Commissioners were indirectly saying, "We should respond to violence in the Inner City in the same way the *Brown vs the Board of Education* Supreme Court legal decision responded to public school inequality thirteen years earlier." According to Harris, the report made a number of recommendations that would assist in making progress. However, Lyndon Johnson feared that John Lindsay, who co-chaired the Commission, was using the report for his own political purposes: that he had his eyes on the presidency, and that Lindsay might be Johnson's competitor in the 1968 elections, just one year later.

In his telling, Harris does not reveal when he became aware of Johnson's fears and preferences, but he concludes the story with the following scene. While the Commission was still working on its report, Fred Harris was invited to the White House for a picture shoot with the president and the newly crowned Miss America for 1967, Miss Jane Anne Jayroe, who was from Oklahoma. As they were lining up for the photo, Lyndon said, "Fred, I'm surprised to see you up; I thought Old John Lindsay had you down and had his foot on your neck." This is a thinly veiled reference to the position calves are held in when they are worked in a corral or an open pasture. After the animal is roped and brought down, one cowboy places his knee on the animal's neck to hold his head down, another braces one boot against the lower back leg and holds the upper leg with both hands to completely immobilize the calf. From this position, a calf can be safely castrated, something the Texan president and the Oklahoma senator both would have known. Perhaps Johnson was closing the loop on his threat about what would happen if Fred failed to be an LBJ man. Senator Harris was on the outs with the president from that point on. Johnson disagreed with the statement of causes offered in the report and did not think he had the political capital to pursue its findings, and the report essentially went unapproved by him.

Although at first glance this story is just more evidence of President Johnson's intimidating character, it is also interesting to view it as a performance story about Fred Harris and the Commission. Despite interference from the very highest level of government, they conducted a brave and praiseworthy investigation and took stands that put their political careers at risk. We tie specific narratological concepts of action to this story in the following sections.

Action and Enactment

The Fred Harris story shows how action is tied to problems—especially how we expect humans to take risks to solve them. One of the reasons that action is such a prominent concept is that narratologists and lay people alike tend to place a high value on it. Stories emphasize the actor's willingness to do something, to take a risk, to move on or move out when others are unwilling or doubt the wisdom of doing so. Autonomous, risky action is more interesting, not only because it is unusual, but also because its outcomes are uncertain (Browning & Boudes, 2005). Taking action is the proof of a character's autonomy; the autonomous actor not only makes choices for him or herself, but also takes action, reaps the rewards, suffers the consequences, and sets an example for the rest of us.

When someone takes action, both the actor and others make assessments of what is taking place, and the character development of the actor is affected by the actions that take place through the consciousness of the meaning of his or her actions (Straub, 2006). We have many familiar terms for such interpretations of actions and learning from them—time on the job, experience, growth, meaning, and a teachable moment—but the direction in this section draws down to a narrower band of analysis. Weick, across his career (1969, 1979, 1995, 2001), uses the term "enactment" to refer to the composite of action and meaning. It is comprised of sensegiving (i.e., what is going on that gives structure to what is taking place), and sensemaking (i.e., the interpretation that occurs as a result of that action). Action is doubly valuable as a narrative concept. First, it is what happens in narratives; actions are responses to what came before. Second, it alters the meaning of the context in which it is taken. Actions are indications of the kind of situation the actor thinks s/he is in. It's like saying that actions are responses to situations and also texts to be interpreted (Taylor & Van Every, 2000). What does it mean? It means, "this could be my big chance," "we aren't dead yet"; it means, "maybe this is the light at the end of the tunnel," it means, "the same thing could happen to me." When we say narrative action is symbolic, we mean that people interpret it as text; they do an analysis of it and make larger interpretations of it. One thing that makes this story compelling is that the invitation to serve on the Commission was, for Fred Harris, both the opportunity of a lifetime and a poison pill to swallow.

Discourse and Action

Discourse is associated with action because it focuses on the content of communication (Clifford, 1988). In Harris' offering of the discourse of this story, despite the larger Commission Project that involved scores of professionals, he puts the spotlight on just four people—Harris' daughter, President Lyndon Johnson, Harris himself, and Jane Anne Jayroe. The story begins with a phone call, complete with a child innocently answering the phone in the kitchen and passing it on to her dad. In offering the invitation to serve on the Commission and in the same breath asking for a loyalty oath from Harris, President Johnson exemplifies both kinds of discourse categorized in this book. It is an example of little "d" discourse in that it occurs in a natural conversation between two people. The same conversation is big "D" discourse because a larger ideology is at work (i.e., whose domestic philosophy is being enacted at the moment of invitation and before any work on the report is started).

Discourse in the Harris story provides a hint for our understanding of action. What Salancik and Pfeffer (1977) discovered about power applies equally well to action. Everyone thinks it is important and everyone has a different idea about what it means. Action can mean a military squad taking the hill or a subordinate taking a stand at a meeting. It can mean having a voice and being willing to speak up when no one else does. In Harris' report of his part in the Kerner Commission, several actions stand out. In addition to the powerful and dominating words of the president that exemplify action, Harris' work on the Commission and his (along with others') willingness to address a problem confronting the country, show the different kinds of action at play in this story.

Agents and Agency

The term "agency" has two quite different meanings for narratology. On the one hand, it is the capacity to take independent action (i.e., it is a synonym for autonomy). On the other hand, being an agent can mean doing someone else's bidding. This second form of agency, familiar to those who study organizations, is exemplified in the nineteenth century by the Indian Agent (Porter, 1986) and in the twentieth century by the FBI agent. The agent is dispersed and perhaps given a territory to be responsible for, and as a result follows a set of purposes and rules established by others that causes agents to perform actions they would not otherwise do. Agents may also struggle with the moral dilemma of determining whether to do what they are obligated to do or what they believe is right. This dilemma of obligation and independence often becomes a point of contention in a story.

The Harris story turns on the negotiation of agency. President Johnson sees Harris as an agent of John Lindsay; Harris sees himself as an autonomous agent. Something that makes this story particularly interesting is the mixed idea of action and agency Johnson imposed on Senator Harris. On the one hand, he was being appointed to a commission investigating the race riots. Harris was a popular and populist Democrat from a conservative and rural state, so his work on the Commission would offer him national recognition for his efforts and demonstrate his identity across the United States for both whites and people of color. The Commission had the additional advantage of being bipartisan, which increased the credibility of the Commission and its findings. On the other hand, Senator Harris was being enrolled as an agent of the president, even though he may have had no inkling at the time about how his loyalty as an agent would be tested.

Action is often related to agency in indirect ways that call for reflection. Ricœur says, "It is the very proposal of 'making history' that calls for the step backward from the future toward the past. Humanity, we have said with Marx, only makes its history in circumstances it has not made" (1984, p. 216). You have to be dealt a hand to be able to play the game. What one does with the hand one is dealt is the narrative and the moral question: it is not merely meeting goals; it is an assessment of what one does with the resources one has (Wildavsky, 1979). The notion of circumstances thus becomes an indicator of an inverted relation to history. "We are only the agents of history inasmuch as we also suffer it" (Ricœur, 1984, p. 216). This is in keeping with the vulnerable nature of the character in the narrative: Sometimes our lives are ironic—the more we push for something, the less likely we are to have it. An agent traverses power relations that have a negotiated order

(Nathan & Mitroff, 1991). Someone acting as an agent interprets the world from his or her own power position in relation to others who are doing the same thing.

Actants, Sequence, and Complications

The Harris–Johnson story has an explicit and identifiable beginning (the problem of race riots in America), a middle (a report is published with much fanfare), and an end (Johnson demeans Harris at a White House photo shoot). Yet, decades later the Kerner Commission is celebrated as a journalistic moment with a seminar in the Lady Bird Johnson room at the University of Texas at Austin, which gives the story still another ending that we elaborate in a section below.

One of the premier writers on narrative action is Julien Greimas, a French scholar whose work has been brought to English-reading organizational communication audiences in the writings of Taylor and Van Every (2000). The work of Greimas elaborates the idea of action by expanding the possibilities for what actors in narratives do beyond protagonistic action. Greimas uses the neologism "actants" to describe the different characters of a narrative and he accounts for six forms of actant positions that are contrasted in three sets of interrelated pairs. First is the Sender and the Receiver, and the actor is capable of being either.[3] The Sender takes initial action; the Receiver is the beneficiary and marks the effects of the action. The second pair comprises Helper and Opponent, which are prominent in mythical representations of stories by such authors as Joseph Campbell (2008) and Paul Ricœur (1985). Third is Subject and Object, which jointly refer to the item of value competitors are jousting over (Greimas & Ricœur, 1989; Taylor and Van Every, 2000). In the Fred Harris story, President Lyndon Johnson initiates the story as the Sender and Fred Harris responds, as he does in the phone call as the Receiver in the literal moment he picks up the telephone in the kitchen, but Harris' daughter who is the innocent intermediary in this initial conversation alters the receivership in this sequence. The Sender focuses on an Object that the Receiver responds to with some kind of support or opposition. These six terms capture Greimas' different actant positions. The Object in this story takes three forms, the membership on the Commission, the Commission report itself, and the potential reputational gains. In the Greimas model, the Sender initiates or enables the event and is the one who causes the action. The Receiver benefits from or registers the effects of the event. Harris is the beneficiary of this event, which is affirmed by his accepting the Commission position. The Opponent retards or impedes the event by opposing or competing with the subject for the Object. In this story, the Sender, President Johnson, later takes up the Opponent position and hints at his possible opposition at the moment he offers the gift of the Commission membership. The Helper in Greimas' model advances the event by supporting or assisting the Receiver, but the Helper role is a side bar or a footnote in the Harris story. The Helper could be New York City Mayor John Lindsay, Vice Chair of the Commission or it could be other Commission members and the staff that did the research for the report. The relatively short length of time to get the report out—it was resear-ched, written, and completed in seven months—can be interpreted as an agent of support for the work of the Commission, but the Helper is largely invisible in this story.

The Johnson–Harris opposition is an archetype for a conflict narrative that shows the action of the players. Taylor and Van Every (2000) have remarked that Greimas' treatment of narrative is particularly economical in that it lays out the bare bones of a proponent and opponent that are overt in the Sender–Receiver pairing. For an action to take place and for a narrative to happen, it is additionally compli-cated by the likelihood of there being some kind of an adversary. Someone else has a different point of view, is a member of a different camp, and has a different set of values, whose actions are rewarded by an ingroup just as much as the proponent's are. This conflict is overt in this story.

In such adversarial narratives, there are really two stories going on, and, as we will address later in the chapter on sequence and locale, when two actors' actions intersect such that there is a conflict, we have the makings of an interesting story. The two stories, the Sender's and the Receiver's, go on simultaneously. And since there are two stories, the value of outcome depends on what story is being told for whose interests. In the Harris story, one interpretation of the president's motives is that he is managing an unpopular war, doubts that he could implement the solutions that the report might advocate, and already has a pet solution anyway. Harris has ambitious political goals and later unsuccessfully runs for the presidency. He is a liberal senator from a conservative state and, as the spouse of a Comanche Indian, he has credibility with people of color in the United States. In this story, action leads to an outcome that has a moral tinge.

In another perspective on actants, the notion of story complication helps us to explain the Harris–Johnson narrative. In Labov and Waletzky's (1997) formulation, and in Labov's (2006) extension, complicated action evolves over time in the con-tinuous chaining out of the event. Action is especially complicated at the point it becomes equivocal, which means that the complication in the story is unclear because the correct path of action is not obvious; it requires an interpretation. Labov and Waletzky (1997) identify six distinct functions in fully formed narratives to set up the complication. The first feature is the *abstract*, which is the overall setting. In the Harris story, the abstract setting is the race riots in American cities in 1967, which follow the sequence of the Civil Rights legislation in 1964. Second is the *orientation*, which signals the direction that the narrative is taking. The orienting action is Johnson's establishing the Commission itself, which is a fact-finding, data-oriented approach to the problem; establishing a commission also acknowledges that the solution to the problem is unclear. Third is the *complicating action*, which identifies what surfaces as problematic. In Harris' account, his relationship with the president is the complicating action. Fourth is the *evaluation of the action*, the first version of moral history. As Harris tells the story, the first stakeholder for the Commission report is the president himself, who did not like what he saw because, from the beginning, it was not what he wanted the report to conclude. Fifth is the *resolution of the action*, which is the story that interpreters walk away with. In Harris' story, the resolution of the action occurs interpersonally when he attends the event at the White House and is verbally attacked at a ceremony that was intended to be a moment of recognition and celebration for his state's achievements. The final and sixth step in a narrative is a *summary or coda*, or how the story is really understood or misunderstood over time. Harris' presentation at the School of Communication in recognition of the fortieth year of the report fulfills this function. In essence, Harris answers: "What really happened?" Franzosi (1998) observes that of these six parts, the complicating action is essential if we are to recognize a narrative. It constitutes the core of the narrative and usually comprises a series of events that make up the complication (Bruner, 1986; Franklin, 1986; Taylor, 2000). Someone is "doing something," and this action, either explicit or implicit, focuses our interest in narratives (Ricœur, 1984).

While a complicating action fits nicely into the Harris story, the contributions from the narratologists on action show that a complicating action can come from several sources. It can stem from the vulnerability of the person doing the action. He or she may have doubts, lack skills to accomplish the object, or may have a vision of the goal that is greater than can be achieved. Paul Ricœur (1965) stresses that one of the interesting things about action is that it is done by a person who is fallible, has the capacity to make mistakes, and who therefore has internal weaknesses to overcome. Because the action takes place as part of a scene that includes other actors, these others, and their own arrogance and doubts, are multiplying sources of complications. Johnson and Harris are no exceptions. One of the special features of a narrative, in fact, is how it draws together or is capable of including all kinds of characters in a single story. For that reason, multiple characters, in all their unpredictable, individual ways, add surprise, complexity, and richness to the story being told.

The Fred Harris story also exemplifies another source of complication that can be added to the Labov listing, which is the social nature of public behavior. Weick refers to this as one dimension of sensemaking (2001). The more public the behavior, the more likely the actions taken by the person will be seen as a model to follow, or one to be portrayed by an opponent as failing to meet the test. Where leadership actions are concerned, in particular, there is a desire for consistency. The social nature of complicated action means that leaders have a wider audience, including others who are close to them, who are viewing their behavior and making an assessment. Even though these members may not take direct action in the scene, they have the capacity to observe and make assessments of the actor's behavior and comment about it. These assessments become a part of the events that require management. Because the actant role can switch easily, in more contemporary notions on narrative, there is the additional consideration of "reflexivity." Not only does a person or agent take action and find out the response to that action from others, but also he or she may change as a result.

Abstract Operations

Actants have in common an arrangement of actions that serve a particular purpose. We are more interested in a narrative when we ask, "What is someone trying to do here?" "What are they trying to accomplish?" "What is the larger issue?" According to Taylor and Van Every (2000), Greimas treats the presence of actors and opponents in narratives as an indication something bigger is going on. In fact, Greimas terms these "abstract operations" (Greimas & Ricœur, 1989) to capture the transmissibility of the point of a narrative—how particular details come to have a larger meaning for listeners and readers. The narrative demonstrates that a larger story concerning value structures is being enacted within the narrative. In other words, stories and actions are really representations of values. Actors do things for a reason, and while we are seeing a story, the larger values that are being enacted by the proponent and the opponent are really what the story is about. The details are the vehicle. This reflective, representational component in narrative is also represented in Ricœur's thinking (1985). An interpretation of the abstract operations shows that the inter-personal political exchanges of commitment and betrayal ("Are you a Johnson man? Yes sir!") are secondary to the larger issue the Commission addresses. What is the cause of, what is the explanation for, African American discontent in the United States three years after the passage of the Civil Rights Act of 1964 that struck down discrimination laws in the United States? What explains the destruction and loss of life in urban America, when there sits in the highest office in the land a president who stands for the hope of equality?

Action occurs in the context of fallibility and possible error. Thus, we are only interested when we don't know what the next sequence is. We don't know whether the outcome is going to be realized; we don't know whether the character will meet the moral test or not. Thus, action takes place in the context of risk that places the will of the person in the narrative on display. Ricœur puts it this way: "Nothing in the world—indeed nothing even beyond the world—can possibly be conceived which could be called good without qualification except a good will" (2004, p. 491). Important in Ricœur's qualification is that what happens in stories is often paradoxical. Good intentions can turn out badly and opponents sometimes provide positive direction that a supporter could not even have imagined.

Action and Symbols

Action is the very center of organizational life. Our hope for control is acted out symbolically and ritually, which is why managers, despite their worry that it is a waste of time, spend time at celebrations, plant openings, and other signs of action and control (March, 1994). All of us, not just managers, put so much stock in the action embedded in narratives because they reinforce our belief that "human destiny (is) subject to intentional human control ... [Through narratives] we embrace the mythologies and symbols of life and could not otherwise easily endure" (March, 1994, p. 65). Points of symbolic communication are marked throughout the Harris story, including the establishing of the Commission itself. But we place special attention on still another moment when little "d" and big "D" discourse (Fairhurst, 2007) come together, and that is at the ritual celebration of Miss America at the White House. Given all the routines for a male politician in the United States, the opportunity to celebrate the achievement of one of his state's native daughters must be a glorious one. In 1967, the Miss America contest was still a popular media event, and a state having a winner represented a moment of celebration and recognition. But what happened during this ritual of Sooner state pride was turned, in a micro-moment, to one of personal degradation as a payback for promise breaking. Harris had affirmed that he was a Johnson man, but his report proved to the president that Harris had, in fact, betrayed him. And while the president could not literally castrate a United States senator, he could do so symbolically (you are down with another man's knee on your neck), and he could do it in front of the beauty queen whom both men were there to honor.

Few stories are so stark and consequential as the conflict between the president of the United States and a US senator. Action is ubiquitous in less significant circumstances. But more mundane instances have all three concepts, taking action, having reasons for doing so, and assessing the moral outcomes, in common with the preceding example. In the next section, we explain how this trio operates in day-to-day affairs by addressing the official requirement for missions, goals, visions, and performances in relation to the practical exigencies of emotion, hope, retrospection, vulnerability, risk, and dramaturgy.

The Nexus of Action, Motivation, and Moral Outcomes

Action, motivation, and moral outcomes—or as Stanley Fish (2010) would call it, learning—are especially tightly connected by the clarity and sense of the mission being undertaken. Ricœur says, "Nevertheless, a new ethics marks the linkage of freedom to hope—what Moltmann calls the ethics of the mission (*Sendung*); the promissio involves a missio; in the mission, the obligation which engages the present proceeds from the promise, opens the future" (1974, p. 408). Whether it is the hero's story of slaying the dragon to save the princess, hiding in the Trojan horse to win the war, or making a dress out of old drapes to bypass the patron's miserliness in the movie *Gone with the Wind*, stories are made interesting when purpose and goals, especially if they are disparate, are at play in the story. The mission of an organization, for example, is simultaneously an effort to organize sequences of action, a way of galvanizing attention, and an attempt to control.

Action is a popular concept in narrative understanding because it stands in for and represents goals, especially when goals are understood to be linked with a particular person who is obligated to act upon them. As Ricœur says, the very term 'action,' taken in the narrow sense of what someone does, gets its distinct meaning from its capacity for being used in conjunction with other terms of the whole network. Actions imply goals, the anticipation of which is not confused with some foreseen or predicted result, but which commit the one on whom the action depends.

(1984, p. 55)

The goal emphasis in this quote is very useful in this book. We are writing about the workplace, and one primary distinction between the workplace and other sites is the goal orientation; that is a key feature of a rational organization.

The awareness of the tie between narrative, action, and goals means that it is sometimes used consciously as a way of placing focus on action. One of the ways of doing this is bringing to the forefront action that leads to an image of the future of goal accomplishment. The vision story can be viewed as a form of modelling. It shows people the future in such detail that it produces a type of virtual experience of it, thereby facilitating a form of vicarious learning (Levin, 2000). For example, in his consultations using narrative, David Snowden generates vision stories in this way: he has his participants review past projects to identify a fateful moment when their project might have failed, which enables them to see how close they came to failure and how they might avoid it in the future (Browning & Boudes, 2005). Through these imagined narrative experiences, people gain an intuitive feel for and visceral understanding of the desired future. This increased appreciation of the future, especially what it could be, helps people to personalize the narrative and assimilate the learning of new behaviors and performance expectations the story makes.

Our concept of action, motivation, and moral outcomes includes the idea of performance because motivation almost always requires some kind of action as proof that something is happening. Stories contain who did what—or at least make that the mover of the story. Motivation is best understood as producing a positive outcome, or at least identifying the source of some person's (extra)ordinary behavior (Franklin, 1986). Corvellec claims that for motivation, a performance must have the following five features to have any meaning (1995, p. 183). First, there is evident production. A motivation and performance story is a tale of pleasing a stakeholder—someone for whom the story will have meaning. Second, motivation in a performance story has clarity; it must be specific enough that a listener can make sense of what the story means. Third, it must have lexical context. Vocabulary and linguistic structure make up the story. Fourth, the story must have legitimization. What is the "buzz" of the achievement? What performance paradigm is being enacted—ascent, decline, or plateau (Browning, 1991)? And, fifth, a motivation and performance story must include the actor's view of his or her own and others' performances. In performance stories, actors are conscious of their own and others' behaviors.

Actors in performance stories must be able to talk about what they've done in a clear and compelling way. This assignment of cause and order in stories is the act of giving them meaning that makes them memorable; individuals remember coherent wholes more than they do scattered fragments. It is necessary to have motivation for memory to be activated. "Organizing events into a temporal progression is the process of meaning creation" (Corvellec, 1995, p. 183). For Corvellec, the interpretation of events becomes the carrier, or vehicle, for distributing blame and credit. As part of the action-motivation-moral outcomes triad, even those who are merely interested in the pleasures of a story are interested in the outcome, and even when process—how things were done—is central, the listener is "interested in the event's result" (Corvellec, 1995, p. 102).

Sometimes, the world as we know it is transformed dramatically as a result of someone's incredible action, and the possibility of such transformation is the foundation of hope. For Ricœur, the hermeneutics of religion is an elevating belief in hope. Action emphasizes the practicality and doability the term implies, but groundless hope is not practical. Ricœur warns against utopian views that are so grand that when they are incomplete, the result is despair. In cinema, we see hope in the eyes of the actor who views a distant horizon. "We must resist the seduction of purely utopian expectations. They can only make us despair of all action, for, lacking an anchorage in experience, they are incapable of formulating a practical path directed to the ideals that they situate 'elsewhere'" (Ricœur, 1984, p. 215). In this way, Ricœur, the narratologist, is in agreement with the industrial psychologist, who encourages moderate goals that can be achieved with diligent work, rather than grand goals that are beyond comprehension (Cooper & Locke, 2000). "Our expectations must be determined, hence finite and relatively modest, if they are to be able to give rise to responsible commitments" (Ricœur, 1984, p. 215).

Ricœur's moderate goals may lead to responsible commitments, but do they lead to a narrative? One feature of contemporary culture is to have a story that is finite and relatively modest; this is truer in the work world than in the personal world. How do you produce a story out of moderate goals? You do so by arranging goals that everyone can meet with reasonable effort, but the combination of which leads to something special, even transformational.

Another component of action, motivation, and moral outcomes is responsibility. Mary Douglas (1992) reminds us that in any culture the most important issue is how blame is assigned. At least in the West, the individualistic nature of agency means that we own what we do. As Ricœur (1984, p. 55) says:

> Actions, moreover, refer to motives, which explain why someone does or did something, in a way that we clearly distinguish from the way one physical event leads to another. Actions also have agents, who do and can do things, which are taken as their work, or their deed. As a result, these agents can be held responsible for certain consequences of their actions.

When we think of the what, who, how, and when in a way that draws plausible links among them, we call it "practical understanding" (Ricœur, 1984, p. 55). The tie of action to practical understanding is useful because action in relation to the plot marks the confluence of actors and events in how the story is resolved.

Action is a dispersed concept that applies to the reader, the author, and the narrative actor. We employ an interpretation and assessment of action and use estimations of what we imagine we would do in the circumstances as a yardstick for judgment (Fisher, 1984). In support of this argument, MacIntyre asserts that we make actions intelligible by giving them an historical character. Since we act out and live out narratives in our own lives, we use the same scheme for "understanding the actions of others," and in that sense, "Stories are lived before they are told" (MacIntyre, 1981, p. 11).

The historical character of action means that it only becomes action after an interpretation is made. While action has an up-front, "just do it," athletic component, it only has meaning when there is an historical trace behind it. Sarbin claims that all stories, from fairy tales to psychological theories, are "compounds of happenings and imaginings" (1986, p. 12). And he means by "compounds" the paired relationships between "happenings and imaginings." Because we are usually working with bounded rationality and "limited epistemic and linguistic skills" that allow no certain, direct, and explicit connection between empirical events, we organize "them into an imaginative formulation that meets one or more tests of coherence" (Sarbin, 1986, p. 12). The occurrence of compounds of happenings and imaginings means that our assembly of them into story form takes place at all levels of interpretation.

Moving from a practical sense of action as it is reflected in goals, we move to a more emotional one, which is represented by hope, an intense personal urge even when there may be scant reason to believe. "In contrast to tones of alienation, anomie, and despair, Ricœur proclaims a revival of hope" (in the translator's preface to Ricœur, 1974, p. xxiii). Hope is in opposition to systemic control and "hope is destined to open what system tends to close up" (p. xxiii). Such desire is bound in the present because, "hidden in the present is the promise of the future" (p. xxii). For Ricœur these emotional concepts connect action with an imagined anticipated set of circumstances. Hope means looking beyond the present as a source of motivation; it is a dream of a future state despite the present outlook.

Motivation is connected to action because we resort to the concept of motives in order to make sense of what happened in the past. White (1980, p. 24) puts it this way: the appeal of historical discourse is that "it makes the real desirable, makes the real into an object of desire, and does so by its imposition, upon events that are represented as real, of the formal coherency that stories possess." In short, the subjective way we structure actions into events is a convenience to make them sensible. It is important to recognize that (some would say all) our efforts to assign motives are retrospective in nature. A powerful and prominent theme of the second half of the twentieth century is the extent to which sensemaking is retrospective, and this certainly applies to the ascription of the causes of action.

Even from the perspective of an actor who sets goals and then sets off to reach them, action and motivation can reverse order. Action can lead to motivation as a result of a "priming effect" of setting up a way of thinking. A person working on a project can be motivated because yesterday's actions proved successful and worthwhile; thus continuing with them only makes sense. Analogously, in Halberstam's (1994) book about the Yankees–Cardinals World Series in 1964, a pitching coach guiding a young pitcher to develop good habits said to him, "Your body wants to do what it did yesterday." The ability of present motivation to arise from past action makes the concept of the gratuitous act (Kennedy & Gioia, 1995, p. 70) problematic.

Motivation that leads to action can come from so many sources, including inspiration, loss, efforts to emulate another person, and innumerable others. McAdams' (2006) recent book on narrative chronicles a series of such reasons for action. For him, action can come from people who have had tragedy in their lives, such as being left alone, living in poverty, being abused, or being overwhelmed in some way. Strength can evolve despite paltry and challenging beginnings. Oprah Winfrey's story is a classic example. Conversely, action also takes place because of privilege. People who are given the opportunity to take on a role in the world take it on as a responsibility to do something special because of their privilege. In short, action can be driven by motivation arising from either difficulty or advantage.

Taking risky action can become its own motivation (Lyng, 2010). In the United States, action is strongly associated with adventure (Scheibe, 1986). For example, prior to marriage ceremonies in the USA, not only do men and women have bachelor parties, they press for an unusual happening within such an event to mark ritually its specialness. Action taking place in the context of risk is developed in the work of Erving Goffman in his book, *Interaction Ritual* (1967), specifically in the chapter, "Where the action is." In this text, Goffman relates various kinds of gambles in which individuals place themselves in dangerous or fateful circumstances: that is, circumstances where things might become problematic and might be dire for the person who fails to negotiate the challenge successfully. Action is central to his approach to risk and the connections he draws between risk and character. Goffman sees the composure, decorum, and skill displayed under voluntary risk as symbolic and representative of one's character. In his earlier work, Goffman develops the symbolic representation of action by calling it a dramaturgical approach, and we will follow that line of reasoning here.

The dramaturgical approach views action in social life as similar to acting on the stage. Rather than being selected because they are necessarily smartest, most efficient, safest, or most morally correct or expedient, actions are chosen because of what they will say about the actor. The actor's motives are primarily to give off an impression, such as of being cool, considerate, or adventurous (Dillard, Browning, Sitkin, & Sutcliffe, 2000). In the dramaturgical view, character evaluation tends to be essentializing and bifurcated. It is essentializing because single actions are taken to indicate a person's overall character. They are bifurcated in that a person's character is imagined to be either extremely strong or extremely weak. Thus, single actions that people take can come to represent who they are taken to be. The dramaturgical scheme includes a series of kinds of character including courage, gameness, integrity, gallantry, and composure. Goffman also writes of "stage" composure that an actor brings to a scene. This emphasis suggests that the presentation of self that a person displays has the capacity to make others believe in her or him. Such examples as "poker faces" or a "con job" that a deceiver must perform to cause the foil to believe they are not being conned fit this type of character.

It would be a mistake to think that this approach to action, motivation, and moral outcome only applies to risk taking by those at the top. Each organizational actor's character is always on display. In fact, organizational actors face a bind in that by being prudent, they can do what is practically necessary, but this will not provide any positive evidence of character. People are required to engage in some sort of action that places their character at risk to even signify that they exist. The kinds of actions that are predictable, such as routines, doing exactly what is said, following protocols, or operating in situations where there is no ambiguity would, from a dramaturgical standpoint, barely qualify as actions. Once again, risk is tied to fallibility. We are impressed with action in stories when characters take a risk, transcend a shortcoming, become stronger, and develop as a character as a result of the action they have taken.

In summary of the discussion to this point, a primary feature of a narrative is that something is taking place. This usually means that some person, some being, is acting. The action that she or he takes is the prime interest of a story. A person takes up a problem—something that needs to be done—that is based on an incompleteness or vulnerability, even a fragility of the actor, so that she or he doesn't know what the outcome is going to be. Thus, the action is a risk—and that risk can be for "oneself" or for many others, such as when military commanders send troops or sailors in harm's way; their actions have effects, possibly life and death effects, on others.

Motive comes into play to allow the reader or listener to make a causal connection about why the action is taking place. The motivation could come from others, such as in an assignment. It could come from socialization or ideological enculturation or some kind of life's preparation that says, in effect, "This is worthwhile for us to do; it is worthwhile for you to do." The assessment of that action over time is the moral of the story. A simple formula for making a moral assessment of the action is calculating a difference score: the beginning circumstance is subtracted from the final circumstance to make the net moral assessment. Is what happened between point A and point B worthy of praise or blame?

Any action can be assessed as being done well or poorly, correctly or wrongly. Therefore, one of the prime uses of narratives is to defend oneself against another's accusation or reproach. This is what happens when a person wants to get out of hot water by giving an account that says, "Although I was attempting to do this honorable thing, I encountered a set of circumstances in which I was unable to do what was expected, so I did what anyone could be expected to do under the circumstances." That kind of account, termed by Austin (1961) an excuse, shows the extenuating circumstances of failed or inappropriate action. Another account, the justification, cites the higher purposes the actor was attempting to achieve or shows that the actions didn't result in much harm or the victims deserved it (Scott & Lyman, 1968). This kind of accounting is also used in investigations and in court testimony where actions have been questioned on the grounds of being immoral or illegal or otherwise inappropriate. The teller of such accounts is explaining why behavior that was thought to be illegal really was not, or was actually honorable, and so forth. With these kinds of accounts there is an air of attack and defense. One person finds fault with another for behavior he or she has exhibited, and the other, now an alleged offender, answers these charges with efforts to restore his or her good character.

Obviously, the ability to account puts a premium on an active memory. Because linking acts and action into meaning is both constant and crucial, Ricœur sees remembering as a cognitive action: "Remembering is not only welcoming, receiving an image of the past, it is also searching for it, 'doing' something. The verb 'to remember' stands in for the substantive 'memory'" (Ricœur, 2004, p. 56). Memory is tied to searching; a memory that is consciously retrieved seems to be valued over the accidental memory—but the accidental memory is more interesting.

To relate the above back to narrative, the accounts we give are narratives we tell to influence the meanings others might ascribe to any and all of our actions. One of the outcomes of action is the summary story-listeners, and indeed, we ourselves, walk away with. As Polkinghorne (1988, p. 14) says, "The products of narrative schemes are ubiquitous in our lives: they fill our cultural and social environment." In this way, action is connected to sensemaking consistent with Weick's (1995) scheme for it. In Polkinghorne's words, "We create narrative descriptions for ourselves and for others about our own past actions, and we develop storied accounts that give sense to the behavior of others" (1988, p. 14). The sense we make about what happened up until now, in turn, influences how we anticipate and design our subsequent actions in the future. For the individual actor, engaging in narratives about action, delving into motives, and assessing moral outcomes changes how he or she might view risk, performance, social requirements, what others said, and how yesterday's actions affect today's motivations. It even affects whether a person awakes in the morning, puts his or her feet on the floor, and has volition for the day. For the individual actor, "vitality" points to living a meaningful narrative. It includes a lively openness to alternatives. "It has purpose. In effect, it has hope" (Randall & McKim, 2008, p. 111). A good narrative has direction; it has a story line (Polster 1987). "It stretches outside itself and into a wider world, to lives and stories of others" (Randall & McKim, 2008, p. 111).

Application: Explanation

In the application section of each of the chapters, we offer an example of a concrete use of the angle presented in the chapter. We select explanation for the angle in this chapter because of its ubiquity in organizational life, in the academy, and for personal accountability. When we construct explanations, we have at our disposal the full range of action, performance, and moral concepts we have been discussing. Explanations can be stories that tell not only what happened, but also delve into the actors' goals, intentions, hopes, and outcomes. Explanations often include exacting descriptions of the circumstances of action, the complications faced, and deliberate efforts to accept or deflect responsibility. As we have seen, the ability to successfully to explain ourselves has tremendous reputational consequences. Moreover, the explanatory power of narratives has been a topic of conversation in history and science for more than a century. The epistemological status of narratives has been in contention since the mid-nineteenth century, when history was carving out a place for itself as an academic discipline and needed to establish what would count as knowledge claims. According to Polkinghorne (1988), for history to be accepted as a discipline it was required initially to provide the same proofs as science. This was unworkable and the definition shifted to history as a quasi-science because explanation required a mix of proofs. It could be accounted for with an event, such as the German bombing of London during the Second World War, and it could be measured and quantified, such as American public opinion toward the war prior to the Japanese attack on Pearl Harbor. From this mixed position, the idea developed that history could not be a science of prediction. Instead, it unfolds narratively, over time. There are surprises, quick turns, and unanticipated consequences. For example, American support for guerilla warriors in Afghanistan, in effect, trained and seasoned a force that would attack the United States on 9/11/01. Since the ironies and turns of history can only be known in retrospect, and since both causes and effects are traced backwards in time, the criteria of prediction and scientific proof that was raised in the nineteenth century for history is not possible. Finally, historical explanation, rather than being established for what it is not, is now compared with what it is. It is a narrative that unfolds like a novel. Fiction and non-fiction share dramatic and flawed characters, plot convergence for an array of causes that are often surprising, and interpretations that privilege one point of view or way of thinking over another. The purpose of an explanation is to take a moment, event, situation, or epoch and account for "Why did it happen?" (Polkinghorne, 1988, p. 44).

Investigating medical costs in McAllen, Texas. This story is told from the point of view of Dr. Atul Gawande, a surgeon and researcher at the Harvard Medical School, the story's protagonist. Beyond his surgical credentials, for the last 10 years of his professional life, Gawande has analyzed the cost of medical care in the United States and searched for ways to make it more effective. Gawande, rather than accepting the first stories he heard (about drinking, obesity) set out to triangulate his sources. In this story, he is the protagonist who goes on against resistance to unearth the truth about a case of profiteering and practices bordering on the unethical. One of his premises is that hospitals and clinics could decrease many costs by simply following standard procedures more carefully (Gawande, 2009a). He has written many examples of this idea that have been published in books and articles and is noted for his relentless effort to combat medical errors. He has also identified successful strategies for merely using checklists to address major problems such as reducing infections in hospitals.

For the story offered here, which we have excerpted from the *New Yorker* (Gawande, 2009b), Gawande won the 2010 National Magazine Award category for Public Interest. In this article, he investigates the delivery of medical care in the Rio Grande Valley of Texas, specifically the city of McAllen, Texas. What drove his curiosity was that in that city, the medical costs per capita are double the national average, and the annual medical costs of $15,000 per person is $3,000 per year above the average income of $12,000. This means that it is not only expensive for the region, it is also unsustainable for the country. Given Gawande's search for understanding medical costs in relation to effectiveness, he says, "McAllen, Texas, the most expensive town in the most expensive country for health care in the world, seemed a good place to look for some answers." One thing that makes Gawande's pursuit remarkable is his willingness to challenge the assumptions of the community of which he is a member. In this way, he risks being a traitor to his class—at least to his profession.

Gawande is especially qualified to examine medical costs, but he also wants to locate his analysis within a culture. He opens up possible answers to the problem by asking anyone who will offer an opinion. When he inquired of a police cadet why costs were so high, he got a knowing explanation: "Just look around," the cadet said. "People are not healthy here." Gawande confirms this by offering that the city had a drinking rate 60% higher than the national average and an obesity rate of 38%. And the number of conditions associated with these problems is apparent in who is treated for what—especially heart disease and diabetes.

As Gawande searched for answers, one thing became clear: over the past 10 to 12 years the cost of medical care for McAllen had shot up dramatically. Previously, costs for the city were similar to the national average, but in the last decade, costs had doubled while the quality of medical care, as exemplified by patient health, had actually deteriorated. As he searched for answers, the raw truth came out in a visit with a panel of doctors who worked in McAllen and knew what was going on. As they reviewed possible causes, "Come on," the general surgeon finally said. "We all know these arguments are bullshit. There is overutilization here, pure and simple." "Doctors," he said, "were racking up charges with extra tests, services, and procedures."

In that period of time, the model for practicing medicine had shifted from the delivery of medical care to a profit-centered practice. One surgeon Gawande interviewed came to McAllen in the mid-nineties, and observed, "the way to practice medicine has changed completely. Before, it was about how to do a good job. Now it is about 'How much will you benefit?'" To explore the validity of the surgeon's claim, Gawande turned to the national medical analysts and found that not only had expenses shot up dramatically, but also the actual quality of health care had gone down. As Gawande would conclude, in this instance more equals less. More time in a hospital, more testing, more medications all have risks and can result in worse outcomes for the patient, not better ones.

As an entrepreneurial model had developed in McAllen, doctors managed to collect not only their fees for providing services, but also a percentage of the hospitals' profits. When they ordered tests or performed surgery, they got an extra cut. As one hospital administrator told Gawande, such an incentive "gives physicians an unholy temptation to over-order." As Gawande pursued why medical costs were so high in the area, he got genuinely surprised responses from the experts in the Valley he talked to. Many knew of one hospital guilty of drumming up charges, but no one knew the extent of the problem. Because hospitals are known to have lots of expenses, their main concern is cash flow. As a result, no one looks at costs in relation to outcomes in a systematic way. But what everyone does know is that "The most expensive piece of medical equipment," as the saying goes, "is a doctor's pen," and when doctors order more medical care than is needed, it is followed without question.

One possible explanation for the high costs was the use of testing and extra procedures to protect doctors from medical liability risks. But the State of Texas had capped the upper end of such lawsuits in the 1990s, and other medical regions in Texas with similar populations were providing medical services at half the cost per patient of McAllen. So, Gawande reasoned, that wasn't the cause.

One explanation Gawande considers is the difference in training for doctors. Some are educated in test-oriented environments; others are trained to defer medical costs if it can be done without risk to patients. Gawande implicates himself as he provides an answer. A few years ago, Gawande's own son had taken a tumble down a flight of stairs and suffered a concussion. The doctor at the hospital where his son was taken decided not to run additional tests because the boy seemed to recover that evening without obvious problems. But Gawande, with his own son's health in mind, pulled rank and insisted on more tests, which the doctor performed. When he later consulted the appropriate medical literature, Gawande discovered that the doctor who treated his son was correct—the tests Gawande had insisted on were not needed.

Gawande acknowledged that doctors are trained in different protocols for testing and treatment. But as he examined the amount of medical expenses being charged in McAllen, he reached the same conclusion as several local doctors who were unhappy about the direction medicine had taken in McAllen. As one surgeon said, "It's a machine, my friend." Some of the agency employees Gawande interviewed told of doctors requesting direct payment in exchange for sending their patients to a hospital. While the hospitals refused to bow to this pressure, it was there all the same. The instances were dramatic. One doctor asked for private school tuition for one of his children; "another wanted sex." With such volatile information coming from his interviews, Gawande's story moves from a study of medical statistics to a highly contentious investigation of professionals committing serious misconduct with potentially disastrous consequences.

Given the power of economic incentives, Gawande pondered on the way home from McAllen why more medical communities did not do the same thing. After all, there was a real fear of litigation, and there were instances where overcharging in one area was used to offset the costs of medicine that went unfunded. Yet,

Gawande holds up an example of two settings where medical care is driven by a different value and with a different set of practices. There is the case of the Mayo Clinic, which delivers medical care at half the costs of McAllen and with much better results. It does so by placing doctors on salary to avoid the problem of doctors trying to increase their income. Additionally, the Mayo group seeks input from everyone in the medical system when making decisions about patients. As one doctor from Mayo says, "When doctors put their heads together in a room, when they share expertise, you get more thinking and less testing." At the Mayo Clinic in Minnesota, "The aim is to raise quality and to help doctors and other staff members work as a team. But, almost by happenstance, the result has been lower costs." Sharing information and working through records and recommendations as a team of doctors and other staff also accounts for the high performance of Gawande's second example, the hospital system in Grand Junction, Colorado. In that system, the doctors mutually agreed upon a program that paid them a similar fee whether from "Medicare, Medicaid, or private-insurance patients." This reduced the incentive to select patients based on how much they could pay. They also agreed to meet regularly "on small peer-review committees to go over their patient charts together. They focused on rooting out problems like poor prevention practices, unnecessary back operations, and unusual hospital-complication rates. Problems went down. Quality went up." Gawande did not presume a local problem with a local solution; instead he identified national examples that could inform and change the way health care is delivered in the United States.

Gawande concludes by asserting that the solution to the medical crisis in the United States is to continue to search for settings that have high quality, low-cost solutions or practices, and someone who is held accountable for the totality of care. "Otherwise, you get a system that has no brakes. You get McAllen."

Conclusion

Gawande's explanation nicely illustrates how organizational action only makes sense retrospectively (Weick, 1979). It only serves as an explanation because Gawande assembles the case from an expert's eye view. Who else would have been able to probe the aggregate data to determine the validity of information? Who else would have developed the rapport with doctors in McAllen to tell him the truth of why this system operated as it did? Gawande's story also demonstrates how oddly innocent and incisive an explanation can be. Although accounting for "What happened here?" would seem to offer a fairly descriptive answer, in this story the result is a blistering indictment of the practices of the characters in the story. Even though the medical practitioners in McAllen are operating within the law, their behavior is reprehensible not only because of the costs of administrative practices and omissions, but also because of the unwillingness of colleagues who know what was going on to say and do anything about it.

The question hanging in the air as we conclude Gawande's story is: When does the story come to an end? Where does it move next? How did Gawande's analysis enter into the health care debate so alive in the United States in the succeeding years? In the next chapter on sequence and locale, we find answers to such questions by addressing the location of narratives in time and place.

4

SEQUENCE AND LOCALE

I shall be telling this with a sigh
Somewhere ages and ages hence:
Two roads diverged in a wood, and I—
I took the one less traveled by,
And that has made all the difference.
                              —Robert Frost

Introduction

The literature on narratives accords great importance to sequence, but attends less than it should to locale. In this book, we utilize sequence and locale together as an angle on narrative appreciation because we consider them both to be essential in locating the action and understanding its import. Sequence is about relationships between one act or event and another; sequence locates particular actions within the context of other actions. Locale, the scenic dimension of stories, locates actions in the particular places, often organizational settings, where the actions take place. Even though the literature underemphasizes locale, the position we adopt here is that stories that have sequences without locales *don't get anywhere*. By this we mean that they are less capable than more well-rounded stories of transporting readers and listeners to the scene of the action and, thereby, having a moving effect on them. Thus, when thinking of history and memory, we should also think of geography (Ricœur, 2004).

Robert Frost's poem most economically captures the interconnection of sequence and locale. It would not have said much had it been confined to the wistful observation that at a certain point in time, he made a consequential choice. The poem is brought to life in two key ways. First, it is enlivened by the image of the woods in which two roads diverged. Second, the temporal setting is extended. From a present point in time, Frost predicts a future emotional telling about his past choice to go his own way when, at a point in the past, he could have chosen the oft-traveled road. The moral of the poem, the importance of making one's own way, is conveyed via the poem's unique time-and-space signature. In Ricœur's terms, narratives are easier to recall because "the order of the places (preserves) the order of the things" (2004, p. 62).

We proceed in this chapter from Hawes' (1973, 1974) insistence that streams of communication should be studied in their spatio-temporal contexts. This amounts to an appeal to embrace the particularity of communication events, something that narratives are especially well suited to do, but a position to which most narratologists have not subscribed. We begin below with a review of several key narratologists' ideas about the centrality of sequence, then refer to Lyotard as a reminder of the importance of the spatial location of action in narratives. We next discuss how narrators construct or *choreograph* movement in time and space, focusing on how stories are punctuated and made coherent within plots. Punctuation concerns separating what is part of the story from what is not and arranging the parts into beginnings, middles, and endings. Plots are recognizable story forms around which particular events and places may be organized or with respect to which a new story may be recognized. A separate section of the chapter concerns stability and change in narratives. The concluding section of the chapter highlights the imagination application for narrative appreciation. With an illustrative story of underworld suspense, we display one of the imagination stories utilized in narrative research.

The Central Role of Sequence in the Narrative Literature

The "inherent sequentiality" (Bruner, 1990, p. 43) of narratives is among their most prominent features. A narrative is a combination of a sequence of events, motivations, and characters that are composed and arranged into an order that has special meaning. The sense of these ingredients of a narrative is determined by how they are placed into the structure of a story—or, in Bruner's terms, in the overall arrangement of the whole into plot or fibula (1990). Understanding a narrative is, in part, a combination of the listener's decoding the plot in relation to the constituent pieces and then reflexively placing the plot back into the sequence to make sense of it (Bruner, 1990).

Sequentiality is fundamental to the very definition of narratives. The meaning of the word narrative itself comes from the Latin *narre*, which means to make known. What makes a narrative distinctive from other ways of making things known, such as maps or dictionaries, is that it "presents information as a connected sequence of events" (Polkinghorne, 1988, p. 13). Collecting a series of events into an integrated whole gives narratives their "follow-ability" (Gallie, 1964). Narratives provide a form of temporal sequencing that involves the collection and arranging of events to be experienced by the listener in a causal manner (Rhodes & Brown, 2006). Causality in narratives, either explicit or implied, separates narratives from other forms of sequence, such as a chronicle, which is a mere listing of events (Brockmeier & Harre, 1997).

Paul Ricœur (1984, 1985) sees the role of sequence as central to the story and, connecting his definition of narrative to Aristotle's, he calls narrative "exactly what Aristotle calls muthos, the organization of the events" (Ricœur, 1984, p. 36). The narrator selecting and arranging what will be included in the story to be told accomplishes the organization of events. Much of the time, this arranging is overtly time-bound. Much of this arranging is done in the service of the plot, which is the moment that the forces in the story come together in a dramatic moment. We will have more to say about emplotment below.

Narratologists use the term "temporal logic" to address how events and actions come together and how understandings are generated as a result of the co-occurrence of events. Co-occurrence of two events can cause us to give them meaning for no other reason than that they are happening contiguously. Jung (1948) uses the term "syncretism" to refer to collecting diverse ideas into a loose, inexact, but meaningful combination. He asserts that if serial events, however dissimilar, intersect in the same unit of time, they will be assigned significance by the individual. Syncretism is a powerful temporal logic that shows up in the relationship among narrated actions and consequences. Narratives are built on Jung's syncretic intersection of forces. Beyond selecting events in a narrative because of their close time relationship, we sequence narratives from disparate and distant events and characters. When we make this arc across time to sequence events, we are usually doing so for integration and the ordering "serves as a lens through which the apparently independent and disconnected elements of existence are seen as related parts of a whole" (Polkinghorne, 1988, p. 36).

The Inseparability of Locale from Sequence

One of the key things we know about stories is that they make little sense, are hard to grasp, and are not very interesting without location in a particular time *and place*. For other communication concepts, a locale and moment are unnecessary for talking intelligently about them. For example, we could discuss a concept such as "organizational satisfaction" as a model or set of features and could extend discussing the idea without necessarily drawing out a particular example of it. There are lots of things to know about satisfaction and how it helps us to understand organizations before a story about satisfaction necessarily comes up. But in narratology, for a story to make sense, some idea of where and when it is happening must be identified— and fairly early. Such an awareness of time and place may be certain or it may be unclear to the actors. Where am I? How did I get here? The eponymous hero of the movie, *The Bourne Identity* is a popular contemporary example of a time and space mystery.

The inseparability of sequence and locale in narratives was demonstrated to the first author in a simple moment of narrative understanding. He asked his graduate students in a seminar on narrative theory to tell a story to introduce themselves at the beginning of the class. One woman in the class revealed her dismay about attending so many weddings in a summer, when none of them was her own. This woman's story of being continually the bride's maid but never the bride brings to mind the movie, *27 Dresses*. As she told it, she described driving to still another friend's wedding, getting lost, and being forced to plead with the change attendant on the freeway to give her the money to continue to the wedding. All the students, like this one, were able to locate and identify who *and where* they were in their stories. This brief telling of stories demonstrated that in a particular moment, it is nearly impossible to tell a story without locating a place and time for that story.

Our thinking about space has been organized under the concept of the local, which owes much to Lyotard's (1984) position that narratology applies almost not at all to the grand narrative or the master story of what is going on, even if actors are operating around a series of values that are consistent, transparent, and felt by every member in much the same way. Lyotard avoids the claim for strong cultures and master narratives by asserting that the local moment is everything to the story.

When Lyotard refers to a *petit récit*, or "little story," the sub-text is about a locality, an experience that occurs in a particular place and is thus limited in its breadth even if it has deep meaning for the actor. The story is dependent on its setting for narrative meaning. Whatever sequential path a story is in, the intersection of that sequence with an identifiable space—in a county, on a farm, in a city, in a nation— is naturally a part of our understanding of the story. This is especially true of stories of risk and fate. An especially drastic moment occurs when the listener is lead to ask, "what if s/he had been a minute later?" The fateful meeting can be the precise moment when two stories intersect.

A study of how relationships between pilots and technicians at a US Air Force base were constituted (Browning, Greene, Sitkin, Sutcliffe, & Obstfeld, 2009) illustrates the importance of spatial location. The authors tell how, near the flight line every morning, technicians conducted what they called the "Foreign Object Damage" (FOD) walk. They spaced themselves a few feet apart and searched every inch of the area where planes had been repaired in order to discover anything that might be left over from repairs that could damage the jet engines when they were started. The technicians even used magnets in their search for very small debris. The FOD walk was visible to all, especially to pilots, whose main work was located in the same space. Through the physical actions they performed in that space, technicians showed just how far they would go to protect the pilots.

One of the effects of local stories such as this is that memories are parochial rather than universal and the listener thus might take something different from a story than the teller intended (Boje, 1998). This point is especially relevant to those who want to use storytelling as a cultural control device. As Boje says, there is often an official story line of interpretation, when in fact members are "processing the many sides to stories to make sense of local change" (Boje, 1998).

The teller of the story accounts for the importance of place in a narrative and can either draw locale down to a specific place (as to a house) or more broadly (as in a city in a country without a name). In maximizing locale, the composer of the story selects and describes a particular place, and then demonstrates the meaning of the place by attaching the rest of the story to it. We quote Ricœur directly to make the point about locale and storytelling:

> This art consists essentially in associating images with places (topoi, loci) organized in rigorous systems corresponding to a house, a public place, an architectural setting. The rules of this art are of two sorts: the first govern the selection of the places, the second govern the mental images of the things one wishes to remember.
>
> *(2004, p. 62)*

Using the reliability of place to preserve order is a thread throughout this discussion of time and place. It refers to the importance of using conventions and meeting listener expectations about what usually occurs in given locales. The importance of spatial location becomes especially apparent when actions expected in one spatial domain are moved to a different one. *Ghostbusters*, for example, a 1984 movie about a collection of unemployed parapsychology professors who set up shop as a unique ghost removal service, was originally conceived to take place in outer space. This makes sense given the unworldly beings they are fighting. The characters have special gear and special clothing fit for that circumstance. But the movie producers decided to move it down to earth and, particularly, into the suburbs of Philadelphia. The result of this special locale replacement was a popular movie. But someone had to say: In what setting is this story more powerful? In what setting does this story make sense?

Much of the work on locale shows how its consideration narrows the story, places it in a local context such that a listener can say, "I see how someone in that place (in the basement of a hospital, in a war zone, in the rural south) would see and act toward the world in the way that they do." One of the versions of the particularity of stories is not only that individual perspectives come from different people, but they come from familiar people being in different places. We would expect someone who has been to Iraq (soldier, news reporter, contractor, native Iraqi) to see that location differently than someone who has seen and judged that war from afar. Such a perspective has to do with spatial relations, position—the place you are in while the action is going on. As distinctive as space may be, it is also malleable. When someone tells a local story, a common response for listeners is to move it to her/his place with new characters and say, "this could happen to me." In these tellings, there is a connection to the story: the person is simply re-placing it.

Choreographing Movement in Time and Space

The structuring of a story refers to the assemblage of components or ingredients the narrator brings to life in the story—the weather, the red phone, the drive toward something, the opponent whose views are flawed, the sponsor, etc. The narrator's reconfiguring of such pieces in the telling is powerful because what comes first has lots to do with all things that follow it. At least that's true in narrative and complexity theory. Sequence in a story that is particularly powerful, that marks the narrative in a particular way, is an example of what newspaper reporters used to call a "bacon-cooler." This is a reference to someone sitting at the breakfast table, reading the newspaper, eating bacon and eggs, and then suddenly stopping—with fork and bacon in mid-air—to focus on something surprising in the paper that grabs his or her attention. Most storytellers hope for such a moment when the sequence and the punch line come together with such force.

One of the brute facts of physical existence is that no two objects can occupy the same place at the same time. Because this is so, the choreographer of a dance must artfully arrange for dancers to encounter, embrace, and depart from each other, but not bash into or miss each other. The dancers enact carefully controlled and stylized collisions. Narrators make similar constructions when they decide which actors will get how close—recognizing that putting some actors together necessarily separates others.

Kenneth Arrow, the Nobel Prize-winning economist, elaborates the original conceptual work on the importance of sequence for decision-making. In his work *The Limits of Organization* (1974, p. 47), Arrow articulates the concept of social choice that affects sequence by saying, "it is implicit that the values of all relevant variables are at all moments under consideration." Choice becomes a part of decision-making not only from the array of thoughts of the content under contemplation, but especially the order in which these items are placed. The ordering of these choices is often called "agenda manipulation" in political and planning theory (Riker, 1982; Sager, 2001), but it is manipulation in the negative sense of the word because people naturally order sequences—whether it is a teenager doing the dishes before asking for the family car or a manager at an approval meeting with her boss who puts the riskiest request on the bottom of the stack and offers it contingent on how the boss responds to the first two less-important proposals during their meeting.

Within a given narrative, every potential ordering is unique. This exclusionary principle of narrative action, which is usually taken for granted, is nicely illustrated by a computer science model called the stable marriage algorithm (Mairson, 1992). Here is how it works in romance: given a population of men and women that is fifty-fifty, the algorithm takes an ordered list of preferences of men and women by pairing their choices with the goal of establishing pairs of relationships that will persist. (Notice it is assumed that, eventually, each woman will be with one man. It is also assumed that men and women prefer some potential partners over others.) The men and the women make a preferential ranking of each other to accomplish the pairing. Each man asking his first choice for a date does this. Then each woman with any offers says "yes" to her favorite and "no" to everyone else.

This completes the first sequence pairing of romantic partners. In the next round, men who did not get their first choice move to their second choice. Women again, after seeing the offers, accept their favorites, including dumping their first choice for a higher preference if it appears in the second round. This interaction continues over a series of sequences until "the dating frenzy subsides into a stable situation" where pairs are established (Robinson, 2004). Relationships become stable because even though a man may not get his first choice, he adjusts to his fate because he has no hope of getting any one better. The same is true for women. Such an algorithm is officially applied to all kinds of choice situations, including how medical students chose and are chosen for internships and the assignment of students to special slots in New York City high schools. The algorithm models the basics of a sequence. Things necessarily happen in an order, and lives are changed by the sequence in which events happen.

In reality, the sequence of choices is complicated by all kinds of narrative features, including the communication that goes on within any given sequence to increase one's standing and the strategies to change the ordering of choices once they have started by increasing the inducements to make one choice over another. The stable marriage algorithm is really only a list of steps, a formula, not a story (Browning, 1992). A narrative of relationship choice will not only contain a list of choices made, but will also narrate the context, especially the communication events, that surround and influence the choices made.

Consider this fictional example from the opening sequence of the popular American television show, *Gray's Anatomy*. In the beginning episode, Meredith Grey (the two spellings of Gray is one of the tricks of the series) shows up for her first day of residency at the hospital in Seattle that she'd hoped for. (In terms of the marriage algorithm, she got her first choice.) As the residents gather in the locker room and walk the halls, they discuss what their placement choices were, how they got to this hospital, and how satisfied they are with the placement. But Meredith Grey is envied because her peers think that her placement was probably affected by family ties—her mother was a famous medical doctor—whereas those who scraped and worked hard for their placement are sure that Meredith had a cushy ride to her placement. But Meredith's life is not cushy. Her famous mother is now demented and only occasionally knows who she is. Most of the time she is unconscious of the medical profession and her accomplishments in it. Her daughter meets her regularly but is pained by the lack of contact or history with her mother. Worse yet, in a moment of anxiety and alcohol before beginning her demanding residency Meredith had a one-night stand with an attractive man she hooked up with in a bar the night before. On her first day in the hospital, she discovers, by meeting him face-to-face, that her one-night stand is a famous doctor in the hospital where she now has her residency. The story augments her placement algorithm with the events and places that led to and from her fateful selections.

Punctuating Narratives

Aristotle provides the simplest yet most reliable definition of narratives when he says they necessarily have a beginning, middle, and end. As Riessman (1993, p. 79) claims, it is not possible to know what these three phases are except in relation to each other:

> The "beginning, middle and end" of narrative are not individual elements of a narrative but are defined in relationship to each other: the beginning can only be defined by its position in relation to the middle and end. For example, we cannot be sure of the significance of events at the beginning of the plot until we know how they are going to be disrupted.

While dramatic three-act plays tend to have the beginning, middle, and end in fairly equal sequences, this is less true of other narrative forms. The beginning may be extraordinarily long, the middle can be brief and poignant, and the ending long and elaborate. Similarly, if there is one, the disruption may only occur in order to be "put right" at the end. An endpoint without events leading toward or away is a conclusion without a story.

The greater the number of salient points demonstrating how actors proceeded from beginning to end, the more mature or well-developed the story is. The well developed story draws readers inexorably toward the end.

In front of this intention of the storyteller and at the root of the expectation of the one who listens to or reads a tale, there is, in general, the conclusion that draws the story forward. The listener anticipates and aims her or his expectation subconsciously towards an outcome. To integrate a story is to be able to "put the end in touch with the beginning, it is to be able to read the beginning as promise of the end" (Adam, 1996, p. 18).

The literature in narrative theory on beginnings and endings addresses when the narrator or actor enters a stream of behavior. Beginnings for some characters in stories can arrive at the middle and be abrupt. The new young wife of one of the old-time friends in the movie *The Four Seasons* comes to mind. Another example includes fresh soldiers, entering a battle, not realizing the requirement for boldness and safety, who step out and get killed when veterans of battle hold back. Beginnings and endings require one to ask, "where are we in the sequence?" What is going on here that requires more or less action in bringing the story to an end? The focus on endings typically resolves the conflict. We regularly talk about satisfying and unsatisfying endings (Abbot, 2008). The ending question in human stories is: when do they really end?

A story from the reconciliation program in Texas prisons (Szmania, 2004) helps to make this point. A young woman befriended two down-and-out men at a gas station in North Texas many, many years ago. To show their appreciation for being given a ride, they raped and shot her, then burned her body to avoid the evidence connecting them to her. But they were caught, convicted, and sentenced to prison. Twenty-five years later, the dead woman's mother and her daughter, who was a toddler at the time of the murder, arranged to meet one of the killers through a prison program that allows victims to meet and reconcile with perpetrators. During that single day, which took months for a third-party specialist to prepare for, the woman's survivors were told her last words on earth and were comforted that she died with forgiveness and dignity. In this case, the story continues years after the woman's death, and in effect, creates a new ending for the story. An awareness of context has much to do with when the story ends. Given this day of reckoning, when does the story really end? What is drawn to a close? Who narrates the final story?

What kinds of stories best typify the beginning, middle, and end sequence? The best are ones that identify the kind of sequence the character is in. Are you in the beginning? Are you the uninitiated? The newcomer? Stories about them are interesting because they seem to be paying more attention to what is going on; their observations are special; the eye of the newcomer sees things in a different way. They may be placed in environments that others are taking for granted. The striking nature of what they see is the basis for their curiosity.

Another kind of beginning sequence is the "honeymoon effect," which means, metaphorically, newcomers to a favorable situation have an initial period where nothing can go wrong—they are placed on a pedestal, all of life is good and things will be fine. We have such periods of non-evaluation for politicians, sons-in-law, managers, leaders, and newcomers to jobs where they are given a pass and are accepted with an eye toward the future, with the understanding that current performance and actions will change over time.

The opposite end of this sequence is people who are finished and are at the end of their phase in an assignment, such as in the military, when their attention is no longer on the present job, but on themselves or their next job. They may still be in the setting, but they are gone. The lights are on, but nobody is home, as if to say, "Don't bother me, I am gone! I am a short-timer; I have 24 days and a wakeup!" One of the stories in *Every Person's Life is Worth a Novel* (Polster, 1987) captures what happens when a person is in an area for a short period of time: he or she has no past or future in a place and as a result has no commitment to the people who live in that time and place. Another kind of ending is the Rebecca Effect, where a person who has died is remembered more positively than she or he was in life. The dead are remembered with special characteristics that are beyond what they had in life. To marry a person who holds such a memory is to be compared in a way that can never have a positive result. The punch line for this is, "Never marry a widow unless her husband was hanged." These stereotypical instances demonstrate that by simply knowing a character's placement in the sequence, we make assessments about her/him and attribute meaning for what a person thinks and does simply because of that placement.

Sequence in narrative contains punctuation that marks when it begins and when it ends, much like the punctuation at the beginning and end of a sentence. But it also addresses sequences internal to the narrative, how they are chosen, and how alternatives are considered. Our clinical understanding of sequences comes from Polster (1987). He claims that a therapeutic intervention is like writing and editing a movie—both settings are time-limited and necessarily time-conscious. In therapy, of all the possible things that could be included in the story, it is important *not* to include the totality. Instead, both the therapist and the movie editor are selective. They draw from the parts of the stream of experience those elements that make a difference, that add to the development and interest of the story, and thus shape the listener's interpretation and understanding of events. Only the sequences that make a difference, or could make a difference, in the understanding of a person's experience are included. Stories are made poignant by their efficiency.

In therapy and in movie editing, the goal is to select particular, pivotal moments. For movies, the question is, "What brings the story to life?" For therapy, the question is how to bring clients to an understanding of who they are through the selective interpretation of the things they have done or that have happened to them in their life history. Polster's therapeutic art is enacted by his use of sequentiality. As he told an interviewer, "one of my simple rules of therapy is that one thing follows another. Now that's a very simple rule, but it means that you stay with something through sequences" (Wysong, 1978). He manages sequences by modulating the bandwidth he employs with the client. When he makes the sequence slow down, he is saying, "this is worthwhile, pay attention to this." In the Wysong (1978) interview, Polster says, "You can do something to make that sequentiality very tight. For example, if you're doing something and I quickly said, 'What are you doing now? What do you feel in your chest? How did you say that? Where's your tongue?'" Making that connection between the content of the story and the feeling of the client is a way of tying emotion to history to produce meaning. When Polster thinks that a loose sequence is appropriate, he uses humor or tells a fantasy; he does something to loosen up the client rather than bear down the momentary attention; he is saying to the client, "don't worry about this; it is not important in the larger scheme of things." Narrative therapy like Polster's that protracts and expands a sequence is a method commonly used for helping clients change their thinking about themselves that results from past events: "the effort of thinking which is at work in every narrative configuration is completed in a refiguration of temporal experience" (Ricœur, 1984, p. 3).

Polster's clinical strategy, as elegantly simple as it is, is bolstered by the research on sequence that shows how the order in which something happens makes an incredible difference—even though we are often not conscious of it. One of the consistent research findings is that the order of occurrence of events in a stream of behavior makes a difference—sequence matters. When D precedes A, B, and C, the outcome is often different than from a sequence that advances from A to B to C to D. For example, the way individual members sequence messages, that is, the way they order their presentation of different parts of a message or present a message strategy, has the effect of increasing or decreasing a message's persuasiveness (Monge & Kalman,

1996). A brief story told by a friend of the authors illustrates how dramatic events and actions come together narratively in a fateful way. Our friend, his girlfriend, and her mother were driving from Spokane, Washington to Coeur d'Alene, Idaho after picking the mother up from the airport. Our friend had an engagement ring in his pocket, intending to propose to his sweetheart later that day. But during the 45-minute drive home, the mother had a heart attack and died in her car seat. He never took the ring out of his pocket because the bent-knee moment for proposing marriage never came about that day and because his commitment to proposing to her drifted by forever as a result of the emergency. Today, they remain friends in distant lives.

In order to understand sequences in our lives, we must construct a story that makes the episode sensible because we normally present ourselves as rational and thoughtful. To support this presentation of self, we must construct a story before we take an action to ensure that the action we are about to take is coherent. We are strategic communicators in that we shape our messages for particular listeners, even though those messages may be inconsistent with each other. (What one might say to a banker when the goal is to assure an investment review panel might be quite different from promising long term presence in the community (Sillince, 2007).) If the story is in any way incoherent, we make it more sensible by putting it into a framework that is acceptable to those who hear it. In other words, "if what we do fits into a well-known, socially acceptable story skeleton, then we can believe that we have acted properly" (Schank, 1995, p. 160). Narrative fidelity and probability are criteria for assessing stories (Fisher, 1984, 1987). Not only is there narrative fidelity (this is what I would expect in those circumstances) and narrative probability (this is what one would commonly expect to happen); as a pair they are kind of an internal/external read of appropriateness all rolled into one.

Appropriateness is a conscious part of stories because the expectations listeners have are difficult to change. Because listeners have such a confirmation bias, they tend to listen to support rather than to disconfirm. "Changing an actual story is very uncomfortable. It involves reorganizing a tremendous amount of information, admitting to ourselves that we were wrong, realizing that we are now uncertain about the relationship, and understanding that our new story may also have to be changed" (Sternberg, 1994, p. 10). The more out of the ordinary one's actual experiences are, the harder it is to find a relevant story skeleton. Communicating the temporal meaning of organizational events is "achieved by imposing narrativity onto those events, [hence] no one narration is necessarily correct, true or accurate" (Rhodes & Brown, 2006, p. 172). Ricœur says that in Freud's terms, to forget is to be unintegrated with a memory, which causes the person to continually act it out as a substitute for recall; "he *repeats* it, without, of course, knowing that he is repeating it" (2004, p. 70).

Dimaggio and colleagues use George Kelly's book on personality theory to make the following point about sequence: "Only when a man tunes his ear to recurrent themes in the monotonous flow does the universe begin to make sense to him"

(Dimaggio, Salvatore, Azzara, Catania, Semerari, & Hermans, 2003, p. 386). The search for likeness and difference in narrative is one kind of sensemaking. "An individual reconstructs the significant episodes in his or her life in the form of prototypical narratives and then uses them as schemata to decode events" (Dimaggio et al., 2003, p. 386). "Brand-new stories rely upon failed expectations about what is likely to happen next by implicitly invoking a story skeleton and then abandoning it when least expected" (Schank, 1995, p. 186). Much of what we assume is creativity is better seen as the adaptation of old stories to new purposes to which they have never been applied before. Insight is often the recognition (note the word 'recognition' means literally, 'cognizing again') that an "old story could have a new use" (Schank, 1995, p. 226). The advantage of an old story is that it harkens back to an earlier narrative from another time, saying, "This story makes me feel like I used to feel—to have the sensory responses I used to have."

The plot. A narrative is composed of a sequence and language used in tandem to form a discursive code (Scholes, 1980). We tend to have less attention for a story that does not coalesce with a plot where all the central features in the narrative come together purposefully. For White (1980, p. 13), the plot means "a structure of relationships by which the events contained in the account are endowed with meaning by being identified as part of an integrated whole." The moment where the plot comes together often sets up the moral theme of resolution for the story.

Sequence is always selective and exclusive within a given narrative, but there are always alternative ways to select and assemble the actions of which narratives are composed. Using Polster's (1987) term, we "punctuate" a story by selecting when it begins and ends. "Although life presents us with continuous activity, we tend to perceive it as discrete events" (Taylor & Tversky, 1997, p. 509). Sequencing includes selecting the events to include in the story. The process of organizing events includes both sequencing and indexing, which are the cues or labels used to recall memories (Taylor & Tversky, 1997). Yet within the latitude for deciding what to include in a story, attention to plausibility and understanding remain important. "A story must obey its own internal laws of probability. The event choices of the writer, therefore, are limited to the possibilities within the world he creates" (McKee, 1997, p. 70). Certainly the presidential biography called *Dutch: a memoir of Ronald Reagan* (1999) by Edmund Morris exemplifies this. The author wrote himself into the Reagan narrative as a personal participant, but it was taken by critics as an attempt by the author to elevate himself when, in fact, he had lived through none of the experiences with Reagan he detailed so carefully. This distraction reduced rather than extended the Reagan narrative.

The ordering of events by linking them into a plot comes about through an intermixing of the various elements of the cultural repertoire of layered stories and creations. Because of this mix of possibilities, narrators are able to take a similar collection of life events and blend them into very different kinds of stories. It is only necessary to think of the differences in one's sibling's stories to conjure examples. "Two people can, by incorporating the same kind of life events into different types of stories, change the meaning of these events. Psychotherapists have used this property of narrative in their notion of 'life-scripts'" (Polkinghorne, 1988, pp. 19–20). This quote is useful because it captures how narrative is used in psychotherapy. A person's life memory is an asset or a liability for one's enactment in the world. One way to deal with bad memories is to take power over and reduce them and to replace them with (one's self) as controller of the story. Perhaps this is what Robert Frost meant to say in the poem with which we began this chapter.

The plot-ordering process operates by linking diverse happenings along a temporal dimension and by identifying the effect one event has on another, and it serves to cohere human actions and the events that affect human life into a temporal gestalt. By being included in a narratively generated story, particular actions take on significance as having contributed to a completed episode. In this sense, narrative can retrospectively alter the meaning of events after the final outcome is known. The means by which specific events are made to cohere into a single narrative is the plot or story line.

The plot is not a prescribed part of a story; instead, it operates reflexively among different events "which discloses their significance and allows them to be grasped together as parts of one story" (Polkinghorne, 1988, p. 25). In other words, sequences interact, and in doing so pose a possible future state. When the plot pulls these forces together, the listener summarizes the power of forces by assessing: what caused what? One thing that helps produce tension in the plot is the possibility of differences among characters about where the story is going. Any experience can be divided or punctuated in various ways. Because two people can link the sequence of events into different chains and create different meaning from the same events, miscommunication and interpersonal conflict can easily arise (Polkinghorne, 1988).

A plot shows us something about the narrative world by changing that world in some important way, as in a plot twist or a surprise. "It alters or reorders the world even as it provides an interpretation of it" (Polkinghorne, 1988, p. 131). The plot often carries the message of the narrative, but ordering and interpretation are reflexive. There is a combination of ordering (what goes where?) and interpretation (what words are used to represent event, phases, and people?).

The nature of a plot sets up a difference between science and a narrative. Science sets out to reduce possible causes as much as possible, because that makes control so much easier. Yet, narratives are more interesting when they are complex and have ample forces interacting, and are both lurching forward and falling back on sequence. "Without the recognition of significance given by the plot, each event would appear as discontinuous and separate, and its meaning would be limited to its categorical identification or its spatiotemporal location" (Polkinghorne, 1988, pp. 18–19). These processes narrow down what a plot is; it is more than a sequence; it is more than what is categorized or labelled as events. It is the combination of forces to assert causal connections among the forces. "In summary, narrative understanding is the comprehension of a complex of events by seeing the whole in which the parts have participated" (Polkinghorne, 1988, p. 22).

Stability and Change in Sequence

We give narratives a sequence because doing so aids in sensemaking. "Perhaps the most essential ingredient of narrative accounting (or storytelling) is its capability to structure events in such a way that they demonstrate, first, a connectedness or coherence, and second, a sense of movement or direction through time" (McKee, 1997, p. 466). One way of displaying coherence is to show how a story reflects tradition, an organization's policy, or an *enfant terrible's* predictable behavior. "The cognitive function of narrative form, then, is not just to relate a succession of events but to body forth an ensemble of interrelationships of many different kinds as a single whole" (Mink, 2001). When we arrange sequences, we bring together characters, events, and time into a plausible explanation.

Consider this cultural example of Native Americans and how Bruner reconstructs historical understanding to fit changing circumstances:

> In the 1930s and 1940s the dominant story constructed about Native American culture change saw the present as disorganization, the past as glorious, and the future as assimilation. Now, however, we have a new narrative: The present is viewed as a resistance movement, the past as exploitation, and the future as ethnic resurgence.
>
> *(Bruner, 1986, p. 139)*

In this example the contents of the sequence are being adjusted to fit a changing understanding that is helpful because it shows that cultural assumptions are part of the emplotment of a sequence. Notice how much narrative probabilities change in the reformulation of where a people are in cultural autonomy and development. "How we depict any one segment of the sequence is related to our conception of the whole, which I choose to think of as a story" (Bruner, 1986, p. 141).

Narrative structure has an advantage over related concepts such as metaphor or paradigm because narrative emphasizes order and sequence, in a formal sense, and is more appropriate for the study of change, the life cycle, or any developmental process. As introduced in Chapter Three, this ordering in sequence sets up the moral judgment for assessing what happened between the beginning and ending of the story and the marked time sequence. Narrative assessments can be miniscule and continuous. One of the powers of the narrative is to slide up and down a scale from "French Revolution" to "would you pick up a loaf of bread on the way home?" But in either instance, whether it is structured as a single moment or a collection of events "depends not on a definition of 'event' but on a particular narrative construction that generates the event's appropriate description" (Polkinghorne, 1988, p. 147). The difference between the beginning and ending of a sequence, whether a grade, a tax form, a work agreement, a decision to stop smoking, or a marriage proposal, is the marker for when the sequence starts and when it stops (Czarniawska, 1998).

Story as model has a remarkable duality; it is both linear and instantaneous. On the one hand, a story is experienced as a sequence as it is being told or enacted; on the other hand, it is comprehended collectively—all at once—before, during, and after the telling. A story can be static (like pulling the lever in a voting booth) and dynamic (like all the political discussions that took place prior to the vote) at the same time (Bruner, 1986). Sequence comprehension is notable because it is an act of the collection and arrangement of facts, which means the dynamic can change before, during, and after a story takes place. Weick's profound understatement about sensemaking, "How can I know what I think until I see what I say?" exemplifies a change in understanding through time sequence dynamics (Weick, 1995, p. 12).

Stasis and Movement in Space

Narratives of and about organizations need not be about people living and working in the same location daily, and even when they are, they are not necessarily static. Organizations and the people within them are often on the move, and a particular kind of narrative, the travel tale or travelogue, is particularly well suited to depict this dynamic aspect of contemporary workplaces. Whether it is the "high adventure" of Edmund Hillary and his team summiting Everest, Malinowski among the Trobriand Islanders of the Western Pacific, Steinbeck and Ricketts in the Sea of Cortez, or a contemporary ethnographer in a Native American community, travelogues have the potential to capture the meaning of locales to the participants, as well as the explorers' preparations to leave, their adventures, their arrivals in new places, and their homecomings. Unlike the linear organization of narratives in time, narratives that capture movement are often circular in nature. Actors depart places, encounter new places, and return home changed by the experience (Clifford, 1997). In the ordinary course of organizational affairs, people occupy offices and buildings, come and go, drop children off on their way to work, pop into the store, hightail it through airports and train stations, and stop into pubs. Narratives are ideally suited to capture this routine movement to and fro. Not infrequently, such daily flows from place to place are interrupted by major organizational events such as hirings, promotions, firings, mergers, acquisitions, relocations, celebrations, or deaths, all of which involve dramatic changes of scenes that are narratable. In short, the actions that compose narratives are not only given context by the other actions that surround them, but also by being situated in particular places where things are on the move. Flight lines, wildfires, shopping malls, therapy offices, and toll booths are, to paraphrase Goffman, "where the action is."

Application

Imagination is a natural concept for narrative sequence because to imagine what to include in a story is to fantasize the details that set up the fidelity of the story. Moreover, imagination is frequently expressed through "symbol, metaphor, myth, dream" to create imagery (Kearney, 1995, p. 173). Visualizing what comes in what order is part of symbolic construction. Certainly imagination threads throughout Ricœur's idea of narrative in that the goal of narrative is to open up a world of perspectives. Much of Ricœur's thought centers on historical imagination where history makes use of fiction and fiction makes use of history; the goal of combining these two is to increase the concreteness of images for past events. This concretizing of imagination is natural for the "intellectual work of interpreting ruins, fossils, remains, monuments, museum pieces, and the like" (Kearney, 1995, p. 176). In Polkinghorne's (1988) conception, imagination and empirical hypothesis testing take the same turn—they are both projections and thus imaginations of the future. Imagination comes into play when interpreters fill in a social context for the objects being reviewed.

The practice of narrative imagination comes with consistent cautions. The goal is to fantasize about events, past or future, that cannot be seen, but to do so with a critical distance from the subject (Kearney, 1995). Snowden, in his work on imagining narrative, places attention on being rooted in an awareness of the embedded self that reaches out to imagination and pulls images to oneself to make connections to possible events. His consulting firm, now called Cognitive Edge, was originally named "Cynefin" (pronounced *cyn-ev-in*), to celebrate a Welsh term that, as noun, roughly means "habitat" and as an adjective roughly means "acquainted" or "familiar." The term more specifically means one's environment or place of comfort or birth (Snowden, 2003). Thus, invoking imagination is enabled by strands of connection of an imaginary world to a present and anchored world of the person.

In her book on cultivating humanity, Nussbaum (2003) identifies narrative imagination as both the ability to think what "it might be like to be in the shoes of a person different from oneself, to be an intelligent reader of that person's story" (pp. 10–11), and the ability to envisage the circumstances that formed that person, including a feel for his/her emotional states and wishes. For Nussbaum, narrative imagination includes making an evaluation that contrasts one's own choices and wishes to those of other people—essentially saying, "how would I have responded to their circumstances? How am I different from them? Would I have faltered or have had the courage to act in that situation?" Chaining out the imaginative understanding of the other extends this action.

Two brief examples of the use of narrative imagination help to clarify the concept. First is King's (1999) interrogation of the abstract meaning of environmentalism. He claims that an objectivist position is limited by the inability to construct a narrative that is intelligible unless it can be presented to a particular audience from a speaker who is contextualized in "one's own 'discursive place'" (p. 25). King uses the example of Third World thinkers who criticize deep ecology arguments "on the grounds they privilege American experience and geography over the conditions found in other parts of the world" (p. 25), which might increase impoverishment by carving out land and excluding people from it by the designation of wilderness. He forces the reader to imagine ecology from a Third World perspective.

Example two is taken from Riessman's (2008) chapter on visual analysis. She makes the argument that visualizing narratives is an act of imagination, and while some images "speak for themselves," most of us contextualize images and make sense of them from the angle of our respective professional fields. Riessman uses photographs of Japanese internment in the Second World War to show how these pictures change one's image of what those conditions were like. In one set of representations, she shows the pictures taken by Ansel Adams, the famous nature photographer, who spent 18 months in Manzanar, a camp in the California desert. He was allowed artistic freedom—with three exceptions: no photographs of barbed wire, armed guards, or guard towers. And while Adams believed the Japanese Americans were "unjustly incarcerated," he failed to address the issue of wholesale discrimination by the limited focus of his pictures (Riessman, 2008, p. 147). Another set of photographs from two other photographers offered a different image of the caution and fear of the internees. The lesson of these two examples of narrative imagination causes the reader to conjure these images—one oral, one visual—to see, if just for a moment, a different context and a different understanding of these two important stories.

In the story below, we showcase the imagination application. The story is a condensed version of one told by Ritchie DiSalvo, who had always dreamed of owning his own pizza shop, and was given the chance to have it, but with strings to the mob attached that play out in dramatic fashion.

Anthony the Hat

This is the story of Ritchie DiSalvo, whose story comes to us from his participation and graduation from Moth Shop Community, a storytelling workshop provided without expense to students from neighborhoods around New York City. Ritchie opens his story by telling of his work life and the colorful customers who frequented his shop.

> One of the regulars in this pizzeria I used to manage was Anthony the Hat. Every time Anthony would come in for lunch he would tell me "Ritchie, you run a great operation here. Place is always clean, food's great, take care of the people nice." He'd say "Someday you have to get your own place, you know, you need to have your own pizzeria one day, you know" and in the back of my mind I'd be agreeing with him cause that was my dream, to one day open my own pizzeria.

The image of owning his own shop was powerful for Ritchie because he had worked as an employee in a pizza shop, but despite being promised a part of the business for his hard work, his boss never came through. Frustrated, Richie tells of an opportunity that arises when Anthony the Hat comes in one day.

> So one particular afternoon Anthony comes in for his usual lunch—two slices with anchovies, fried garlic knots, a calzone, and a Diet Coke, I could never understand that—and he says, "Ritchie, I got this proposition for you. I want you to come and

> *work for me. I'll take you under my wing and I'll let you make some real money."*
> *And it happened to be a bad day at the shop that day … so I was like "let me take a*
> *shot with Anthony." He tells me "I'm setting up this operation downtown. I have my*
> *friends in the back taking some illegal bets on sports and a few numbers in the back,*
> *and your job would be to stay up front, run the operation up front. All you need to do,*
> *Ritchie, is you'd look out for police, you know, take care of the buzzer, let in the*
> *clients, press the code if you see the police, and in the morning when my workers come*
> *in make sure everybody has that little metal plastic wastepaper basket filled with lighter*
> *fluid and make sure everybody has matches." That was my job. Piece of cake. And I*
> *says "No problem, Anthony."*

Ritchie began his work for Anthony and it was going wonderfully. Not only was the business thriving, he was being introduced to a culture he could only imagine. He says:

> *Every night after work we'd all go down to Eddie LeBlanc's social club down on*
> *Sullivan Street, start off with a little cappuccino, we'd go to Nick & Eddie's on Sullivan*
> *Street, we'd go to La Dolce Vita, every time we'd walk in the restaurant the seas*
> *would part. The waiters would trip over themselves to take care of us because Anthony*
> *the Hat was there. Eddie LeBlanc was there. Frankie California was there … From*
> *working behind an oven all these years this was kind of a nice thing. People would stop*
> *at the table, give their respect to Anthony, buy us a bottle of wine, and just move on.*
> *It was kind of nice, I started feeling like King Kong after awhile.*

The shop was making money and Ritchie was enjoying the riches, then one incident changed everything. He introduces this part of the story in this way:

> *And as fate would have it and it usually does, I look out of the corner of my eye one*
> *afternoon and I see cops coming with hammers, and they were pretty close so I was just*
> *able to get the code in and one of the guys so I knew they would get to work in the*
> *wastepaper basket and no evidence and everything and we'd be cool. So now, they*
> *must've known the operation, they must've known somewhere to come in the back*
> *because they just bolted past me and they broke down the door and they wanted the*
> *guys in the back to try to get the papers and stuff like that. So with that, I was able to*
> *walk out of the place, you know, I just kind of scooted out of there and went down the*
> *block, got down in the subway, and I'm going like this, "Man, why didn't I stay*
> *sweating behind this pizza oven rather than come aboard with Anthony?" But I didn't,*
> *and I was running down the train station, with no job.*

Ritchie laid low for three days, but he got a call inviting him to a meeting at the Woolworth Building and was surprised to find that rather than being punished for running away, he is being offered the cash to start his own place. Here is how Ritchie offers the details:

We walk in there and he hands me a brown bag, and I says "What is this, lunch?" He goes, "No, what are you, a wise guy?" and he says, "Open the bag" so I open the bag and there's 38 thousand dollars in there. And I says, "What is this for?" and he says "See the man over there? That's the owner of the pizzeria that's going to be your pizzeria in a couple of minutes." "This is pretty good, this is nice of you Anthony, and I'm sorry I yelled at you before, sorry I got a little excited." He says "Go sit down by the lawyer, put everything in your name, and you are the owner of the pizzeria." I'm saying "I can't believe, this is unbelievable Anthony, this is too much for me, this is a beautiful thing. This is my dream, working many, many years."

Ritchie got his pizzeria in Brooklyn, developed his own product called the "Baby Calzone," put a neon sign in the window in the colors of Italy, placed antique coke bottles on the tables with fresh flowers in them daily and the money rolled in throughout the school year when lots of students frequented his place. But in the off season, when student purchases at his shop subsided, Ritchie could not make his weekly payments to Anthony, and in a dramatic scene, he put the collector off. After three weeks of failing to make payments, he was desperate and went into seclusion at his sister's house on Long Island. In short order, Anthony's gang caught up with him and "invited" him on a car ride. Although reluctant to get in that car with the gangsters, he wanted to get harm away from his sister's house, so he did as told and got in car. There, sitting in the back seat was Anthony the Hat and another scary character who drove Ritchie's fear up even more. He continues:

We get on the Long Island Expressway, we're riding for five minutes, ten minutes, fifteen minutes, and nobody's saying a word. The silence is deafening and my heart is about to come through my chest. … We're driving, my head is down, and I try to speak to Anthony. I tell him "the store … the summer … " and he don't want to hear about it. So at this point, I don't really know what's going on. We're just driving and nobody's saying a word. So finally Anthony speaks and he goes, "Ritchie, you remember the IOU that we signed in my lawyer's office?" and I says "Yes" and again I try to tell him this and the summer came and corner of my eye I see Anthony going like this [reaching into his pocket] and my stomach is flipping, my heart is racing, my head goes down even further, and he comes out with the IOU and he goes "Remember this IOU? That you signed in my lawyer's office?" and I says "Yeah Anthony, but the summer" and everybody starts laughing and he rips it up and goes "Ritchie you're a stand-up guy. When you get the money, you take care of it, if you don't get it, don't worry about it. You look a little sick though, you all right?' And I says "Yes, I'm fine, but I have a date tonight Anthony could you get me home immediately?"

Ritchie got his ride home, eschewed free dinners, and committed to working hard to make his own money. He offers the advice to "work hard, do it yourself, don't count on anybody."

Imagination is evident in several of the sequences of Ritchie's story, from his dream of owning his own shop while toiling over an oven in a shop of a manager who promises everything, but over time, delivers nothing, to imagining how he will beat the cops by pushing the buzzer that alerts the boys in the back that the law is on the premises, to fearing that his life is in such danger that he hides out in another town, to taking a fateful ride in Anthony's car down the expressway thinking that his life will be snuffed out in the next second. The interplay between sequence and imagination is potent in this story. Ritchie's retelling of this dramatic story, including reliving the fear for his life in the car ride on the Long Island Expressway, is heightened by his artful reimagining of sequence, right down to the word-for-word quotes of what Anthony and he said.

5

CHARACTER AND IDENTITY

Introduction

In 1888, a French newspaper, mistakenly thinking the scientist and inventor had died, published Alfred Nobel's obituary, headlining it, "The merchant of death is dead." The obituary read, "Dr. Alfred Nobel, who made his fortune by finding a way to kill the most people as ever before in the shortest time possible, died yesterday." This was a reference to Nobel having invented nitroglycerin. Actually, Alfred's brother, Ludvig, was the one who had died. Mortified upon seeing how he would be remembered, he changed his will to bequeath most of his fortune to the establishment of a series of prizes for peace, literature, and the sciences that now bear his name. The prizes were established eight years later, when Nobel actually died and his will was unveiled.[1]

This known but underappreciated story dramatically illustrates the dynamic and multi-faceted nature of character and identity. Alfred Nobel had a rare chance to peek into the future to observe the public and presumably final assessment of his character. The grand philanthropic activities in which he engaged in the name of peace and learning were an attempt—ultimately successful—to transform what the public would come to think of him. Nobel's story is an archetype for character and identity because his character assessment and identity are negotiated between those who evaluate his character (i.e., how others view him) and Nobel, who redefines how he views himself. The example highlights the dynamic, as opposed to static nature of both character and identity. In post-structuralist thinking, character is mutable, changing in relation to others. Character is changeable in the same way that the demands and stresses on a person change over time (Polkinghorne,

1988; Bruner, 1986). In the Nobel case, of course, the sequence in which these events happened greatly affected actions taken and the ultimate interpretations made. The Nobel story highlights how the timing of assessments affects the ultimate interpretation of a person's character.

It is additionally instructive because it provides an early example of the application of celebration, which we address at the end of this chapter. Celebration is honoring others' lives and achievements. In this case, Nobel's life was denigrated, not honored, and his reaction was to redirect the meaning of his life—and the appreciation of it by others—when he established annual prizes for those who perform above the standard he was able to set in his life. His life example redirects our attention away from the retirement speech with the gold watch and the rubber chicken banquet (i.e., the kinds of events readers might associate ordinarily with celebration) and toward a wider definition, including self-celebration, of what qualifies as a celebration.

Given the importance of the narrative in representing character and identity, this chapter joins these concepts and shows how they operate in relation to each other in the dynamic way current conceptions of character and identity in narratives promote. To develop the ideas for this chapter, we will first introduce the concepts of character and identity, then address how the narratives that affect character are managed by the individual. We turn next to how a narrator constructs a character. We showcase Erving Goffman's (1959) approach to the display of character, and then explore how vulnerability, risk, and effort within narratives affect our reading of them. The application section of the chapter pertains to how the concepts of character and identity come into play in narratives celebrating individual lives. We offer a series of narratives that show how we celebrate character in large and small circumstances.

Character

The most important feature of character is its assessment component; any character appraisal requires answering the question, "What is the 'quality' of this person?" (Ricœur, 1984, p. 50). The possibility of a quality person implies a non-quality; for each character feature, there is an opposite, a binary, or in the language of Gestalt therapy, a polar opposite feature that can be the downside—or asset—of any given character trait (Polster & Polster, 1974). For example, the boxer who wins championships because he persists in the later rounds to best his opponent may be the same boxer who persists in too many fights and is left with a life-long injury as a result. One of a character's problems is knowing when to adapt and when to persist.

Character assessment is inescapable. As Ricœur says, "this is the one division that characters submit to almost without exception, goodness or badness being universal criteria of character" (Ricœur, 1984, p. 50). These assessments of goodness and badness become evident in numerous forms, including a feeling of simpatico with another (i.e., identification), the lack of registering any feeling (featurelessness and blandness), or even a sense you'd rather be somewhere else (e.g., "get me away from this person"). In some instances these character assessments are functional and have material meaning, such as when you are buying expensive used equipment from another person and you have to believe their report, "let the buyer beware." In other circumstances, the assessment may not have specific importance or meaning, but simply takes place as a part of conversational exchanges. All the same, "The quality assessment of character is universal" (Ricœur, 1984, p. 47).

Identity

Operating in contrast to character, which is a judgment of another from the outside, is identity, which answers the internal question, "Who am I?" (Ricœur, 2004, p. 81). The formula for answering this query is extracted from a person's memory, because answering the identity question requires a particular recall: "In remembering something … one remembers oneself" (Ricœur, 2004, p. 96). For example, when we listen to a golden oldie song or watch a movie from decades ago, we tend to do so because they remind us of the way we felt, of who we were when that entertainment was popular. In instances of such recall, the scene might include a friend or romantic partner from the period. When we remember ourselves at a given point, we also reconstitute the groups or individuals who were our cohorts. Such temporal memories are the stuff of identity construction.

For an example of how past memories help construct the contemporary self, consider this story. A father drops off his daughter at the front steps of the schoolhouse on the first day of public school. The young girl is both frightened and stubborn and resists the act of walking up the steps and going to her home classroom alone; "She's beside herself." As he sits in the car and watches her eventually ascend the steps, a tear comes to the father's eye because his daughter's emotion reminds him of his same fears and tears of his first day at school. In a research interview that focused on what parents learn from their children, he reports seeing his own history in the vulnerability of his child.

The intersection of memory and identity becomes controllable when the actor narrates his/her own story. Such opportunities for narration occur in three phases that we will cover in more detail in this chapter. But briefly, we initially establish who we are by answering for the past: "This is what I did." The advantage of establishing one's identity from past memories is our capacity to select events, people, and outcomes that present us in a particular light. The tone of the past can be celebrative: "Look at all I have done," or it can be tragic: "Look at what I have risen above—can you help me?" But in either case, our presentation of a past sets a tone for the reception we want to establish.

Second, we offer a projection of the future in the form of a promise: "This is what I will do." The promise we make for the future has the effect of establishing expectations. A basketball player who has routinely hit a high percentage of his three-point shots in the past and is transferring to a new team is usually promising the same (or better) three-point success for that new team. These two narrative components, the past and the future, are stated from an existential view of the present: "This is who I am." Such a view places the responsibility for the hopes and joys and sorrows on the person, which reaffirms the individual nature and the changeable nature of identity. As Ricœur (1984, p. 96) says, "First memory does seem to be radically singular: my memories are not yours." The value of a story is more toward personal meaning than it is toward verifiable history (Polkinghorne, 1988).

How are the past, future, and present handled narratively? To accomplish an account of the past and for the future from the vantage of the present, the narrator invokes Barthes' "functionality" of causal relations. In a concrete situation, one might say, "I presented this project on time today because I worked hard on it last night," or "I am late for this meeting because there was an accident on the freeway." These accounts are at play as actors report on their ownership of the present to the extent they internalize (this was caused by me) or externalize (this happened out there) causality, or, as a social psychologist would say, "locus of control" in their stories.

Control of the Narrative

To showcase this point on who controls the narrative, look at the chain of attributions in the story below of a blue-collar worker's strategy for what would appear to be the mundane task of getting to work in the morning. The story concerns a man named Hobart Foote, who lives in a cramped trailer near the Illinois–Indiana border with his wife, two teenaged children, and a dog. The one visible book in the trailer is the Holy Bible, looking as old and scuffed as Hobart himself, who's 37 and looks older than his years. The trailer trembles with the pervasive, nearly continual clangor of nearby trains—"Gary-to-Chicago-bound, freights off the sidings of the nearby steel mills, switching and coupling cars." His narrative begins and ends each day near the tracks.

Hobart works as a utility man at the auto plant. He's been there for 17 years. Notice how he establishes his identity and how it changes as other forces enter his life:

> *I'm from Alabama, my wife and kids are Hoosiers. I was gonna work a few years and buy me a new car and head back south. Well, I met the wife now and that kinda changed my plans. I might've been working in some small factory down south or I might have gone to Detroit where I worked before or I might have gone to Kalamazoo where I worked before. Or else I mighta stuck on a farm somewheres, just grubbing off a farm somewhere. You never know what you woulda did. You can't plan too far in advance, 'cause there's always a stumbling block.*

As he relates who he is, he also makes it clear that his future is not entirely of his own making. His identity is that of a man of struggle, and this theme continues as he relates the daily cycle of his experience. His day begins around four thirty, when the clock radio goes off:

> *First thing comes to my mind is shut my eyes just a few minutes. Yet I know I can't shut 'em for too long, I know I gotta get up. I hate the clock. We lay there and maybe*

listen to them play a few records. And she gets up about five minutes till. Of course, I say, "Get up! Get up! It's day, get up!" I tell you, after goin' on 17 years, I don't want to be late. You're one minute late clockin' in, they dock you six.

His awareness of the workplace controls over him is evident even as he emerges from slumber and he enrolls his wife in the urgent movement to prepare to leave the trailer. His morning rituals, almost automatic, rarely vary:

I get up after the news comes on. Sometimes it's five to five, sometimes its five o'clock. The assembly line starts at six. I go to the washroom, comb my hair. That's routine with me. I have to get every piece in place. Drink maybe a cup of coffee or a half a cup of coffee. Maybe a whole piece of toast and sometimes I might eat two pieces of toast— depends on how I feel. In the meantime, I'm watchin' that clock. I say "I gotta go, it's eight minutes after. At twelve minutes after, I gotta leave here." You get in the car. You tell your wife, of course you'll see her tonight. It's routine.

But as he continues his morning routine, his logistical challenges really begin—trying to beat the trains at intersections, developing alternative routes to avoid stoppages— so as to avoid having his paycheck docked. It's become almost a game to him:

We do have a train problem, goin' from here to the assembly plant. I cross one set of tracks twice. Then two other sets of tracks once each. Long freight trains, going from Chicago to Gary. I have waited as high as ten, twelve minutes. Then you're late.

If I see a train coming I keep going. It's a game you're playing. Watch the stoplight, catch this light at a certain time and you got the next light. But if there's a train there, I take off down Cicero Avenue, watching the crossings. Then if I make her okay, you got a train over at Burnham line, you got a train there you gotta watch for. But it's generally fast. [Takes a deep breath.] Well, these tensions … It don't bother me, really. It's routine.

(Terkel, 1972, pp. 168–69)

Hobart's story is causal; it contrasts with many of our own experiences and the concreteness of the images he offers to account for his life; the extra snooze, the cursory listen to the news, a morning ritual of coffee and toast—all of this bound by the punch clock at work that waits for no man and is ready to penalize him harshly for every minute he is late. One can imagine the satisfaction (and dread) of raising that stiff paper card and pushing it down into the machine until he hears the "click" that registers his presence on the job. This sound and other sounds around him are constant reminders to him, both in his home that is rattled by the trains, and in his car as he listens for the location of the oncoming trains so he'll know how to race around them. He makes the sound work for him when he strategizes to find an intersection that allows him a passage through as he presses toward a job that has no interest to him other than one thing: it is his contribution to the most important thing in his world—meeting the material needs of the family that he speaks of so dearly.

How Characters Change

The initial presentation of characters in stories is either general—we only know them vaguely at the outset and the details are filled in as the story develops (Czarniawska, 2010)—or a sequence in the story is presented to show that initial impressions are completely wrong. Both vague and initial wrong impressions serve stories well because they allow for revelations that surprise and change the mind of the listener as the story unfolds. This shows how our narrative understanding of characters changes and grows over time. As Robichaud says:

> When a character appears for the first time, we do not yet know very much about it. The qualities that are implied in that first presentation are not all 'grasped' by the reader. In the course of the narrative the relevant characteristics are repeated so often—in a different form, however—that they emerge more and more clearly.
>
> *(Robichaud, 2001, p. 125)*

Just as stories change, a dependable and stable sense of what is going on is communicated by repetition. Character presentations are circular because we are continually trying to align the story with a history (Polster, 1987). Characters become reliable when what we know about them is reinforced repeatedly in "the construction of the image of a character" (Robichaud, 2001, p. 125). Tom Wolfe's (1979) presentation of John Glenn, the astronaut, in his book, *The Right Stuff*, is a useful example. The theme of the first cadre of astronauts for the United States showed them to be wild and woolly guys, hard-drinking, and woman-chasing throughout their training and their space missions—with one exception, John Glenn. He, instead, was dedicated to his wife and drove his aging Datsun to see her as many weekends of time off from training as he could. Later, when she was pressed into the public relations spotlight against her will, Glenn came to her defense without regard for whose feelings it might ruffle—including the president of the United States.

The requirement for consistently showing strength of character for one's dependability, one's willingness to follow through in all circumstances, sets up an interesting dynamic with change. This is what makes change in characters so interesting—how does that person achieve both tradition and stability while making changes in character simultaneously?

Facts in Support of a Character

In addition to repetition, inserting facts and data from different sources additionally fulfills a function in the construction of an image (Robichaud, 2001). Such accumulation of different information might come from multiple sources—if all these different groups believe this, it must be so. "The accumulation of characteristics causes odd facts to coalesce, complement each other, and then form a whole: the image of a character" (Robichaud, 2001, p. 125). The idea of a character as an accumulation of characteristics is accurate, especially when we assume that this accumulation is, itself, changing. Think of the recipes individuals have for judging character: "If a man would cheat on his wife, he would cheat on me at work." "If he has sacrificed for his country by going in harm's way during a war, he will be reliable when he is in public office." "If he has run a company successfully, he can run the government with the same sense of accomplishment."

The more data that is piled up in support of a particular assessment of character, the less energy the listener spends wondering about it. As the picture gets affirmed, we relax our judgment of character. But the resolution of character and the ambiguity about her/him means the tension that uncertainty provides will be directed toward another part of the story—essentially saying, now that we know the character, what circumstances is s/he in?

In the following narrative that the authors of this book developed as they drove across the southwestern part of the United States, note how the story unfolds naturally in the conversation and how the circumstances of the character unfold in the telling:

Bud: *I have this wonderful story. Have you ever heard of Aimee Mullins?*

Larry: *No.*

Bud: *Aimee Mullins is a Paralympics track athlete who has 12 pairs of legs.*

Larry: *Wow.*

Bud: *And she's been on beauty-fashion shoots with all these different kinds of legs. She has those kind of legs that have those springy—those J-shaped legs that you can run really fast on. I saw her give this lecture on TED. You can't help but stare at her legs the whole time. You don't exactly know what the deal is. At first she's just talking along. You eventually realize that her legs are longer than they should be. Then she tells this story about telling one of her friends that with her various legs she can be anywhere from 5–8 to 6–1. She's drop-dead gorgeous. Her friend said, "That's not fair. You shouldn't be able to do that." Her friend saying that made Aimee realize something. She said, "Now I see. This is no longer about deficiency, this is about augmentation." Isn't that a great story?*

Larry: *Yes.*

Bud: *"This is about augmentation."*

(From the transcript of a road trip conversation of the authors)

Aimee's story is so dramatic because it is so visual. Here is this beautiful physical creature who is made whole by the attachment of equally beautiful and decorated artificial legs. She tells her story with confidence and grace. In another presentation at TED, she even included an instance of self-doubt. Since she had almost run out of the socket of a leg during a particularly hot preliminary race, she worried, "What if my leg comes off in this race?" But as she tells it, her burley coach replies, "Aimee! Get out there and run your race. If it falls off, put it back on, get up, and finish the race!"

The Aimee Mullins story shows that the narrative is something actors themselves reflect upon. It is not just an accumulation of characteristics, but rather a picture constructed retrospectively that comes to grips with the circumstances a person has been dealt and the various ways he or she has responded. Moreover, the morality is not from the standpoint of the individual, a uniform goodness or badness, but rather a long and only partially remembered series of circumstances that needs to be sorted out. According to Polkinghorne (1995), this is why we live longer than sheer biological necessity: we spend our later years, if we are lucky, in life character review.

The Narrative Construction of Character

Character that is developed in relation to other characters brings to bear all that we know about how we are formed, how we constitute ourselves, and by the reflections we see in the eyes of others in responses to our self. George Herbert Mead's famous formulation assumes a conscious self that is established only to the extent that it can be communicated to others; at the same time, by accommodating the attitudes of others, one establishes personhood in relation to others (Mead, 1959).

There are four principles that work in concert to construct the image of a character: repetition, accumulation, relations to others, and transformation (Robichaud, 2001, pp. 125–26). This set of character ingredients can be developed as follows. As we have already offered, repetition is represented classically in the John Glenn character in Tom Wolfe's *The Right Stuff*, where Wolfe shows Glenn's willingness to drive a dilapidated compact car 300 miles each weekend to be with his wife, whose health conditions needed Glenn's support. This theme about John Glenn is repeated throughout Wolfe's book. Accumulation is useful because such accumulations can arc over to change; accumulation can be the small thing that tips the scale; accumulation can be like heat in the summer—the fifteenth day of 100-degree heat in Texas is much different than the second day, even though the thermometer reads the same. But accumulations can also be as small as a constant replenishing of resources, as when sales for a company are not dramatic, but are dependable and steady, or when a high jumper inches the bar up slowly, in fractions, as discipline and skill take hold. Accumulations, positive or negative, count because unless a system (person or organization) is replenished and given new energy, accumulations amount to extractions from it, which can drive the actor to poverty. At the same time, small increases in things done right can also tilt a structure (person or organization) in the right direction (Weick, 1984).

Character is established via "the presentation of the nature of the people in a story" (Bal, 1997, p. 59). Bal sees characterization as the presentation of motives. "We understand a person if we understand what makes him act the way he does" (Bal, 1997, p. 59). This supports the idea of characterization as being who we are as seen by others, but identity as what we tell about ourselves. How does characterization (as seen by others) relate to identity (as seen by the self)? To know people well is to have an insight into them; to be able to accurately read them is to know what makes them "tick." Such an interpretation is in contrast to a surface reading of a person in the moment.

The principal means of presenting a character is through what s/he does and says. These two, action and dialogue, are the same means we have for understanding characters in real life (Bal, 1997). Action and dialogue applied to the Gremias model means that there is a traditional sender/receiver (as in a communication model) and a secondary level (supporter/opponent) as well as a stage three, which is the ultimate unfolding of the narrative. How long does it take? With whose account for what happened? With what results? What is the effectiveness of the communication and interpretation of the good and bad news?

Character and identity meld into recognizing how the person in the story is known. The leading dimension of character is action. Ricœur's statement about poets who develop dramatic characters applies to narrative development as well. He says they operate historically as though their character constructions are "persons engaged in action" (Ricœur, 1984, p. 48). The poet's awareness carries over to narrators in that the easiest way to identify a character is to show what they are doing. We fail to recognize characters when they are standing still; we are averse to cardboard or flat characters (Kennedy & Gioia, 1995). We are attracted to them when they are engaged in action, when they are making choices. Such dynamism is a product of the person's character—the restrictions s/he has faced, the opportunities s/he has been given, the hand s/he has been dealt.

Transformations are the result of the forces operating on a character—either the ones sought out or forced on her/him. Transformation is illuminated by McAdams' (2006) notion of the actor doing something of risk (emotional or physical) that s/he has not done before and that requires her/him to let go of an avenue to performance that has served well in the past. Transformations are a makeover; they can be as familiar as the movement from adolescence to adulthood, from active professionalism to retirement, or performing well in a role or a task that the actor and those around him/her had never anticipated. Complex change can arise from the repetition of a few, moderate forces that interact in novel ways. Of course, it can be difficult to know if a change is actually occurring or if the narrator is pursuing a vested interest to make it appear so. How can you judge the story when the actor is the narrator?

Character and Action: Goffman's View

We single out Erving Goffman's perspective on character because he uniquely treats character like a risky game. Gambling is Goffman's core metaphor for action. After discussing the concepts that go into gambling games, such as the plays, the odds specifying what can be gained and lost, he moves into a treatment of the phases of the action. In Goffman's account, the first phase of the play is bet-making or squaring off. This is the phase in which the players commit themselves to the gamble. The second phase is the determination, such as a coin toss in the simplest case, in which causal forces acting on the gamble produce the outcome (e.g. heads or tails). The third phase, the disclosive phase, is the span of time between the determination of the outcome and the participants learning who won. In coin tossing, this is generally instant and the suspense brief, but the disclosive phase could be lengthy. The final phase, termed settlement, occurs between the disclosure of the outcome and the exchange of gains/losses as the result of the gamble. In short, it ends when the loser pays up and the winner takes his/her gains.

After the discussion of these phases, Goffman proposes that action is primarily about matters being problematic and/or consequential. He then catalogues many sorts of gambles in which people assume risks that can be to their persons or their resources. Activities that are both problematic and consequential are termed fateful. The centerpiece of Goffman's approach to action is people engaging voluntarily in fateful activities and the consequences of engaging successfully or unsuccessfully for the actor's character.

Concerning character, Goffman thinks that day-to-day life, including life in organizations, is fairly devoid of fateful action. This being the case, people turn to competitive sports, non-competitive risky sports like skydiving, slight competitions in activities such as bowling or vertigo rides, and what he terms "ordinary social milling," by which he means being in the same place with rich or notorious people. In such circumstances people have to carry off a certain identity in possibly problematic situations with possibly large consequences. By engaging in this kind of chance-taking, people can develop the capacities they need to be able to show audiences to the action that they can behave appropriately and effectively under the stress of fatefulness. When they are at risk, actors show characteristics such as composure and effective use of their skills under conditions where the costs would be great if they did not.

Goffman observes that properties of character are always judged from a moral perspective, because "the capacity to mobilize oneself for the moment is always subject to social evaluation" (1967, 218). Whether or not someone can mobilize him or herself successfully in fateful action indicates his/her strong or weak character, and being frozen at the switch, like a deer in the headlights, represents a character that is fearful of action. Part of the fatefulness of this action is that audiences judge behavior in the extremes (as indicating strong or weak character); they generalize or make determinations about a person's character on the basis of single performances. Therefore, failures can have instant and catastrophic consequences for an actor's character.

The idea of character for Goffman (1967) is articulated specifically in several forms of character including courage, gameness, gallantry, presence of mind, and dignity. He highlights composure, which is characterized as the skillful execution of tasks and the ability to stage confidence while in the midst of action. As an example,

Goffman mentions the self-possession of a person who is about to be executed, a time when grace and composure would be most difficult to sustain. Despite the near universal assessments of his despicable character, Saddam Hussein's execution may be a case in point. He reportedly said, "let's do this thing" at a time when his execution committee were jockeying for a piece of his clothing. Likewise, no one could muster as much composure as St. Lawrence who, when placed upon a burning hot gridiron, is supposed to have said, "This side is done. Better turn me over."

As may be evident, character relates explicitly to actors' reputations. Surveying these reputational consequences, Goffman proposes that observers make assessments of character on the basis of single trials that show strong or weak character; a single failure in action can make it impossible to restore more favorable reputation. Character judgments can be very durable: "once a man's price has been discovered and paid, he no longer has any reliability left and might as well accept bribes that are small but frequent" (Goffman, 1967, p. 236). In economics, this is called a "sunk cost"; the price has been paid and cannot be recovered.

Action is appealing, according to Goffman, because of its ability to display character. A character display provides a motive for engaging in action in the first place, which is to show that one can act well under pressure. This enables or even obliges people to engage voluntarily in risky action that has the potential to transform them. The character of the self can either be reinforced or recovered by engagement in successful action.

Character is comprised of both the stable characteristics attributed to a person and the more ephemeral, dynamic attributes that are put on display in action. Character, then, for Goffman, is basically an illusion, composed both of strictly unchanging qualities and yet also of something precarious and mutable. We carry facets of our character with us from one situation to the next—factors that provide continuity to the social scene about who we are and what we do as well as our practiced, skilled behaviors. At the same time, we can voluntarily subject ourselves to action, thereby making our character mutable and at risk.

This relationship was articulated in Goffman's earlier book called *The Presentation of Self in Everyday Life* (1959), where he essentially equates etiquette with morality. In other words, we can stabilize the impressions people have of us by following a set of practices in a style that leaves the impression that we are moral people who can be expected to behave appropriately. For instance, whatever one's assessment of his politics, it would be hard to say that President Obama did not have his eye on public office fairly early during his public career. His having avoided ever writing a word associated with an ideological position while he was editor of the *Harvard Law Review* and later a university professor shows that although he wanted to demonstrate leadership by being in leadership positions, he did not want to make a commitment to ideology that would hurt him at a later time by narrowing the constituencies to which he might appeal. As he was advised, run for office before you have a set of commitments that can be revealed, deconstructed, and held against you.

The Obama point notwithstanding, in "*Where the action is*" Goffman (1967, p. 260) explicitly writes, to the contrary, that "careful prudent persons must … forego the opportunity to demonstrate certain prized attributes. After all, devices that render the individual's moments free from fatefulness also render them free from new information concerning him, free, in short, from significant expression." The downside of prudence and behavioral orthodoxy is that nobody notices, in essence. That is the value of the paradox of character Goffman sets up. We have to show ourselves to be the kind of a person society needs, and simultaneously distinguish ourselves as individuals. A response to this paradox between need and distinction is to seek out various kinds of practical risks through which to display character because, in them, the consequences of failure would be less severe.

Should someone take a practical risk, the determination of the success or failure of the risk might come rapidly or eventually. One thing that distinguishes much chance-taking is that the play and the point of determination occur close together. One knows fairly quickly whether a gamble paid off. This contrasts with other risky activities, such as deciding to go with one product rather than another or taking a stand on a politically charged issue, in which the success or failure of the gamble may be unknown for years or may always be indeterminate. In effect, this is the micropolitics of character.

This argument is extended with the notion of idiosyncrasy credits (Hollander, 1958), which supports the idea that because people have for some time behaved as preferred and met people's expectations of them, they have accrued a bounty of social capital that enables them to take risks. A leader's past obeisance to rules, in other words, is a reason to trust him or her when s/he proposes risky actions.

Goffman essentially divides the world into the safe and the risky, associating workplaces with the safe. "Serious action," he says (1967, p. 261), "is a serious ride, and rides of this kind are all but arranged out of everyday life." But they are not absent. Goffman goes on to say that "Serious action is a means of obtaining some of the moral benefits of heroic conduct without taking quite all of the chances of loss that opportunity for heroism would ordinarily involve" (p. 262). A virtually cost-free form of risk is purveyed through vicarious experience, which Goffman refers to as "living once removed." An example of this would be the sports fan wearing an athlete's jersey, jumping up after the athlete has scored and saying "we did that." Identification with vicarious experience, Goffman proposes, is facilitated by focusing on a single actor (as opposed to a group) and by allowing the action to be fully realized in a certain, limited span of time. This suggests something about the emotionality of vicarious experience: there is a rush in this which means that you see me do something and you say, "Yes, that's what we're trying to do."

The rush or exciting part of it is what gets away from the calculation. Action is really driven by some sort of passion, which arises from emotion created in the circumstances. Vicarious experience, essentially, transports people out of their safe, workaday environments, placing them in these problematic and consequential circumstances where they have to take gambles. But in the end they only suffer the consequences of failure if they identify with the character.

One of the reasons we are interested in narratives aligns with this treatment of action and character by Goffman. Narratives enable us to see what happens to a character, maybe even ask, "Would I have taken that risk?" or "Do I have the skill that would be necessary to pull off that gamble?" without suffering the consequences of taking risks ourselves. We may even gain knowledge from others' achievements as a result of being the recipient of the story. This is vicarious learning.

Vulnerability and Effort

Paul Ricœur asserts that one thing that makes action interesting is people's fallibility and their doubt. They are limited in many ways, so when there is perfect prepara-tion for an action and it goes off without a hitch, then it would not be a story, it would be a report on a set of procedures that would be summarized by saying, "this is what we got done." It is only when a vulnerable character who has doubts takes a risk that the problematic dimension of action really comes to the fore and adds to the interest of the story. The possibility for human will in these situations helps explain why we are interested in the forcefulness of a character who actually takes risky action that moves something in a particular direction.

One way to understand the character is to locate the narrative grade s/he is climbing or descending (Browning, 1991). This aspect of character addresses the direction of the narrative slope (Rand, 2000). A narrative with a positive slope—things are going well, life is successful—while not easy, has the advantage of building on past successes. In narratives and in complexity, positives accumulate, good things lead to good things; relations amplify achievements that produce pleasant surprises in a synergistic fashion (Maruyama, 1963). But as Charles Perrow (1984) points out, the same formula for the things that go good is in effect when things are going bad. Just as $2+2 = 5$ in synergistic terms; $-2+-2 = -5$. This negative synergy of dual negative forces joining up is part of the formula Perrow uses to characterize accidents, or as he calls them, "normal accidents." The crisis (personal or global) that negative synergy creates is regularly used to display and understand character, because relevance is part of the consideration. The greater the consequences of failure, the greater the importance is placed on getting everything right. Therefore, someone who is able to hold things together when failure would be catastrophic, especially when others lack the ability to do so, is especially prized.

The Dynamic Nature of Character Narratives

Yet it is difficult to keep the dynamic nature of character in mind because we treat momentary evaluations of character as though they were frozen in time. Even when we talk about what a person does with his/her narrative and the responsibility they have for it, it is important to remember that we enter life as part of an ongoing narrative. "When we enter human life, it is as if we walk on stage into a play whose enactment is already in progress—a play whose somewhat open plot determines what parts we may play and toward what denouements we may be heading" (Lainé, 1998, p. 34). The presence of a character in an open plot means that the dramatic scene of entering human life is dependent on the time and place of entry, which makes a narrative beginning an astrological moment. But character assessments in such a moment may be well known in advance by others. Those in place ahead of the actor, who know the background, might include teachers, older siblings, coaches, counsellors, religious leaders, and of course parents. They have been in the world that precedes the actor and as a result have seen the actor learn, make mistakes, gain, and grow (or stumble) with an awareness of these events that the young actor cannot be conscious of. "Others on stage already have a sense of what the play is about, enough of a sense to make negotiation with a newcomer possible" (Lainé, 1998, p. 34).

All of this means that we enter a world of "possible selves" (Markus & Nurius, 1986) that includes the triad of features we have mentioned here: a sense of where we have been, a sense of what we might become, and a "now" self of who we are. The negotiation among the past, future, and present are aided by the questions of time and narrative (Ricœur, 1983, 1984). In Bruner's conception, the individual is forced to rebuild permanently the equilibrium between what s/he was, what s/he desires to be, and what the environment demands at present (Bruner, 1990).

We develop the character that others evaluate through the identity resources available to us. Anthony Giddens promotes the ongoing view of narrative to show that "the very idea of personal identity is not to be found in behavior, or—important though it is—in the reaction of others, but in the capacity to keep a particular narrative going" (cited in Gergen & Gergen, 1986, p. 103). What actions are necessary for keeping an identity story going? Part of what drives a story along is our possible hopes and sorrows as revealed by what we want to be or by a legacy we fear. What will I leave behind? As one might wonder, "What will become of my gun collection when I'm gone?" This self-directed query may refer not to a collection's value, but to the possible harm it might bring to others. What part of our character is flung into such a void, a future beyond us that will be left behind? Is it a torment? How does the moral achievement of child-raising affect our last narrative in life?

The identity narratives people construct represent their efforts to come to terms with a past, future, and present to provide a sense of unity in the face of an uncertain and chaotic world (Brown & Humphries, 2006). Of course, the institutions of which we are members fill in part of the uncertainty of identity construction. Institutions are a source of identity support, thus they have "encompassing tendencies" (Brown & Humphreys, 2006). For organizational communication, the fidelity between the version of life presented to the public and the actual communication within the organization is never an exact fit. An organization's own identity and character is achieved by celebrating its membership in ceremonies that cause members to value the organization and preserve its cherished identity through subsequent actions.

Communicating "This is who I am" is a life-long occupation. Joseph Campbell told a story near the end of his life about the mental work he was doing to move to the final step. In that conversation with Bill Moyers, Campbell said that the transformations keep coming—adolescence to adulthood, and end of career to retirement. The self-abstracted person, so clearly seen in adulthood, is one who has acquired a biography and thereby can tell his or her life story. A person thus is defined as "a self-narrating organism" (Ezzy, 1998, p. 239).

We agree with Ezzy that the most important part of narrating the self is the consciousness of temporality. "One of the most important consequences of a narrative conception of the self is that it incorporates temporality" (Ezzy, 1998, p. 239). Temporality is a code word for fate and hope; it means that narratives are more interesting when they emplot an intersection of forces. As an example, think of the development of women in the professions over the last 50 years and how much their opportunity to participate has changed. Now intersect that narrative with the collapse of the economy in the years of 2008, 2009, and 2010. What construction of narrative temporality is possible from these two forces?

The narrative about the past that is interpreted in relation to a future means that the events from which we construct a meaning for today are based on some sense of continuity from the past that serves us until the novelty of tomorrow "necessitates a new history which interprets the new future." In this scheme, we borrow from our history and make interpretative forms that look like Bakhtin's (1981) use of the novel to explain social life. We borrow from fiction sequences and ideas that allow us to interpret a past "in light of new experience that brings potentially contradictory information" (Ezzy, 1998, p. 243).

According to Ezzy, Ricœur emphasizes narratives of acting and living in the world in such a way that our past and futures are recalculated in the present. Ezzy makes the claim that "life is a nascent story" (Ezzy, 1998, p. 244). Life as a nascent story, of continual development and rebirth, is "living the ethnographic life" (Rose, 1990), a life of interpreting the world of what you see and know. Living the narrative life is to believe the purpose of life is experience and the meaning we make of it. In aesthetics, that means combining meaning with style (Brummett, 2008).

The term "narrative identity" as Ricœur (1991) uses it suggests that it is a subjective and a dynamic force: "what we call subjectivity is neither an incoherent series of events nor a stable substance; as a result it is a dynamic force." Narrative identities are multiple, processual, unfinished and thus are under continual reconstruction because they try to corral "the disordered nature of life and because we cannot be sure how the story will end" (Ezzy, 1998, p. 245). If complexity is chaotic and a narrative is unfinished, it is continually made and remade, or in Weick's (1969) term, accomplished and reaccomplished.

"A narrative identity provides a sense of personal continuity through time grounded in social networks and larger institutions" (Ezzy, 1998, p. 248). The continuity across time that networks provide means that it only takes a little organizing of social support groups to affirm the self. Organizations are important, apart from networks, for the support they provide in terms of resources and for the formal system of approval that comes with formal evaluations.

The narrative integration of lived experience and preexisting plots reflects the influence of power, social organization and the "politics of storytelling." Further, routine activities, regularly used props, and a stable, or predictable, physical environment are also important sources of a sense of personal identity (Ezzy, 1998, p. 248). Such resources as these to make a narrative dependable are plentiful in organizations. The exchange for members is to keep up the routines the organization directs, whether sales or administration.

Application: The Celebration of Others and Their Deeds

Becoming more aware of premises about character and identity in stories enables us to develop and express our appreciation for, and celebration of, the lives, actions, challenges, and accomplishments of those around us. Stories that apply concepts of character and identity often celebrate others, giving expressions of high regard and offering homage for the person's unique contributions. Celebratory narratives about others honor them and express gratitude for what they have done.

The following narrative from a university student nicely illustrates celebration for the person being honored, his grandmother:

> *July 19th, 2009 was my grandmother Kim's 79th birthday. For this momentous event, family from all over the world came over to my mom's house ... To celebrate, my mom put out lush red roses, she hung a framed photo of my grandmother over the mantel, fresh food was laid out on the dinner table (perfuming the whole house with the scent of Korea), bottles of alcohol lay in a tub of ice, and there was soda for the kids.*
>
> *My grandma's birthday means a lot to me. Since I was little, she was always there for me and when I would get mad at my parents, she would always be on my side. When I was eight years old, I left the faucet running for almost 20 minutes and somehow the sink wasn't draining, so the kitchen floor was drenched in water. I remember my mom being so angry that she grounded me for a week. She scolded me for being so careless and forgetful, then made me mop up the mess. While I was getting in trouble, my grandma was there calming my mom down and defending me. She even took the mop from my hands and made the kitchen cleaner than it was before. Not even two days into my punishment, my grandma snuck me out of the house and took me to the zoo. We got snow cones as soon as we got there, then went exploring. I remember looking at the giant elephants, reptiles, and screaming monkeys. There were numerous occasions like that in which my grandma would come to my rescue.*
>
> *Growing up, she always made sure I was healthy, well-fed and happy. She would sacrifice everything she had just for me. Thinking back, there have been times she would give me money to buy things that I really wanted, even though she wasn't wealthy. She was always so generous with what little she had, and I would feel awful taking anything from her, but she would hide money under my pillow, or in a dresser, then tell me about it later over the phone.*

Every year on July 18th I'll give her a call or visit and spend time with her to show how much I appreciate her. This year, though, things were different. On her 79th birthday, family from all over the world gathered to celebrate my grandma's birthday, but this year she wasn't with us. She passed away a few months before her birthday. We decided anyway that we would celebrate her life and show our appreciation for her kindness, generosity, and positive, optimistic energy. For many of us, her death was unexpected, so this was a way to get closure and say goodbye.

Such a tribute operates something like the opening of presents on Christmas day, in that each gift selects and acknowledges parts of the recipient's character that merit celebration. In this example, Mrs. Kim is honored for standing up for the storyteller and for her generosity towards him. Not content with adjectives such as kindness and generosity to describe her, the narrator relates how she rescued him, participated in the labor of his punishment, violated his parents' prohibitions, and secretly stashed money for him under his pillow. A particularly nice feature of his tribute is that it relates two kinds of celebration for his grandmother: his personal tribute and the family gathering on the occasion of her birthday.

The distinction between celebrating a life with and without the local, personal stories that illustrate the target person's uniqueness can be seen by contrasting the above story with the following tribute. In this case, a man's daughter is honoring him for making more of himself than might have been expected:

My dad was raised in Indiana on a farm, by a mother who was a hard-working nurse and a father who held many positions and jobs. The second child of three, he was born into a working-class family. He grew up as a farm boy, and he watched his father work hard but never achieve stability. He watched his mother struggle to juggle a full-time career and the requirements of being a mom of three. He struggled in school and was considered a slow reader and a slow learner for his age. He watched his brother, who was a troublemaker, show no sign of initiative, but all signs of educational success.

At the age of 14, it would seem that his life and character were destined to be similar to his father's. He had struggled in school and sometimes followed in his brother's footsteps, even when they led to trouble. Any one of his teachers would have told you that he would be lucky to marry, find a job, and live a modest life. He would have agreed.

His transformation from a downward to an upward slope in his life was not a drastic one. He began to work on small engines with his father, and he learned how intelligent his dad really was. The appearance of simplicity and commonness was far from the truth. My dad quickly moved from small tinkering to rebuilding entire car engines. He learned patience and perseverance through this hobby.

As high school graduation neared, he began to wonder if the self he thought he was was the same as the self he wanted to be. He thought about what kinds of people went to college. He knew he didn't fit into this mold, but he also knew that education was an important part of his future. Somehow, with average grades and writing ability, my dad made it into the university. His struggles didn't end there. His parents were unable to finance or even contribute to his education, but he was able to find a working-student program where he worked every other semester. The semesters he wasn't working and, during the summers, he went to school. He found that the character others began to know him as was similar to the person he wanted to be.

He graduated with an engineering degree and eventually was hired by Chevron. The people who know him now see him as a successful, knowledgeable person. My dad is quick to agree, but he also remembers the identity he once knew, as a slow, destined-to-fail farm boy. His self-constructed identity is the reason for his success. The person he is today is honorable and respectable, and I am proud of his determination and strength in the face of adversity. I owe a great deal of my positive attributes to his character.

In this celebratory narrative, the arc of the person's life is represented as a series of expectations, efforts, milestones, and accomplishments, but the points along the way are not narrated in detail. For instance, no particular incidents of his father teaching him about engines are related. When did he learn that his dad was really intelligent? He appears to have done well in college. How did he do that? Who helped him along the way? In the preceding story of the Korean Grandma's seventy-ninth birthday, the storyteller filled in the detail about his grandma's character by relating incidents that happened between them. We see the grandma making choices to rescue a child, countermanding parental demands, and sacrificing her own wellbeing for that of her grandson. Both are worthy applications of concepts of character and identity, but only the latter offers a local, sensitive portrait of the celebrated person's life.

Another sense of appreciation that may arise from deeper immersion in narratives of character and identity is a tendency to celebrate the lives and actions of persons who would ordinarily not receive such recognition. Stories of character and identity often herald "unsung heroes," persons close by whose actions are praiseworthy but are usually overlooked. The chaplain's story (Isay, 2008) of the people in a hospital basement blessing surgical instruments, included in Chapter One, is a nice illustration of such a sense of appreciation. Where ordinarily the surgeon's actions would be characterized, in this instance the actions of those far from the limelight were heralded. They bring to the moment something of their own identity and self-concept. Not only do they do what the organization needs them to do (provide antiseptic medical instruments) but at the point they pick up and bless the instruments, they are adding their own beliefs and hopes about what will eventuate in a good surgical outcome. As in the preceding examples, the chaplain's story expresses both her high regard for and her gratitude to them.

A related sense of appreciation pertains to seeing and honoring the distinctiveness of the characters of those with whom we interact. Part of being appreciative is to know things about another person that we had not seen previously. This is a rather strong form of appreciation, the kind of thing that is strived for in intercultural communication. The goal is not merely to observe or tolerate others' differences from oneself, nor change one's assessments of other people and groups, but to see and interact with others as unique individuals. An outcome of stories about character and identity development is to see and value others' distinctiveness rather than seeing them more remotely as members of a group. The following tribute a student offered to one of her fellow students narrates how she came to know that the focal person, a sorority sister, was not just another pretty face:

> When I first met Sarah, all I knew about her was that she was a gorgeous, thin, blonde sorority girl from Houston, Texas. I was to be her pledge trainer. It was my job to teach pledges all the things they need to know about college and sorority life. I took 50 of the new girls on a pledge retreat to Camp Champions, in Marble Falls, Texas. The first day, we were getting ready to leave, everyone had come to the house, had gotten their coolers loaded on the bus. We were counting and found we were missing people. We found that Sarah was missing. So we called Sarah, and she said, "Oh my gosh! I slept through my alarm. I am so sorry. I'll get ready right now." We said, "No worries. We'll bring the bus and pick you up right outside your dorm." We called Sarah again once we got there and she said, "Okay. You know, I am still getting ready. I'm sorry." So I decided to go up to her dorm room to help her pack and put her things together, because this entire bus of 50 people is waiting for her to come so we could leave for our retreat.
>
> Well, I got up to her room and she was slowly packing, kind of hesitant, and I asked her, "Sarah. What's wrong, is everything okay?" And she said, "Yeah. Yeah. It's fine. I just slept through my alarm. I wasn't ready. I'm sorry. We can go. We can go." And so we were running down the hall, getting in the elevator, and I noticed that Sarah was tearing up. I said, "Sarah, don't worry about it. No problem. You are here now and we are glad you are coming with us." And she looked at me and said, "No, no, no. It's not that. I-It's just that—my senior year in high school I was in a horrible accident on a charter bus. Four of my best friends died." And that's when I noticed that she had these horrific scars all the way down her left arm. Tears were welling up in her eyes and she said, "You know, I just haven't been on a charter bus since that day."
>
> My heart just sank to my stomach, and I said, "Sarah, by no means do you have to get on this charter bus right now. Everyone will understand. I can drive you. We can drive behind the bus. You don't have to get on it." And she said, "No, no, no, Natalie. If I am going to do it at any point in time, this will be a great time, with all my new sorority sisters, all these people who care about me. It's been a year now. It's been enough time. I'm going to have to get on one eventually. I want to do this today."
>
> From that moment on, I thought of Sarah in a whole different way. When I first met her, all I had was a bunch of characteristics to describe her from the outside. That day, she showed me part of her identity and who she was, this strong, vivacious, girl who loves life and was given a second chance at life after her accident and she hasn't taken it for granted for one day.

In this narrative, not only is the distinctiveness of Sarah showcased by relating the relationship between the current bus trip and the deadly one she previously took, but also the dialogue that occurred between Sarah and the narrator was related. We learn that Sarah was initially reluctant to explain why she was stalling. We learn that she declined Natalie's invitation not to get on the bus. We learn that she understood the trip as an opportunity to put the crash incident behind her or, in other words, to shrink the size of one story and replace it with another, better one. So, we not only glimpse a person being justifiably timid, but also a person facing her fears and accepting help. By virtue of this included dialogue, we also glimpse the identity of the narrator as a thoughtful, helpful, sensitive student leader.

Conclusion

Identity and character narratives are ontological narratives (Somers, 1994; Ezzy, 1998) in that stories constructed by the self are designed to communicate the coming into being that results in constructing the nature of the person. An individual's identity is how he or she situates him or herself in the extended temporal sequence that makes up a set of beginning circumstances, a life, and a legacy. One's character is who one is taken to be by others and the moral assessments they make of one. Character narratives are epistemological in the sense that they reveal what one person has come to know about another. Both these ways of coming into being are mutable, at least to a point; it is never too late to start a good reputation and it is never too late to learn something new about others that changes their character for us.

That, in the end, might be the prime lesson of Albert Nobel, merchant of death and originator of the Nobel Peace Prize.

6

INTEREST AND MEMORY

In the glow of the running lights, most of the crew looked like refugees, huddled, wearing blank faces. Among them, Tom West appeared as a thin figure under a watch cap, in nearly constant motion. High spirits had apparently possessed him from the moment they set sail, and the longer they were out in the storm, the heavier the weather got, the livelier he grew. You could see him grinning in the dark. West did all that the captain asked, so cheerfully, unquestioningly and fast, that one might have thought the ghost of an old-fashioned virtuous seaman had joined them. Only West never confessed to a queasy stomach. When one of the others asked him if he felt seasick, too, he replied, in a completely serious voice, that he would not let himself. A little later, he made his way down to the cabin, moving like a veteran conductor in a rocking, rolling railroad car, and got himself a beer.

West was at the helm, the tiller in both hands, riding the waves; he was standing under a swaying lantern in the cabin studying the chart; he was nimbly climbing out onto the foredeck to wrestle a jib and replace it with a smaller one. And when the captain decided to make for shelter, very late that night, at a little harbor with a passage into it that was twisty, narrow and full of tide, it was West, standing up in the bow, who spotted each unlighted channel marker and guided them safely in.

Introduction

The character sketch with which we begin this chapter is from what we consider to be one of the best organizational narratives, *The Soul of a New Machine*, by Tracy Kidder (1981, pp. 4–5). The book narrates the successful development of a new mini-computer by a team led by Tom West, the person depicted as "a good man in a storm" in the selection above. This sketch of Tom West epitomizes for us the interesting and memorable narrative. We appreciate it so much because it marks so many stark contrasts between what most people would do if they found themselves in a storm at sea, and the competence, force of character, and joy Tom West was able to muster. We also appreciate the author's selection of this story, from everything he knew about Tom West and his team, as an experience to be remembered and celebrated about him. It is not about his leadership aboard ship, but rather his casual, flowing, masterful accomplishment of whatever needed to be done. Something about this opening story compels us to remember it now, nearly 30 years after we first encountered it.

This chapter is about what makes stories interesting and memorable. Memory and interest are combined into one angle on narrative appreciation because these two concepts can account for both the present attention and the long-term recall a powerful narrative can invoke. We center the chapter on five challenges the story-teller faces as he or she tries to come up with something that will not be judged to be dull and forgettable. We offer several stories as examples of the challenges being handled well. The application for this chapter, which we discuss at the end, is to use narratives to transport hearers or readers: that is, to move them to the scene of the action and make a long-lasting impression on them. In essence, the transportation application is about invoking extremely high degrees of interest and memory in the hearers' or readers' experience of the narrative.

Five Challenges

It is tempting, when seeking to explain how narrators can arouse interest and provoke memory for hearers, to determine a set of ingredients which interesting and mem-orable narratives possess. A fairly credible list developed with that approach might include such concepts as context, novelty, surprise, suspense, and relevance. We think making and explaining such a list would oversimplify what it really takes to make interesting and memorable narratives, because doing so is not just like adding in the necessary ingredients in a cooking recipe. It is more like knowing the right mix of ingredients, balancing the tastes of some off with the tastes of others, giving the whole concoction time to come together, and stopping at the perfect time. So, to register this greater degree of difficulty in constructing interesting and memorable narratives, we offer here a set of five challenges that the successful narrator must meet if he or she expects to be listened to intently and give listeners something to remember.

1. Connecting with, yet departing from, context. Stories use known and remembered circumstances and historical persons as a launching pad. The action in a story is a departure from what ordinarily happens, but it needs to be grounded in these normal conditions. Something has to trigger the story; it has to begin some-where. The source of the triggers for drawing interest in a story can be as varied as from the nature of *who* is interested in the story (some people are ready to hear; some people search for an answer), *whose* turn it is to tell the story (contention over who has the right to be the voice of the story), *what* is being said (its discursive nature and style) at what *moment* (there is a time and place where every thing comes together (plot convergence)). Interesting stories hold these things in common.

Any content, even a bland numerical representation or algorithm, can start to add up to a story when a context is provided. When people say they don't want to be treated like a number, they are saying they want the numbers about them to be understood in context of the situation. They want a story about them. One finding about nursing homes in the United States is that the more patients are visited, the better the care they received from the staff of the institution. In addition to monitoring for quality, and knowing that someone cares for them, as reasons for assuring the best of care, when visitors came, the elderly shared stories with their family members. The staff began to overhear a story of who their client was; once the patient had a story, they became more of a person and received of better treatment (Brown, 1982).

When narrators begin stories, they do not merely represent circumstances and people. There is much more to establishing context than that. They actively select memories, composed of emotions, details, causal relationships, and dialogue, to evoke memories of a place and time and give people a history. Since these memories are to an extent durable, they can be used to interpret present actions. By invoking them, the narrator sets up a familiar point of departure, like a home territory, from which the action (e.g. a quest) can emerge. This context is a summation of a state of affairs that prevailed when the real action in the story begins.

Since many fine narratives are constructed improvisationally in spontaneous conversation, it is not automatic for the narrator to remember moments and images of the past that can serve to establish context. A premise of narratology is that the past is held together through memories—the unwritten, tellable experiences of people. Memory is involved at the global level (when the culture of the organization is represented in stories) and the personal level of individual story memory (what am I thinking about what to tell?). Memory is one of the ancient canons of rhetoric and refers to what a speaker recalls to place in his/her oral text; if one wants to develop a story that has an impact, then memory of what to say becomes part of composition. In narrative speaking, one can't compose what one does not have in the head. If a speaker is beginning to tell a story, s/he is usually operating extemporaneously as s/he searches the mind for details and order. What to say in what order with what emphases is dependent on the narrator's scan for information. Memory, then, is constantly in play and is so important that it is "one part of the virtue of prudence, which figures among the major virtues, along with courage, justice, and temperance" (Ricœur, 2004, p. 64).

Memory's importance is reaffirmed when it is absent. We understand our own normal practices more concretely when they are compared to a person for whom narrative recall is missing. A person who has no narrative has no memory. The consequence for unconscious narratives is that they do not allow for an "inner voice" to guide a person's behavior, thus the person has an inability to "interpret and adjust to signals and to negotiate a place for oneself among them" (Dimaggio, Salvatore, Azzara, Catania, Semerari, & Hermans, 2003, p. 391).

The cognitive conception of the person is that s/he is responsible for knowing who they are and accounting for themselves. Harré and Secord (1972) say that to get to the cognition of a person, why not ask them? Memory operates with interest in story development because it is cognitive; one way of remembering stories is by tracing their cause and effect. "It is not simply the images of things that return to the mind but the intelligible ideas themselves. In this, the memory is equated with *cogito*" (Ricœur, 2004, p. 99). For a narrative to exist, it must have a space in a person's memory, and placement is aided by sorting that includes both a chronology and causality. The causal interpretation of the past amounts to reality itself for the narrator, since reality consists, not of occurrence "but that, first of all, they were remembered and second, that they are capable of finding a place in the chronological ordered sequence" (White, 1980, p. 23). Part of the ordering sequence to aid memory is constructing schemes for how people relate to each other. "Memories of the past, myths, dreams and day-dreams are stored in a pool of stories providing an individual with models for how relationships are articulated" (Dimaggio et al., 2003 p. 386). Ricœur adds to this the notion that memory is an image and thus a perception. "If a memory is an image in this sense, it contains a positional dimension that, from this point of view, brings it closer to perception (2004, p. 48). Making the tie of memory to perception means that memory is associated with human needs (hungry people have different images of food than content ones; children without money overestimate the size of a quarter). Given the array of things that affect memory, it can be conceived of as a mutual causal system; numerous things are in play, powerful main effects may offset each other so much that a side issue— the color of the sofa, the depth of the pile of the carpet—becomes causal in the story (Maruyama, 1964). The memory of causal linkages is both selective and limited (Ricœur, 2004). The order of presentation of events in a story is best organized around setting up the context, building to the point of the story, delivering the punch line, and moving away to give the listener a chance to incorporate the point of the story into his or her thinking. This search for cause and effect among an array of possibilities is a cognitive process.

Presuming limited capacity as it is represented (March & Simon, 1958) means that a good narrative is partial. How much to remember is additionally complicated because it is sometimes important to shrink memories (repress, forget, sublimate) that do the person harm and, in effect, forget them. They might also be replaced with stories of autonomy. This calibration requires bringing to the forefront the memories that reaffirm the person as an interesting character and independent self and moving to the background the non-supportive stories. The speaker has to believe in the story. (Weick would call this part of the story: "Respect for the self.") A big test of the story is whether the person wants to live and defend the story told; as we elaborate in the identity chapter when we say, by my story I am answering, "Who am I?"

Memory for stories is not simply a matter of recall because memory is selective even when all the information is available. Tales shared at a family reunion tend to be a remix of familiar stories. Remembering some events over others means that a person completes a kind of early editing in story construction, which is one way of assuring emotional distance. "The memory is, in fact, capable of recalling joy without being joyful, and sadness without being sad" (Ricœur, 2004, p. 99). This suggests the amount of emotionality included in the contents of a story or in telling a story is a cognitive choice—people can be trained to open up and shut down memories depending on what is needed for a competent narrative. Another component of a limited and flexible memory is the presumption that minds are dormant until something triggers them; a stimulus must exist before there can be a response. Stories can spark an emotion, change the senses, give a shock of adrenalin, or induce a softer, tearful feeling. Narratives arouse the listener to attend to what is being said. Stories are not automatically interesting; it is not a matter of presenting the facts; they can be boring, somewhat interesting, or, in the extreme, fascinating. Polster (1987) invites us to take the banal and transform it into fascination by looking for the turn in a person's life that shows its dynamism and distinctiveness.

One thing to make clear about the idea of context is that it does not mean only the background information given at the start of the narrative. An important part of context is the situation or event into which the story is introduced and back to which the storyteller and audience return when the story is finished.

Our approach to narrative presumes an informed audience, a selection of listeners who would know the wider relevance of the memorable story, which means that the necessary amount of context is in keeping with Grice's (1975) concept relevance, causing the listener to ask, "now that you have my attention, what does this mean to me?" Since attention is a scarce resource for narratives in organizations (Cohen, March, & Olsen, 1976), what do you do with it when you have it? You can't have stories all the time. When is the story told and what is the telling used for?

Part of the meaning of the term "context" is the situation or event from which a story emerges. It is important to remember the conversational, interactive character of story contexts because the fact of telling a story changes the context. The impact of telling stories and having others react to them is generative: "telling stories generates further stories in the listener's mind" (Dimaggio et al., 2003, p. 391), thus memory stimulates memories.

2. Balancing the novel with the familiar. The easiest way to create a memorable story is to surprise, to provide an angle, a point of view that is unexpected. Yet stories need also to capitalize on the familiar. There must be something in it you have not heard before (a new story); or have heard before with such fond memories that you want to revisit that time and emotion again (sentimental story). Like most other forms of communication, a story requires a mix of the novel and the traditional. What is surprising is a sudden, unexpected departure from the familiar, providing a contrast between what is expected and what actually happens. In another artistic domain, New York University set designer and drawing teacher Sal Tagliarino drills into his students that "contrast equals interest," and the same definitely applies to narratives. It is not simply that something unexpected happens; it is also how the familiar is drawn upon to set up the unexpected.

To get a feel for the importance of the familiar we need only consider that some stories are told recurrently specifically to affirm a belief or value the listener already has. This is why religious and other ideological stories may be tiresome for most, but not the true believer. For them, the problem is not how to believe, but how to keep the belief alive in narrative ideologies which are belief systems that are held together completely by stories. We all value having our beliefs affirmed, especially on matters of value, taste, and competence. We never tire of stories that reaffirm our belief systems.

Surprise is fascinating because it takes the listener from the unknown to the known in a moment like an epiphany or an insight, in which, by definition, surprises come in a flash. When the listener gets the point in an instant, you've had an interesting story.

The OED definition of "novelty" simply states that the term refers to "a new or unusual thing" or to "a new matter or recent event." Narrative is a tool for registering novelty when the story contrasts with a previously understood condition or state of affairs. Narratives are especially useful for registering such change because they universally depend on something changing—a problematic—for a story to count (Franklin, 1986). Good stories are an interruption in present thinking, a surprise, which causes the listener to pay attention to it, identify with the event, or with a character in the story. The listener might say, *That could happen to me; I could be that person* (Snowden, 2003).

Novelty is determined by surprise, especially when the surprise wipes out our past expectations for sensemaking. "What is going on here?" is answered with a violation of expectations (Weick, 2001). Surprise is extraordinarily useful to surface because it allows us to probe what people take for granted, what point of view they have that shows what they expect. This suggests that surprise not only transports the listener to something new, it brings into sharp relief the nature of the difference and the listener's past assumptions about it (Snowden, 2003). A surprise brings to the fore what we presumed would happen, "what is taken for granted, what is expected to be the case" (Snowden, 2003, p. 46). Surprise breaks what is expected in a given case, in part because expectations are so strong in organizations, especially in relation to organizational sensemaking (Weick & Sutcliffe, 2007).

Narrative's ability to turn assumptions into a shocking, jaw-slacking surprise allows us to probe our thinking about such relevant topics as success and failure because they are the stimulus of stories of beginnings, in religious stories, and in personal identity stories (McAdams, 2006). Seeing things in a new way becomes a communicable story.

The advantage of telling stories of near failure is that they are often tales of warning: "this could have happened to you" or "this might have happened." Snowden makes narrative the central idea of his consulting about future possibilities—both the kind to seek out and the kind to avoid—and he occasionally asks the following question in his seminars: "What spreads fastest in your organization—stories of failure or stories of success?" He says the usual answer is "failure" because we realize that stories of failure are more valuable than success stories (Snowden, 2003). Because people tend to agree more on what is going wrong than what is going right; what are called "best practice" efforts in fact rely on the ability to identify *both* past successes and past failures (Browning & Boudes, 2005). What is interesting in a story need not be entirely new if it can bring a new perspective and lead to refinement of held knowledge; sometimes a small percentage change in a work formula can cause significant differences. Remembering successes and failures is one way to identify such differences.

Stories that depict emotional arousal reinforce "long-term memory; in particular declarative memory" (Dimaggio et al., 2003, p. 390), which is a feeling about the past that is certain enough for a person to speak it or to "declare" it, to say this was the way it was. Declaration also implies that one form of memory is the act of telling the story to someone. If we don't tell the story soon enough after the experience or often enough immediately after the experience or if we don't tell the story at all, the experience cannot be coalesced into a gist since its component pieces begin to mix with new information that often continuously rolls in (Schank, 1995, p. 115).

In narrative theory, interest builds in three ways to draw the audience to the story. Novelty can arise from *mystery*, where the audience knows less than the characters and remains involved to find out what happens. It can come from *suspense*, where the audience and characters know the same information, but they don't know when the provocative event will occur. Or the interest can arise from *irony*, where the audience knows more than the characters, but is surprised by how the story comes together and remains engaged to see how and when the characters realize what is going on (McKee, 1997, pp. 349–51). These three narrative types generate interest because they draw a spark, a moment of awareness, that redirects attention toward the point or message in the story. A story provoking an emotional reaction in a listener is therefore one that "will impress itself better in his or her memory" (Dimaggio et al., 2003, p. 390).

Given our attention to stories of the workplace, we identify various kinds of ironies in organizations, ones that can be managed skillfully to elicit interest and make a compelling and memorable story.

Ironies of variation are important for narratives because we use stories as containers for memory, and one way of doing so involves the sort of items that are a necessary part of the story. Ironies of variation question what is multiple and what is singular; what is integrated and what is held together with a single force (Bakhtin, 1981). What seem to be assorted and mixed matters are in reality composed of a single element. What seems to be a single thing is in reality composed of heterogeneous elements—a family reunion of people with the same last name discovering that living their lives produced different outcomes and values. What seems to be stable and unchanging is in reality unstable and changing: for example, the skin on the human body looks stable, but completely replaces itself every 30 days. What seems to be unstable and changing is in reality stable and unchanging.

Aristotle (1981) proposed that stories present events as causally connected. Steps toward an outcome and outcomes themselves must seem necessary in some sense. The causal implications of an event may not (and often should not) be obvious when the event occurs in the story, but subsequent events should seem inevitable once they happen. By framing events in a certain way, stories make strong statements about their causes. The story that uses irony of cause replaces what we thought was the cause of a circumstance with another, novel cause. For instance, a force that appears to function ineffectively as a means for the attainment is in reality effective. It is commonly believed among urban managers and police forces that replacing broken windows in worn down factory building reduces crime in an area. Potential criminals see a place well kept and move on down the street. Opposed to a practice that appears to be effective is one that one assumes is effective but which is, in fact, the opposite. Runaway medical costs in the Rio Grande Valley of Texas, as developed in Chapter Three, support this premise. Such an irony grabs us because it rolls over our own sense of what-causes-what.

The classic story of the design of the typewriter keyboard illustrates this (see below). It keeps the readers' interest by explaining the systems and circumstances that led to an inefficient design, the QWERTY keyboard. Most people take it for granted and assume that it survived over time because it made the most sense. In truth, there were a variety of politically motivated reasons for its success and the failure of the Dvorak keyboard.

> You might expect the keyboard is designed so that most of the typing is done on the home row. You would be wrong. Only 32% of strokes are on the home row; most (52%) are on the upper row, and 16% are on the bottom row. A new version of the keyboard called Dvorak has nine of the most common English letters—including all five vowels and the most common consonants (T,H,N)—on the home row, while the six rarest letters (V,K,J,X,and Z) are on the dreaded bottom row. Therefore, 70% of typing strokes remain on the home row, with only 22% on the upper row, and a mere 8% on the bottom row. Thousands of words can be typed with only the home row.
>
> The QWERTY system is an inferior method. Over 3000 English words utilize the left hand alone. This overuse of one hand extends to our weaker fingers. The QWERTY makes almost as much use of the weakest finger (pinky) as it does of the second strongest (right third). The outcome of all of this is typing that is unnecessarily tiring, slow, inaccurate, hard to learn, and hard to remember. A good typist's fingers cover 2 miles on a QWERTY keyboard, but only one mile on a Dvorak keyboard. Dvorak typists hold most of the world records for typing speed. QWERTY typists make about twice as many mistakes as Dvorak typists. A beginner using a QWERTY keyboard needs 56 hours of training in order to reach 40 words per minute. The same person needs only 18 hours using a Dvorak keyboard … In short, the QWERTY keyboard is a perfect example of obsolete technology and process. So why do we use it? Why is it the winner?
>
> The QWERTY typewriter did not win because it was the best invention then or now; rather it won for other reasons … The QWERTY system was clearly less "fit"

or effective, but those buying the typewriter perceived it to be a better way. Because one company, E. Remington & Sons, started mass-producing a typewriter with the QWERTY layout, more typists began to learn the system, which meant that other typewriter companies began to offer the QWERTY keyboard ... Soon everyone began ordering this new tool and inertia built up. The power of the status quo took over, and Remington continued to use the QWERTY – even as newer typewriters evolved.

(Denton, 1999, pp. 76–77)

This story is interesting because it shows how technological questions affect our practices long after the original reasons for them have passed. QWERTY is also interesting because it is dissipative—a choice was made, and long after the reason for it passed, the commitment to it remained. Ironies of cause are engaging because one dimension of human intelligence is the ability to predict outcomes from causes. When a story has a tripwire about causes, it both shatters and attracts the listener.

3. Juxtaposing the liminal and the persistent. Another source of interest is liminality. We use Turner's meaning of *liminal,* "betwixt and between" (Turner, 1987), for this section because he focuses on people and situations that are in the throes and phases of change, and to be liminal is to be an agent or actor in an open and changing environment. Narratives are dependent on the transition to "what's next" because responding to the future and having a plan for the future is a relevant decision for any given day. Narratives are able to register change because they are adept at capturing a sequence of events, from beginning to end, and infusing them with meaning. It is important to ask not only what is going on now, but also what is changing. How soon will things change? Managers and leaders often complain about how much change is taking place, but their power and value actually come from their ability to respond to uncertainty (Pondy & Mitroff, 1979). The more uncertain one is of the future, the more one seeks experts. Uncertainty often compels us to respond by making rituals to mark the transition from one state or status to another. Models of progressive steps usually allow for contingency when they have "if, then" assumptions within them. *If-then* statements are analytic when they contend, "If such and such can be achieved or is allowed to happen ... then such and such will follow." And if such and such follows, then we should see an increase in positive outcomes and a decrease in problematic ones. Narratives are filled with such contingencies and when they are there, there is more interest than a machine-like response to regularity. "If I fail, then my father will reject me" or "If I succeed, then my father will love me more" (Baldwin & Sinclair, 1996, p. 1131). The sense of anticipation and expectation creates an interest in what is happening and what will happen next. Multiple, continuous thresholds of meanings and symbols characterize liminality.

If liminality is about what's next, persistence reaches beyond what's next to commitment and investment in keeping a story going. Persistence refers to a continuing and vigilant interest in seeing change through to its conclusion. To be interesting, a story requires both a spark that draws the attention and a continued investment in what comes next. One of the reasons that Weick and Sutcliffe (2007) emphasize vigilance so much is how quickly training effects dissolve without continued reinforcement. Stories serve as reminders—especially if we never tire of hearing them. What is the extended or deliberate interest? Liminality for listeners means that they are so caught up that they are lost in the flow of the story, in their curiosity about what will happen next.

The following example is narrated by an actor who suffered in a liminal and in-between position for a protracted period of time. As a bonus, this narrative also illustrates the moral irony that what he thought was bad turned out to be good:

> *My library career began with a nine-month gestation period as a trainee at the Bodleian Library, working (if that is the word) mostly in underground stacks, deprived of natural light but made tolerable by the presence of a lot of young ladies. The "scholarly" work took place upstairs; the scholarship may have been impressive, but its practitioners as a whole were not. In those days it was a restful place. I learnt nothing there.*
>
> *Next stop was Glasgow University Library, with its guard-book catalogue, its antiquated building where I nearly knocked myself out several times against overhead iron beams, and its overwhelmingly female staff, one of whom I married. Here I learnt to speak Glesga (though I never fully mastered it—one of the janitors used to tell me jokes; I knew he had reached the punch-line when he laughed, so I did too), and probably did learn a little about management.*
>
> *The 12 following years, at Southampton University Library, are imprinted on my soul. The first seven were spent under [Miss H.], who dropped into the job during the war. In retrospect, I realise that she was a very insecure and neurotic woman, who should never have been in charge of anything. She was a mistress of demotivation. She had an unerring eye for the trivial and irrelevant, a general scorn for readers (who included the entire staff of the university), and a fear of her own senior staff, which manifested itself in bullying, rudeness, and dissatisfaction with whatever was done. As a result, we did as little as we could. We were dying to get out of the place, but since we were given no responsibility our applications did not read well. She retired early, at the age of 55, having worn herself out by antagonising everyone; when she announced her coming departure, we all sat stunned until one of my colleagues said with monumental tact "Well, we would all agree the place won't be the same without you," to which we all wholeheartedly assented.*

But for this character, the pain of his supervisor eventually had a positive outcome. Here is how he continues:

> *Life under Miss H. was misery. However, I owe four things to her. First, I knew that her idea of a library, as an organisation to which everyone had to adapt, was wrong; so I started to think what a library designed around people might be like. This way of thinking has never left me. Secondly, I learnt in the hardest way how continuous criticism can damage, even destroy, people by eroding their energy, their wish to work,*

and their self-belief. Thirdly, to keep myself sane I became involved in university affairs, becoming president of the local Association of University Teachers and later an elected member of Senate. For the same reason I joined several extra-university bodies, and discovered I could be a reasonable chair, secretary and speaker. Finally, she left me with a fund of stories of her absurdity and iniquity, stories which have served me well ever since.

(Line, 2005, pp. 156–57)

This story is interesting because it takes the envisioned logistical tedium of re-stacking and checking out library books and gives it a personal context and an effect over time. It is easy to conjure all the ways Miss H. might have selected the needless, the trivial, and the observable as points of control over the powerless staff who had no way to escape her. Without any physical cues, the reader is on his or her own to paint a picture of her in the mind's eye. The storyteller's assignment of the distributed costs of her petty and soul damaging behavior—even to Miss H. herself—is interesting because the behavior continues even though its failure is evident; persistent blindness is interesting. When the storyteller tells of the learning hatched in the years of monotony he experienced, he offers us an irony: I learned in spite of her; I learned to do the opposite of what she did because the tolls of her practice were so obvious.

This story rings true because the context he describes is so familiar—dreary library basements with low ceilings, women professionals in service roles, self-important professors, and little chance of change. It is easy to accept his interpretation of the negotiated order—a theory that accounts for an individual's particular location in a structure and how s/he handles it. The story is a moral irony because, despite his distaste for Miss H., he learns a moral lesson about being good and bad from her and transfers the hard lesson to his own practice.

4. Matching the uncertain with the reliable. An interesting and memorable story has to have uncertainty, but at the end the uncertainty of the story needs to resolve back into some reassurance that we have the capabilities and resources to handle what comes next. To a point, chaos is interesting; the bombing of Pearl Harbor is interesting because of the mass uncertainty that surrounded it—What is happening? Who are they? How to respond? Is there a future? Things that are changing are interesting, whether it is roles, resources, rules, environments, personalities, or group compositions that are at play. Stories are interesting when they capture the world in flux. There are lots of things going on; lots of possible different outcomes; something is at risk. The archetype is the love story in times of war. Interest matches variety with variety. All-encompassing concepts must be understood with all-encompassing concepts. Ultimately, the challenge of an interesting story is to show how actors grappled with uncertainty and created something reliable.

Since organizations differ from other structures in the amount of control they display, they are especially interesting when the expectations for control are violated (Davis, 1971). What seems to be a disorganized (unstructured) phenomenon is in reality an organized (structured) phenomenon. A story about sharing information helps to make this point. In this story, the CEO of the company does something out of the ordinary, which has the effect of changing the entire system of how the company communicates. Here is the context for the story: the CEO of a small firm decides to open the company's entire financial records with its employees to explain why they have to eliminate overtime, wage increases, quarterly bonuses, and new equipment. The employees learn how to understand the records and, as a result, begin questioning the costs of doing business instead of merely looking at the profits of the company. With open communication the company was able to figure out how to deal with the company's financial crisis.

> *Because of an economic recession, Hugh Aaron, the CEO of a small closely held plastics manufacturer, told his employees that the company must eliminate overtime, wage increases, quarterly bonuses, and the purchase of new equipment; even his wages were being cut. The announcement was spurned with suspicion and resentment. To counter the snickers of doubt and innuendo, management decided to share the company's entire financial records with its employees.*
>
> *The decision to open the company's records was difficult, because such information is usually kept from employees. But the biggest problem was helping employees understand how to interpret a profit-and-loss statement. A manager who enjoyed teaching held daily sessions with small groups of employees to explain basic accounting and finance.*
>
> *Some employees were still skeptical and accused the company of keeping two sets of books for ulterior motives. In response, the company's outside accountant and auditor attended the next session to validate the figures and to explain their fiduciary responsibilities.*
>
> *Gradually the employees' skepticism changed from questioning the profits to questioning the costs. They wanted to know, for example, why the company spent $4,000 each quarter on laundry expenses. When they were told it was for the uniforms they carelessly tossed into a laundry heap each night, they suggested buying washers and dryers and laundering their own uniforms. They also questioned why the company spent several thousand dollars on a Christmas party and suggested that it be eliminated. Each employee was given direct responsibility for making policy decisions that affected him or her, including the janitor, who chose the most efficient and economical broom to buy.*
>
> *Although some employees could not see beyond their own narrow interests, open communication helped most of them see and accept the company's financial crisis. Open communication helped the company survive in difficult times.*
>
> *(Cherrington, 1994, p. 571)*

This is an irony of control because what appears to be in control of the information is out of control of the outcome. Placing all the performance information in the hands of the leader is a traditional indicator of control because it places the leaders in a position to know what is going on and everyone else is in the dark. This is called the circularity of control because information is passed among a few people.

Giving up control and giving information to others has the effect of placing everyone in control, which, in this case, has the effect of controlling performance. Ironies of control are fairly common: open classrooms in educational institutions appear to be unstructured, but the lack of walls and doors creates an openness that often leads to control because of the amount of gaze and monitoring this arrangement allows.

What seems to be an organized (structured) phenomenon is in reality a disorganized (unstructured) phenomenon. A classical bureaucracy that controls the wrong thing or is unresponsive to the environment exemplifies this kind of irony. The following story from IBM service engineers helps make this point. What appeared to be tightly organized and predictable was, in reality, unstructured. This story shows how cost-cutting changes implemented by an executive recalibrated field engineers from being highly valued to neglected. Their manager assumed that the field engineers would remain loyal and took several steps to extract resources from them in a way that demeaned their sense of value and professionalism. The story shows how actors who appeared to be controlled were instead actors who showed signs of not only independence, but also creativity in terms of how they displayed their independent value.

> In those days, IBM's major competitive advantage was its thousands of field engineers. These were the people who installed computers in customers' offices and then took care of maintenance and repairs. They were an uncommonly committed group who would do whatever had to be done, at all hours of the day and night, to keep customers' computers running. IBM salesmen made sure that customers understood the value of those field engineers. They were a powerful argument for placing your orders with Big Blue.
>
> Paradoxically, those same field engineers were also a potential Achilles' heel. Despite its size, IBM was (and still is) nonunion. But if a union were ever to attempt to organize IBM, the two most logical points to attack would be workers in the factories and field engineers. Both did the kinds of work that unions understood, both were the kinds of workers unions had successfully organized elsewhere.
>
> IBM management was aware of this vulnerability and went to considerable lengths to convince its employees that they had no need for "third-party intervention"—its euphemism for unions. Partly because of that vigilance, the unions never made a serious attempt to organize IBM. But the vulnerability remained. One of the premises that IBM managers neglected at their peril was that the field engineers could be relied on only if their loyalty to the company were undivided.
>
> Although no one questioned the value of the service provided by the field engineers, a debate arose within management about its cost. One executive in particular became identified with the view that it was extravagant, and that customers would be equally satisfied if certain excesses were eliminated. He pointed, for example, to expensive parts that field engineers carried with them, even though they were seldom needed. Eventually, he was put in charge of all field engineering operations and told to reduce costs without harming customer satisfaction.

He undertook a variety of cost-cutting programs, many of which were quite effective. However, the payroll was by far his biggest cost, so that's where he looked for the biggest savings. He decided on two changes:

First, he slowed the rate of hiring so that new computers were installed faster than new field engineers were deployed to service them. The result was a rise in the average work load. Second, he slowed the promotion rate for new supervisors, so their "span of control" (the number of field engineers reporting to a given supervisor) also increased. The result was a gain in productivity. More work was done than before, without a corresponding increase in manpower.

But when grumbling arose about the pace of the change, the executive denounced the complaints as unjustified and ordered his staff to ignore any further griping. He thus managed to cut himself off from information on whether the field engineers were still as loyal as ever.

About a year later, a small notice was inserted in the want ad section of the New York Times, *stating that IBM field engineers were available for hire and giving box number for replies. To the discerning eye, it was a subtle but unmistakable hint that the loyalty of the field engineers should not be taken for granted.*

The ad was neatly clipped out and taped to a blank sheet of paper, which "mysteriously" showed up on the desk of the division's president. It had its intended effect. The president promptly investigated, discovered an alarming slide in field engineering morale, and immediately replaced the executive who had slowed the hiring and promotion rates.

(Gellerman, 1998, pp. 34–35)

The amount of structure exerted and the effects of that exertion are common narrative themes. People listen to stories for practical information on the effects of structure.

5. Uniting practical and aesthetic relevance. Stories are interesting when they have something for us. We have to care about something in the story. When we care about what happens, stories provide vicarious learning, which occurs when someone hears something valuable that saves him or her the trouble of direct experience. Stories are practical. Narrative knowledge takes many forms; socialization, cultural knowledge, "the ropes," "how things are done here," who to trust and who to watch. "So what?" Labov (1972, p. 366) states that, "Every good narrator is continuously warding off this question." This means that a component of interest is relevance; what does your story have to do with me? One of Grice's (1975) components is relevance, although he couches it in a different language. Grice's version of relevance applies to narratives at several levels; within the story, the question is what does any particular clue have to do with the previous one? The kind of relevance could have to do with the relevance of the story in relation to the discourse it speaks. What does that story have to do with a theme? That is why topic change is a major negotiation; there must be a reason for a segue.

This is nicely illustrated in the following example, contributed by one of the authors' students:

About ten years ago, my family took a vacation to Kona, Hawaii, and stayed in a secluded resort that was paradise. Each family had their own tiki hut over the ocean and were completely secluded from the real world.

My mom, sister, and I had a blast kayaking, snorkeling, learning how to hula dance, painting coconuts, and swimming with the stingrays. The three of us girls were used to being a family of three and it didn't discomfort any of us to know that my dad wasn't taking part in these activities. He was at the hotel's concierge desk using their internet to check emails, voice mails, and fax important decisions back to his office. We were used to him leaving dinner to take a phone call or missing the hula dance lesson performance because that was the only time the client could meet with him because of the time difference. Needless to say, my dad filled the traditional gender role and wasn't a huge part of my life other than paying for things.

My dad has taken the stereotypical version of being a father, being the sole provider and allowing the mother to provide emotional support while he provided financial support. There was an unspoken understanding between the four of us in my family and we were all content with the way our family operated. We were scheduled to stay on the island for fourteen days to do nothing but enjoy the sun and relax. My dad had acquired so much vacation time from working so hard that we could've stayed for two months on that trip, but he could only leave his project for a limited period of time.

Seven years later, I was running for Student Body President for my high school back in Colorado. I was so, so, so nervous because it was going to be a close race against two of my closest friends. The morning that we were allowed to begin campaigning, my mom and I strategized when we were going to put up posters and who was going to pass out the buttons while my dad went to work. When the morning of the big day arrived, my dad came in and woke me up and said, "Hey Jess, I've already put car paint on your car that says 'Vote Jessica – A Step in the Right Direction' and I was just thinking, if we leave now we can stake our claim for your posters in the good spots where more students pass by."

I was shocked! My dad helped me campaign by doing, instead of by paying, and I realized what a difference it makes. I always thought my mom would've been the only one helping me that morning, and I was pleasantly surprised that she wasn't. Apparently, the night before the campaign, my dad made a vow to my mom that he wanted to take more of an active role in our family's lives. As ironic as it seems, my dad has held this vow to this very day and I am fortunate enough to have two parents that play active roles in my life, and I wouldn't have it any other way. The term "work/life balance" has an entirely new, different meaning for me now, and I have a new appreciation for the phrase, "You don't know what you're missing until you've had it."

Application: Transportation

The purpose of an application is to summarize the point of the angle articulated in the chapter and move it toward a particular use in such a way that the listener picks it up, examines it, tries it out, and exits with a new way of applying narratology. We are using the concept of *transportation* narrative to apply the ideas about memory and interest because to be transported to another plane through a narrative means that an interest in the story must precede such movement and that a narrative must be stored in memory to have enough of an emotional impact to change the transported listener. One of the reasons that Green and Brock (2000) offer for the power of stories, as opposed to traditional means of persuasion, is that stories capture memory out of the sharp details offered in the telling. The lesson for the storyteller whose goal is to transport listeners is that memory arises out of interest. To make use of the precepts we have offered in this chapter means that to transport is to have liminality, to have specific and unusual circumstances, and to connect with a reality in which the listener can imagine her/him self.

We have chosen what Green and Brock (2000) call the transportation narrative for this purpose because such a story has the ability to hold interest and engage memory, to move listeners to another moment and site, to be entranced by the story to such an extent that they are transported out of the consciousness they are presently in and removed to the site of the story. In fact, such a feeling is common. Consider these examples: A person gets to her feet and steps in front of you in a movie theater to go get popcorn and you can barely let her by, you even crane your neck to look around her, because you are so entranced with the flow of the movie that you refuse to lose contact with the screen, even for a second. Or you are reading a book in a quiet place and are asked by someone who enters the room for your attention, yet it takes two or three tries, finally with increased volume, for him to garner your awareness. These examples of being lost in the moment are the essence of the transportation narrative.

Green and Brock elaborate the transportation narrative in this way. They make a case for the new conceptualization by asserting that this form of narrative is an overlooked mode of persuasion. For all the attention given to the attempt to form and shape a careful persuasive message, the story is a far more frequently used mode of influence. They state it this way: "Novels, films, soap operas, music lyrics, stories in newspapers, magazines, TV, and radio command far more waking attention than do advertisements, sermons, editorials, billboards, and so forth" (Green & Brock, 2000, p. 701). They claim that the dynamic of transporting the listener to a new time and place generates imagery in the mind's eye that increases one's emotional involvement in the story through the vividness of story details—and this is true whether the story is fact or fiction (Green, 2006). Part of the power of the transportation narrative is its obliqueness. The listener is absorbed in the story, and rather than seeing it as an attempt at influence, s/he is simply engaged in the story's details and takes in both the details and premise of it. As opposed to communication specifically designed for persuasion, the listener is so absorbed and emotionally involved in the story, s/he is less likely to refute the message (Green, 2004). Psychological experiments completed by Green (2004, 2006), including one study completed with her dissertation advisor Brock (Green & Brock, 2000), found that the more a person is transported by a narrative and is attentive to the story's elements, the more s/he reports beliefs that are consistent with the story's message. The story below is a transportation narrative because the writer is merely completing an observation assignment for a writing course. She is required to go to the local airport in Austin, Texas and write about what she observes when attending to people arriving at, or leaving, the airport. Here is her brief ethnography.

The Pink Stuffed Teddy Bear

We all recognize this person in airports—the suit-clad, harried businessman, barking orders on his Blackberry cell phone while all-importantly forcing his way through the security line with his black leather briefcase—as if his travels and destination are superior to those travelers around him. When observing the departures area of the Austin airport, I looked with annoyance on this man, tempted to disregard him and focus my attention elsewhere—to a more obviously interesting individual or occurrence. However, as this man is passing through security, his carry-on bag (of course, since he is a businessman, he does not waste time on checking a bag) is selected to be searched. As he impatiently glances at his watch with haughty annoyance, something furry and pink emerges from his bag and catches my eye. It is a pink stuffed teddy bear.

The sight of this pink teddy bear immediately causes me to alter my opinion of this man. I begin to imagine his family that he is leaving behind for a business trip—his young daughter sad to see her daddy leave, and, as a way of showing her love, she selflessly gives up her most prized possession (the bear which she sleeps with every night) to keep him company. The visualization of this man as a father causes me to see him in a new light—he is uptight and domineering in the business world, striving to earn money to support his family whom he dearly loves, and is in a rush to be efficient and accomplish his business trip in order to return home. This incident also brought me back to my childhood—my blue and white striped blanket named "Petey" was my prized possession. Whenever my dad would leave for a business trip, I secretly would place "Petey" in his suitcase and write a note in crayon telling him that I loved him and that "Petey" would keep him company until he got home. As a young girl, this gesture was an immense sign of love, because a night without my blanket forecasted an evening almost completely void of sleep. Therefore, I envision that this professional businessman is one of the most loving, involved fathers—just as my dad was—and he immediately earns a place of compassion and respect in my mind.

As the businessman gathers his belongings after the inspection and begins to head to the gate, I see him take a second glance at the pink bear, allow a tender smile, and place it securely back in its safe place in his bag. As soon as he zips up his bag, the impatient mask of agitated superiority resumes its previous position, and his voice can be heard over the constant flow of travelers as he places a new, important business call. Although the moment has passed, this brief window allowed me a glance into this man's life, which completely changed my perception of both his motivations and his intrinsic characteristics as a person. Taking the time to fully observe an individual allowed me to withhold my immediate stereotypes and truly construct my perception of the story behind one's actions. This lesson not only has made me more aware of those around me, but has also allowed me to be more forgiving in my judgments of others.

The contrast between what the observer saw and what she expected creates the surprise in this story—what she saw in the suitcase of the busy traveler. Her transportation story begins with a bland and familiar experience of the security line at the airport and her monotonous opposition to the man she is observing. But the moment a teddy bear sticking out of a briefcase catches her eye, her view of what she is seeing not only changes, it transports her to her own experience, her own childhood love for her dad, her own sacrifice of sleep so that the guardian blanket travels with him rather than comforting her sleep as a child. Her concluding claim for transportation—that she will be cautious about presuming the character of those she sees—surfaces just as quickly as the object of her observation returns to the harried businessman she saw in the first place.

7

THE BEAUTY OF NARRATIVES IN THE WORKPLACE

aesthetics (n.): "the study or theory of beauty and of the psychological responses to it."
—*Webster's New World College Dictionary*, 4th ed.

Introduction

The *beauty* of a story—if indeed it possesses beauty—is one thing, if not the major thing, that separates the story from other kinds of communication in organizations. Those other kinds, such as reports or lists, are relevant communication in organizations, but it's rare, indeed, that they qualify as aesthetic documents (Czarniawska, 1998). But a lack of agreement is part of the definition of beauty in the first place. White (1996) uses Kant's conceptualization to say we find things beautiful that we cannot necessarily articulate. He uses the term "purposiveness without purpose" (p. 202) to account for when we are drawn to something that we cannot explicitly account for. Again using Kant, White (1996, p. 202) adds still more complexity to the term when he says that "beauty is necessary," which means that when we see something as beautiful, we expect others to necessarily see it in the same way and are surprised when everyone does not. Certainly that is true for the beauty of stories, and a theme we have emphasized throughout this book applies once again at this place. Since everyone has the right to tell a story and the right to critique a story, we also have the imperial right to say someone else's story is boring and for them to find ours, even ones that we have carefully crafted, guilty of the same fault.

In contemporary culture, we know aesthetics primarily from its opposite: anesthetics, as in anesthesiology, which is meant to deaden all senses. This is why it is remarkable that some people—redheads, for example—can still perceive remarks made about them by the operating team even when under deep anesthesia, and will require a

20% larger dose of medication to knock them out. The focus on senses is in keeping with the ancient Greek definition of the term; in the eighteenth century, German scholarship expanded the term to focus on beauty (White, 1996). Our development of this theme in this chapter makes use of both trends.

Part of the power of stories can be found in our common assumptions about child-rearing and aesthetics. According to the political philosopher Alasdair MacIntyre (1981), children who are deprived of stories are unscripted and anxious in actions and words. Stories are aesthetic in that they allow for the exploration of feelings, identity, and meaning. The capacity of a narrative to engage our feelings and to capture important cultural information about identity and worthiness places it at the center of most of our lives. Stories are beautiful communication; they have the capacity to engage the senses that respond to quality. Conversations and human action are enacted narratives. A narrative includes what someone is saying or doing about an event—located in a context (Deleuze & Guattari, 1988). Stories are basic to placing oneself in the world—whether it is about the knowledge of a farm operation or the beauty of seeing workers toss broken tile from the roof of a near-by building. Prior to moving to Strati's initial example, we will summarize the contents of this chapter that we take up immediately after his story. We follow Strati with a statement on the meaning of aesthetics, four stories demonstrating aesthetics, and then an application we call "elevation" that sets up a final story that demonstrates the connection between the idea of elevation and an aesthetic story.

Strati's Accidental Aesthetic Observations

Strati (1999) is the foremost speaker for the aesthetics of organizations, and he captures it well as he relates a story of his own observations. He relates this happening one afternoon: his immediate purpose is to observe teamwork and decision-making processes at a board meeting of an Italian business firm. But he finds what he hears dry and repetitive, and his eyes are drawn away from his official task to an event outside the meeting room.

Here is what Strati observes: imagine an elevated view of a city in Italy. Imagine the red-tile roofs, backgrounded by cascading hills that create an unmatched depth of color and simplicity. Outside Strati's window, he notices a repair job taking place on a nearby building. He is drawn by an array of images. First is the natural beauty of it all: something being accomplished, human figures working high on a rooftop in the Italian sun. Beyond the natural beauty are the workers themselves, who, for safety's sake, have developed a rhythm to their work and a sure feel for what their fellow tile-layers are doing. Only experts at survival belong here, and they make it look easy. Aesthetics in this instance is an example of action, and what better example of action fused with senses could there be than twisting and turning one's body to achieve balance on the roof? If a worker on the roof is slinging a tile to be caught by a fellow worker on another part of the roof, he has to correctly recognize the readiness, reach, and flexibility of the other person, who must operate on the receiving end of the tile throw with an equal sense of awareness. Strati observes that this coordination needs to be accompanied while gingerly walking around on the roof, being aware of its different feel of stable and soft footing, consciously moving rhythmically and carefully—when a misstep might send you sliding off the building to the terrace below. For Strati, the dance between tossing and catching red tile on a precarious roof stands out as beauty in the workplace.

But an additional angle for Strati's story of aesthetics is the contrast between his response to what he sees outside the room and the meeting his senses are obligated to attend. By stealing a view, taking time out from the task at hand, by accepting an insight that leads to a feeling of pleasure—all this feels to him like a romantic moment of aesthetics. He especially sees a beauty and elegance—both to what is going on up on the roof and in his mind. If aesthetics are expressions of the senses to things of beauty, Strati shows us that it can be anywhere, that it is in the eye of the beholder, that it can be as passing as a moment and as eternal as the pyramids of Egypt, and that things outside us, distant from us, can be taken in and become a part of ourselves when they are aesthetic. The simple visual, physical features make this an easy story to appreciate for its beauty. Strati's tile story shows that aesthetics' accomplishment can be indirect; the point is made obliquely. He begins this tale by saying he is actually being paid to observe the decision-making process at a business meeting, but since his client placed him away from the meeting and near a window, he is drawn to the drama and physicality of workers deconstructing a roof on a building in the plaza. Stories are often compelling when they are a little off, when they provide an oblique view. When stories are at their best, they meet a requirement for relevance in conversation, but this same significance is what empowers the observer to at first be focused on one thing but then turn to another, overlooked, scene to interpret.

Narrative theory is important to aesthetics because analytic philosophy is unable to sustain claims of universal validity and objectivity. Analytic philosophy does not deal with the diversity and particularity of the real world. Even the tile tossing story is a moral story: if you do not have the coordination for this job, stay off the roof; you could kill someone.

The most common meaning for aesthetics is how some visual object or event is seen and then communicated to another in an artful way. Thus, a major emphasis of this chapter will be how people offer accounts for objects and events they have seen and heard that cause others to remember and appreciate them as stories. We will include diverse meanings of aesthetics because their differences add to the complexity of the wider project of interpreting the literature on narratives in organizational life.

Our focus will be on how a tacit understanding is communicated—how something is translated into something beautiful. Narratives are capable of capturing the complex dialogues centered on the issues of how cognition, perception, and intuition relate to "structures, communication, and images, especially how these are enacted in a role"; this display of the "aesthetic" as a grand term is shared as an instinct "across the arts and sciences" (Kemp, 2005, p. 308).

We connect beauty to the title of our book, *Stories of Life in the Workplace: An Open Architecture for Organizational Narratology* because action is so important to organizations (Weick, Sutcliffe, & Obstfeld, 2005), and there is a line of work celebrating the action dimension of aesthetics. Narratives, like organizations, are at their best when they suggest movement, and they both fail when they get stale or repetitive. We use the term "life in the workplace" because we see people in the workplace as broadly defined, ranging from hourly temp workers to directors of non-profit organizations; it includes people holding 8–5 jobs in an office building, as well as entrepreneurs. Certainly work life includes people whose work is entirely produced on a computer, and for that reason their stories can take place anywhere.

Work does not necessarily mean drudgery. In *SeinLanguage*, Jerry Seinfeld's collection of amusing life stories, the famous comedian notes that when a comic asks the question, "You got work?" and the answer is "Yes," he's happy for his colleague because, for a comedian, having work is a gift, not an obligation. Seinfeld's conception of work developed from childhood observations. He begins with reminiscences about his father:

> *When I was a kid my father used to take me around with him in his truck. He had a sign business on Long Island (New York) and he had a little shop called the Kal Signfeld Sign Co.*
> *He really did.*
> *I'd ride in the van with my sneakers up on the dashboard and it was there that I first learned one of life's great pleasures, watching other people work.*

But the person he most enjoyed watching was his father, a natural comic:

> *There has never been a professional comedian with better stage presence, attitude, timing, or delivery. He was a comic genius selling painted plastic signs that said things like "Phil's Color TV" and cardboard ones like "If you want to raise cattle, why do you keep shooting the bull?"*

But if his father was a comic genius, he was nonetheless nearly a failure as a salesman. Even so, he was undeterred. In fact, he counted his sallies as a comedian to be far more important than making a sale:

> *The thing I remember most about those afternoons is how often my father would say to me, "Sometimes I don't even care if I get the order, I just have to break that face." He hated to see those serious businessman faces. I guess that's why he, like me, never seemed to be able to hold down any kind of a real job.*

For Seinfeld, seeing his father enjoying being comic more than being a conventionally successful worker taught him that being satisfied with your life can take a form other than traditional "success." Seinfeld goes on:

Often when I'm on stage I'll catch myself imitating a little physical move or a certain kind of timing that he would do.
    "To break that face."

In fact, Seinfeld, as a child, was so impressed by his father's comic genius that he began to identify with other comedians:

I was proud to be the only kid in my neighborhood with a complete Bill Cosby album collection. He was my favorite comedian and the first black actor to star in a series. But to me, he was the first adult on TV to wear sneakers on a regular basis.

Significantly, Seinfeld himself took to wearing sneakers on his television show. He closes his reminiscence with this observation:

My father lived to see me start to make it as a comedian and he was always my most enthusiast supporter. He taught me a gift is to be given.

In Mr. Seinfeld's case, the gift he gave was the gift of laughter, the gift of making another person smile or unbend.

Aesthetic Stories

The gift of aesthetics can take many forms in the workplace—for example, a chef pleasing a discriminating diner, or a writer pleasing a discriminating reader, or a therapist using her insight to help a client transform meaning. The stories covered below show the range of aesthetic possibilities, from the delight of a newly designed hamburger that arises out of a car crash, to the joy of translating one's musical discipline into interracial friendships over jazz, to an unexpectedly happy incident while working in a hotel, to the joy and surprise of dreaming up a new way of refining petroleum, to a consultant and a manager stumbling across two lovers who could not wait to get home, to a workplace conflict that Rachel Upton is tortured by and how her discomfort is such a contrast with the beautiful gardens her company has cultivated outside her window.

The first, a story of the senses, begins with an adolescent boy's crazy idea and a crazier SUV ride in the middle of the night, followed by despair that morphs into creating a cheeseburger for a food trailer, a story that remains strong for the narrator long after the story concludes.

The Hat Creek Cheeseburger

At the end of my sophomore year of college I was out at my ranch in Mason, Texas. I had taken a few buddies out there to celebrate the end of the year. We were out there to fish and do some off-roading. The second night we were out there we got so bored that at two o'clock in the morning we decided to go do some driving. We all packed in my Z71 Tahoe and set out to the field. There were six of us in the car, plus the dog, Buck. I was flying along the dirt path, getting airborne from the small mountains that covered the area. I was having a blast, the guys were cheering me on, so I kept pushing, every run was crazier than the last. At about 3AM I told the guys we would just do one more, then we were heading home. My buddy Kipper was joking when he said "Famous Last Words" but he couldn't have been more right. I gunned it to 65 and everyone was hootin' and hollerin', then I took a sharp left and everything went silent. The next thing I heard was a ringing in my ears. I opened my eyes and I was staring up at the ground. I was hanging in the driver's seat, my seat belt keeping me firmly in place. I reached for my knife but it was gone, so I looked over and saw an empty passenger seat beside me. Then it all faded to black. Everyone ended up being okay, with only minor injuries, aside from one guy breaking a couple ribs. Even the dog was fine.

My car, however, was totaled. I had taken out a four-year loan on the car and I'd only paid a year of it. The insurance company didn't cover the accident so I had to eat up all of my savings to pay for the stupidity I'd displayed that night. So there I was, start of summer, no car, no money, and a job that was thirty minutes away from my house, with no feasible public transportation. I had to quit my job—I'd worked at it for five years—I didn't know what else to do. I had a bike, but no car, so I had to find something nearby my house. So I applied several places but the only place that would hire me was this little food trailer called Hat Creek. I wasn't very excited to work there but I had to take what I could get.

They stuck me at the cash register, that was all right, I didn't mind dealing with people, but after a few weeks I really started to want to cook. I would cook myself burgers on my breaks and put in so much time and effort with them. I ended up crafting a masterpiece that, to this day, I still have one a week at least, even though I don't work there anymore. What I'd do is I'd start off by cooking the burger with the mustard already on it. I'd add pepper to the mustard side and a pinch of salt to the flipside. I'd melt a layer of cheese on the patty and then I'd grill bacon, jalapenos, and onions and put them on top of the cheese. After that, I'd melt another piece of cheese on top, so you'd have like a cheddar sack, with bacon, onions, and jalapenos in the middle. I'd toast the bun, and then I'd add lettuce, pickle, tomato, and ketchup at the end. One day, my boss tried one and he loved it so much that he added it to the menu. It became the most popular burger that Hat Creek sold and now they make all the burgers the same way that I do, with the mustard, salt and pepper being cooked into the patty, the bun being toasted, and if you get grilled items, they'd put a cheese sack on there for you. The trailer ended up becoming extremely profitable, so much so that they were able to open up their first store about six months after I started working there.

The experience taught me that I have the ability to take something that exists and make it better. It gave me the desire to always be improving, always be working toward something in every aspect of my life.

This is an aesthetic story because the cheese stack stimulates the reader's mouth to water by the author's cooking steps and the object of beauty in front him each time he makes a cheeseburger. He was not only creative once, he treats himself each week to revisit his original construction. Every time he does it, it makes the reader wish s/he was in his shoes. The story is also beautiful because it arises out of necessity; he has no job, a big bill, no transportation, and a boring position at the cash register in a hot food trailer. But out of this comes a creation that inspires our story's author to this day. In summary, this story is about improvisation, of being in process, in the flow. Eisenberg asserts (2006), as does White (1996), that one of Weick's key contributions to organizational theory and his incessant focus on "becoming" that the person and his role in life and in the organization can change, especially when s/he is in a structure that encourages and takes advantage of the person's natural move toward the future.

Jamming with the African Americans

The following narrative, by John Kao, comes from his 1996 book *Jamming: The Art and Discipline of Business Creativity*, which uses jazz as an extended metaphor for exploring both the sources of creativity and how to foster and control them in the business world. Here he explains how he, a classically trained pianist, came to learn about jazz and why it's now so important to him:

> *I unexpectedly came by my passion for jazz in an unusual setting. My parents decided not to risk my future in the wasteland of a New York City public high school, and instead sent me to a more rigorous institution, the Riverdale Country School. To make sure I would benefit from that change, they enrolled me as a boarder.*

Once there, Kao, a first-generation American of Chinese origins, found himself drawn into a group of African American students, all of them his dorm mates, who were impressed by his knowledge of classical music—he had been playing piano since age four—and who felt that he might become as fascinated with jazz as they themselves were:

> *At night, after lights-out, we all gathered for a bull session, often about music. Addison Adams, smoking a large, obviously illegal cigar, would unlock his closet, where he kept his jewels: a large collection of jazz albums from Blue Note, Riverside, Prestige, Impulse—all the best labels. I'll never forget the night I first heard John Coltrane's gloriously sweet ladder of notes that accompanied the legendary crooner Johnny Hartman in their version of the ballad "Lush Life."*

As a result of such moments reminiscent of the movie *Dead Poets Society*, this small group of like-minded friends founded a jazz club at the school:

We were a bunch of prep-school bohemians, reading European literature, playing poker, smoking banana peels, and be-bopping along to the coolest, "most best" music in the world.

Kao and his group even managed to get the school to invest in some hi-fi equipment and to sanction their club as an official school activity. In this way, Kao recalls, jazz became "the soundtrack of my life":

The tunes vary, dictated by circumstance, or by my own inspiration and desire. Likewise the rhythm, the bass line, the tonal center. All are in some sense up for grabs, ready for improvisation. And I play this music, not in isolation, but with a host of other players whose contribution makes a difference: colleagues, family, friends, partners, clients, strangers. ...

But whether I am alone or with others, my practice of life and the conduct of my thoughts and actions are the practice and conduct of a jazz player: I proceed by improvisation, by jamming.

"Jamming" traditionally means the ability to operate within a set pace or rhythm that one would expect from drums or a bass guitar coupled with the ability to improvise unique melodies and displays of striking creative sounds. Kao expands that definition by applying the "jamming" mindset to all aspects of life:

At its heart, jamming is about improvisation. When we have a great conversation, we are jamming.

(Kao, 1996, pp. 30–31)

What Kao misses in this last statement is the acknowledgment of an appreciation for music that caused the feeling of identity and community among Kao and his pals in the first place. While conversation can be jamming, it is not necessarily borne of motives and values, rather it arises from common experience, like listening to or doing music, playing pick-up basket ball, or other kinds of experiences where acting together, behaving together, doing together, is a predecessor to feeling anything (Eisenberg, 1990). The title of this story, "Jamming with the African Americans," shows how aesthetics can grow out of an accidental combination of forces. His parents do not send Kao to school for the purpose of increasing his ethnic exposure, but that's what happens when this classical musical disciple merges with the African American students as they introduce him to jazz. As we noted in Chapter Two on open architecture, expanding narrative appreciation, is like music appreciation especially in the form it takes in Kao's story. Jazz improvisation can be done because the musicians are following a held-in-common understanding of the tune they are playing that resides in the melody, chord structure, and rhythm of the tune as laid out by the musician who calls the tune. After playing once or twice through the sections of the tune, the musicians take turns improvising. This front-of-the-stage moment is more than an effort to show technical sophistication. When it works, and it doesn't necessarily work, the improvising musicians are able to surprise listeners by coming out with sounds unexpected for the sonic context. That is what we hope people who appreciate narratives and understand open architecture can do with this book. The next story is about a service job—much like many of us have held before; there is a requirement for a smile and consideration, even when it is difficult. But note how guests changed the service experience.

Hotel Guests that Change the Experience

I work at Hyatt Summerfield Suites; a small eighty-room hotel located three blocks from Carlsbad State Beach. I work at the front desk as a front host, checking guests in and out of the hotel, answering telephone calls, giving directions to local attractions, recommending good places to eat and things to do around Carlsbad, and resolving any guest problems or complaints. Since Hyatt Summerfield Suites is located one mile from a business park, Legoland, the beach, and the Carlsbad Premium Outlet shops, we get a mix of business and leisure guests staying at our property. I have worked at Hyatt Summerfield Suites for a little over two years, and within that time I have learned that guests like to complain about anything and everything. On my regular evening shift from 3 pm to 11 pm, I get a minimum of twenty guest complaints. Ranging from complaints about rooms not having enough towels to guests refusing to pay their bill at checkout because they were just not satisfied with their room or hotel stay, many guests find something to mention just to get their bill adjusted to be less. I have learned how to deal with guest complaints, and how to calm guests down when they are yelling in my face, and screaming profanities at me. But, one cold winter night things were different.

December 12, 2010 was a cold, windy night with rain pouring down from the sky. I was working my usual evening shift. Around 10 pm, a large family of two adults and five children walked in dripping wet. The mother was carrying her three-year-old son as he was asleep in her arms. Her two other sons, ages ten and twelve, were walking behind her. The father was struggling with the family's luggage and trying to carry their two daughters, ages five and seven. As they approached the front desk where I was standing with a smile on my face, I could tell that this family had just endured a long day of traveling. I politely greeted them, "Welcome to Hyatt Summerfield Suites, how are you?" The mother replied in an enthusiastic tone, "We're tired and exhausted, but we're excited to be here. This is a lovely hotel." I was shocked; she seemed to be in a good mood and high spirits, despite the tired look in her eyes.

I quickly asked the mother for her last name to begin the check-in process. I assumed the family of seven wanted to check in as quickly as possible so that they could head up to their room and go straight to sleep. I was wrong, the mother replied, "Mrs. Stumpfhauser," and continued on, "You have a Southern accent, don't you?" she said to me. I was baffled; Ms. Stumpfhauser was making small talk with me. This was very rare. The majority of families who come in late at night, with kids, always tell me to check them in as quickly as possible and don't say a word to me other than their last name.

Ms. Stumpfhauser, who insisted I call her by her first name, Elizabeth, had a Southern accent similar to the one I had. I asked her where she and her family were from, and it turned out they were from Blue Ridge, a town located in Georgia. It was the same city that I grew up in. Elizabeth, her husband John, their kids, and I all began talking about back home. "Did you go Blue Ridge Elementary school too?" their seven-year-old daughter Marissa asked me. "Yes! I did go there" I replied. Marissa began to giggle and talk to me about her second grade teacher, Ms. Wilson. It turned out that Ms. Wilson was also my teacher. "It's a small world," Elizabeth said. The Stumpfhauser family and I continued to talk about our favorite restaurants, friends we had in common, and they informed me of all the changes the town had gone through since the last time I had last been there five years ago.

It is unheard of to have a family come in after a long day of traveling and be as pleasant as the Stumpfhauser family was. They didn't let how tired and jetlagged they were get in the way of being nice, polite, and genuinely pleasant to be around. This was not a typical response from families—or really, any other guests. After talking to the family for over twenty minutes about our hometown, I told them they better go to their room and rest up for their big day at the Legoland amusement park the following day. All five of the kids got huge smiles on their faces and began to giggle; you could see the excitement in their eyes. Since this family had been so pleasant I decided to upgrade their room. I upgraded them from a studio room to a family suite; essentially doubling their room size and giving them an ocean view. "This is too nice of you, I can't tell you how much we appreciate your kindness," John, the husband, replied. As I finished the check-in process by having them sign the appropriate papers, assigning their new room, and making their keys, John and Elizabeth continued to thank me and express how genuinely appreciative they were for the larger room and ocean view. The kids were ecstatic as well. They had never seen the ocean before and were excited to have a view from their bed. They could look out of their hotel room window and see the ocean anytime they wanted to. After I gave the Stumpfhauser family their keys, they all turned the corner and headed towards the elevator up to the fifth floor.

The Stumpfhauser family stayed at Hyatt Summerfield Suites for five nights. Throughout those five nights I saw them as they would come and go. We would chat and have respectful interactions like the one we had when they were checking in. Continually thanking me for the upgraded room and beautiful ocean view, the family was always pleasant. I'm very used to guests entering the hotel and being rude, demanding, and needy. The Stumpfhauser's were the furthest from that typical experience. I wish all guests staying at Hyatt Summerfield Suites were as nice and pleasant as this family was. It definitely makes my job easier and much more enjoyable when I'm able to have such nice interactions with guests.

Dreaming of Refinement

Given the world energy problem, oil companies face the challenge of generating more cost-efficient ways to refine crude oil and produce a full range of petroleum distillates. In addition to the environmental hurdles that must be overcome, the cost of constructing a refinery is almost prohibitive. This story is about Doug Farmer, an engineer at an American oil company, who worked on this very problem. To solve it, according to J. Mauzy and R. Harriman in their 2003 book *Creativity, Inc.: Building an inventive organization*, "Farmer imagined the flow of crude oil as it entered the refinery, before it went through the various processes of reduction to emerge as separate gas and oil products" (p. 48). Here is how Farmer himself explained his problem-solving approach:

> *I wanted to think about flow in a different way. The flow of traffic came to mind. I tried to forget about refining petroleum and just pictured myself standing in the middle of the street, about six lanes one way. I could look down the street in my mind and see, a quarter mile away, six cars stopped at a light.*

Once having imagined the cars and the six-lane street, he saw the traffic begin to move:

> *The light changed, and all six cars started. They were all coming in my direction. By the time the traffic had gotten to me, two of the cars had pulled off to park, and two others had turned corners; only two of the original cars passed me, one on each side.*

As he sat there thinking about those cars, and wondering what possible relevance they had to the flow of an oil refinery, he had a brainstorm:

> *Suppose an initial cracking vessel could separate out huge portions of crude oil and shunt them off to one of our already-built refineries, like the cars that turned off onto another street. Then we could take what was left—the better, really expensive portion of the crude—and build a specialty refinery for it. I spent much of the night working on drawings of how this could happen.*

Mauzy and Harriman note that "when people are asked to think about the flow of oil, they compare it to the flow of other liquids—'like water, only thicker.'" But "by making a more far-fetched connection through dreamlike thinking, Farmer arrived at a new idea about the flow of oil that could save his company a lot of money."

The imagination in this story arises from the ability to fantasize about a new way of distilling petroleum products. It, like science in general, is a mental activity that is like a gift from a Muse, one who inspires springs and wells, of bringing forth from places unseen. If creativity is bringing two things together that were previously not combined, then thinking of petroleum refinery as a six-lane highway qualifies.

What we like about this story is that it illustrates how a creative individual can solve a problem that had defeated all kinds of conventional thinking but also how his telling of the solution illustrates his way of approaching his work. Mauzy and

Harriman sum up his free-thinking attitude by quoting a famous line from *Hamlet*: "There are more things in heaven and earth, Horatio, than are dreamt of in your philosophy" (Mauzy & Harriman, 2003, pp. 48–49).

Caught in the Act

What can we want to say about aesthetics—the component that "philoso-phizes?" Lots of stories do not meet the criteria of the heroic myth of trial, opponents, enablers, and outcomes. Sometimes they are merely seedy. If aesthetics have to do with the arousal of the senses, then stories of sex place themselves in a position for consideration. Our experiences are more like the evolving ones that Boje offers. For him, narratives are scattered, polyvocal, and do not necessarily come together to make a piece of art. But exceptional to this is the lived narrative, which he comments on personally in his "getting it on" story. Here is Boje's account of his experience as a consultant, where he is told the following story offered by the manager who has retained him:

> *I was here around 2 A. M. to visit the night crew. I had met just about every one else in the company. After talking a bit with the guys in the loading dock, I went to my office. As I approached I saw a light on. Then, as I came closer I could hear someone in my inner office. As I look through the outer door, I saw pants, and shorts and shoes all about before. I passed the secretary's office and opened in my office door very quietly and very slowly. There on my new leather couch was my Vice President of Marketing and one of our best sales reps going at it. They were embarrassed. I was embarassed. I said something like "oh excuse me," and waited for them to get dressed.*

Bewildered by what to do with such an unusual circumstance and wanting to get help with personnel issues from Boje, the manager asked the following questions:

> *What would you have done at this point? What is your recommendation? I (Boje) told Doug that given what he had told me the VP's excessive drinking and the embarrassing exchange at the party for their key corporate accounts, it was time to cut this guy loose.*

This is fairly direct talk for a consultant, who usually avoids direct intervention into company affairs, and instead, acts as a guide for decision-makers to improve the overall quality of the decision. But Boje makes the intuitive choice to answer the query directly, to make a recommendation:

> *Doug agreed: "I ask him to write a letter of resignation." Now what they do about the girl? Fire her too? Listen to her side? Perhaps, she is the victim? Are they in love? She is our best sales rep. If she goes, some of our key accounts go with her. Our competition would love that. I told Doug, "I would hear her side and see what were the circum-stances." That is what I did. I decided that who she slept with was her business, but*

not on my couch. "Am I fired?" She asked? I told her she is not fired. I did not have to say much, she was thoroughly embarrassed.

If stories are sufficiently intense, we forgive them for their lack of closure and accept them as a moment in a life rather than a report on a life. It counts as a story because it is easy to imagine the power and passion involved for the participants. Consultants rarely get involved in such provocative material, which may be why Boje chose to tell it.

Leading to Failure

Rachel Upton sat at her desk, shifting uncomfortably, and peered out her office window. For perhaps the first time since she had taken her new job as director of Learning, Empowerment, and Development (LEAD) at Prestige—a large, successful telecommunication company in the Southeast of the United States—she noticed the nearby gardens, famous locally for their variety of plants. She wished she were strolling through the beauty and tranquility of them right now, able to divert her attention from the seeming turmoil of her department, which had seen more than 85% turnover in the past 12 months. She had hoped for and expected to create significant change in the department by bringing greater visibility and credibility to it. She had hoped her director's position at LEAD would be the next step in building her résumé. The gardens weren't much solace, though, as she recounted a conversation with one of her former employees, Gabriela.

That conversation seemed to be a turning point. Gabriela was the first to leave LEAD, and 12 more of Rachel's employees left in the first year of the new department. Although her boss, Carlton Kellogg, human resources executive director, had not asked questions at first, he was beginning to put pressure on her to "stop the bleeding," as he put it. Carlton was concerned that the rash of departures was not only affecting morale at LEAD but that it was also creating a stir throughout the company. Through the rumor mill, Rachel heard that Carlton was worried that undue negative attention was being drawn to LEAD, risking the department's potential—and his reputation.

Thinking about it now, Rachel was reassured that she made the right decision, severely reprimanding Gabriela for her work performance. Prior to her meeting with Gabriela, Rachel had even talked through the decision with Wanda, her consulting team manager. They discussed how to get the right message across to Gabriela, clearly and strongly. Both agreed she was potentially a "troublemaker" and "not with the program." Wanda even asserted that Gabriela might "poison the well" by furthering the growing division between Rachel and Wanda and the rest of the department. They both suspected that Gabriela had been confiding in several of the new hires, and it made them wary (May, 2003, pp. 419–20).

Rachel's story qualifies as aesthetic because what is more arousing, more engaging of the senses than public recognition or humiliation, than blood and poison?

As James says, "Aesthetic development concerns the way in which the very complicated feelings and emotions, which are bound up with all the variations of personality and character, can be adjusted to the objective world" (2000, p. 34).

In what appeared to be a chance to demonstrate her professional prowess by launching a program designed to liberate and showcase the talents of others in an organizational training program, instead is an opportunity gone wrong—bogged down in petty politics, side-choosing, doubt, and charges of incompetence. Her story moves from being "chosen" in that the opportunity she was given goes to the deserving, to being "blamed" and weighted down with an impending failure. Now, lay over this an image of humor. Such programs are sometimes given the "Dilbert" cartoon treatment, where lofty words of empowerment and enrichment are treated sarcastically, as though nothing like them has ever happened before and only the ideologically foolish could believe that such a thing could ever take root.

One thing that marks aesthetics in a story is uncertainty in the protagonist, the choices she makes and how she interprets what is going on, that, in this case, is ironic. One possibility for irony is the role of those who believe too much and those who believe too little, and as a result of their disbelief, make believers into fools. "In irony there are often fools as well as *cons*—both known as *alazons*" (Kenny, 2003, p. 667). In this case, Rachel is the fool who tries to uphold a social principle and her opponents are the rogues who exploit the fool. The rogue exploits the fool who is otherwise "no more deserving of what happens to him than anyone else would be" (Kenny 2003, p. 667).

Rachel's is an aesthetic narrative because it is both organized enough to give us a sense of what is going on, yet uncertain enough that we are intrigued about other facets of the story. How could this go so wrong so quickly? Utilities are stable systems with decent pay scales and little risk. Training and new programs are often seen as a reward in such mature companies because they give employees a chance to stay abreast of new ideas. Why is this value not operant here? Why the lack of cooperation on a program that promotes cooperation? Part of what makes narratives aesthetic is their capacity for sensemaking (Weick, 2001). A narrative "is a meaning structure that organizes events and human actions into a whole, thereby attributing significance to individual actions and events according to their effect on the whole" (Polkinghorne, 1988, p. 6). The attributions of significance and their effect on the whole is aesthetic in this story; abstractions become real; pain becomes palpable.

Application: Elevation

This application is called elevation, which refers to the ability of a story to raise the stakes for a person by opening up possibilities and changing expectations through altering the context and the conditions one is in. In the elevation application elaborated below we show how a story that is based in fact can increase possibilities when it shows how conditions have changed beyond what could be expected. The conceptual base for it includes our own work on positive organizational scholarship (Browning, Morris, & Kee, 2011), the therapeutic approach to possibility therapy that uses Rogerian validation as a means to raise the expectations for potential (Bertolino & O'Hanlon, 2002). Also included is the quality movement that makes use of goal-setting and continuous improvement as mechanisms for elevating the performance of individuals in work organizations by identifying elaborate levels of aspiration. These show the most one could expect when a future is portrayed that values and creates opportunities for performance (Peters, 2003). Elevation is about narratives that show what can be done, not by merely imagining what is possible, but by offering a concrete, dramatic example of creating conditions that cause people to rise up and do more than they ever have before. An especially applicable idea for the elevation application is McAdams' generativity script (1985, 2006), which involves a person first creating something of value—a book, a painting, a piece of furniture, or even an organization structure—then releasing the item of value into the larger community. The key movement for the person in the generativity script is releasing or giving up control. It requires an awareness that, despite the high level, or even heroic, achievement that a person has accomplished individually, for the next step of accomplishment to take place, the person must release the effort and take the chance that others will join in and pick up the achievement to extend it to a wider purpose.

The story offered below tells the tale of Bill Strickland, who was an under-achieving African American child in Pittsburg, Pennsylvania, who happened to peer into an art classroom as a high school student in an inner city school to see a potter's wheel moving around and forming objects. Bill was drawn into the open door, almost magically, and asked a question. Here is his recall of that moment. "And if you've ever seen clay done, it's magic, and I'd never seen anything like that before in my life. So I walked in the art room and I said, 'What is that?'" And he said, 'Ceramics—and who are you?'"

From that moment between a curious child and an art teacher comes an agreement to work in the art studio for the next two years. Bill finagles permission from his other teachers and receives a pass to spend time in the studio mastering ceramics. The teacher appreciates the developing talent he sees in Bill, yet he knows that in the circumstance of the inner city the chance of survival still remains slim for Bill. So he says to him, "You're too smart to die, and I don't want it on my conscience, so I'm leaving this school and I'm taking you with me." Bill is subsequently admitted to the University of Pittsburg on probation and says with pride that decades later he is now a Trustee at that university.

The arc of the story that Bill Strickland tells is that over the years from the 1960s to the twenty-first century he developed, in one of the most crime-stricken inner cities, an arts and vocation program called the Manchester Bidwell Training Center that produced incredible successes for a high percentage of the people who came there. His guiding principle has been consistent throughout. If you treat people with dignity, if you build and offer an environment that shows not only that they are valued, but that they deserve the very best, they will perform up to the environment they are in. From recognizing they are being valued, they will extend their grasp beyond the space in front of them and do more and better than anyone dreamed.

One symbol of specialness and recognition for Bill is the presence of a fountain, which at first appears to be a simple if odd request. He had seen one in other buildings he admired, and Bill has insisted on and placed one in front of or within every structure he has built. He says, "I think that welfare mothers and at-risk kids and ex-steel workers deserve a fountain in their life. And so the first thing that you see in my center in the springtime is water that greets you—water is life and water of human possibility. And it sets an attitude and expectation about how you feel about people before you ever give them a speech." His insistence on the very best, rather than merely the functional or the adequate, chains through all the buildings and programs he designs. A good example is the handmade furniture he arranged for from a designer and builder from Koto, Japan. He says, "I felt that welfare moms and ex-steel workers and single parents deserved to come to a school where there was handcrafted furniture that greeted them every day because it sets a tone and an attitude about how you feel about people long before you give them the speech." In the slides Bill shows of his school and its equipment are fine-grained artfully designed wood tables, dining rooms with fresh linens on the tables, and computer training rooms with the most recent equipment available.

Bill's impulse for aesthetics is thematic throughout his story. Once the fountains were in place, he had the idea to bring live flowers into the settings he designed. And rather than making a plan for them or establishing a team to consider the idea, he simply acted. He says, "I went out to the greenhouse and I bought them and I brought them back and I put them there. You don't need a task force or a study group to buy flowers for your kids. What you need to know is that the children and the adults deserve flowers in their life. The cost is incidental but the gesture is huge. And so in my building, which is full of sunlight and full of flowers, we believe in hope and human possibilities." And this statement offered by Bill in his speech about what he has done over the last 40 years typifies his philosophy: "Create beauty and light. Show the natural, powerful aesthetic of the world to those you are trying to serve and help, and they will respond to it with their very best."

Since the school focuses primarily on vocational training and the arts, his examples range across a series of vocations. With the help of the Heinz food company, he established a world-class kitchen for culinary training. Trainees learn to cook and bake the best, from puff pastry to paté, and they then sit at beautifully decorated tables to enjoy eating what they have learned to make. Bill is especially proud of the gains made for all races and backgrounds of people. He retrains out-of-work steel workers and welfare mothers, and he describes with pride how they relate to each other. "We have students who sit together, black kids and white kids, and what we've discovered is you can solve the race problem by creating a world class environment because people will have a tendency to show you world class behavior if you treat them in that way."

The context for this story is Bill Strickland telling it in Monterey, California in 2002. It is a speech he has given many times and he simply arrives and says, "I have a box of slides to show you, and I do this because I have realized that you remember a picture long after the words have been forgotten." Also included in this speech is the presence of the great jazz pianist, Herbie Hancock, who sits at a piano behind Bill and extemporizes jazz music while Bill tells his story. The setting is unusual because both sounds—Herbie's music and Bill's storytelling—are so loud and so compelling that you fear having to make a choice of what to attend to, but in reality it is possible to take both in at the same time and to experience them as going delightfully and harmoniously.

Bill Strickland's aesthetic tastes infuse the whole story, showing in his own learning, the crafted story, the photography program and the culinary arts program at the school, and the partnerships he has developed over the years with musicians drawn to his program and making a creative offering to it. Here is how he tells the story. Dizzy Gillespie offers to perform at his school and shows up for a sound check on a Wednesday afternoon, and Bill says, "Dizzy, why would you come to a black-run center?" To which Dizzy says, "I did not believe that you did it and I wanted to see it for myself." Bill replies by noting what a gift it is for Dizzy to come honor the program. And Dizzy replies, "No, you are the gift, and I'm going to allow you to record the concert, and I'm going to give you the music."

And still another jazz great drops by and makes a contribution. Bill says, "But I met a guy by the name of Quincy Jones along the way and I showed him the box of slides." And Quincy said, "Where did the idea for centers like this come from?" And I said, "It came from your music, man, because Mr. Ross used to bring in your albums, when I was 16 years old in the pottery class, when the world was all dark, and your music got me to the sunlight."

Bill's story of his personal achievement—to save himself—and to extend that into a structure for others makes it a perfect fit for the generativity script (McAdams, 2006). He went beyond his own recovery and discovered, in doing so, that he could replicate it for others. He captures it perfectly with these words, "Remember, I'm the black kid from the '60s who got his life saved with ceramics. Well, when I decided to reproduce my experience with other kids in the neighborhood, the theory being if you get kids flowers and you give them food and you give them sunshine and enthusiasm, you can bring them right back to life."

After listening to Bill Strickland's story and transcribing it for this book, we are drawn to Strati's conception of how the telling of a story is part of its beauty. In the statement below, he is talking about the person who accounts for organizational life as an observer. And Strickland's use of his pictures are central to his telling. Strati says it like this:

> The charm of a story, the beautiful way in which things are described, the evocations and the allusions conjured up by the listener in order to understand the story, and its seductiveness, these notions leave fragments of organizational life impressed on the researcher's memory. If the story is beautifully told, it will act as a structuring factor in the relation between researcher and interlocutor and transform these encounters into part of the organization's aesthetic dimension.
>
> *(Strati, 1992, p. 576)*

Strickland's themes are aesthetic throughout, from his introduction to pottery, to designing buildings to show respect for and increase the respect of those who enter the door, to the food, flowers and fountains that he insists on at every turn, he is a walking promoter of the aesthetic dimension.

8

COMPLEXITY AND CONTROL

Introduction

This story is from Weick and Sutcliffe's book, *Managing the Unexpected: Resilient performance in an age of uncertainty* (2007, pp. 3–8):

> *The Cerro Grande fire in New Mexico in May, 2000 originated as a prescribed burn, intended to reduce the severity of potential fires by eliminating sources of fuel. What went wrong? The conditions on the ground were miscalculated, which led to a smaller detachment of firefighters being deployed and other small deviations from normal practices used to contain prescribed fires. The fire was started later in the day than planned, which meant that the crew was exhausted rather than fresh when matters began to go south. Part of the firefighting crew was kept on duty longer than usual, which further diminished its effectiveness at noticing small events at the edge of containment. The first burn boss was unable to convince dispatchers to send a relief crew as soon as it was needed, because dispatchers deferred to authority rather than to the fire boss' expertise. They required him to wait until their supervisor came on duty. But when the supervisor came on duty, an argument ensued about who was to pay for the relief crew and whether the fire fit the technical standards necessary to warrant another crew. Although the crew was eventually deployed, it arrived at least three hours after it was needed and the helicopter sent to reinforce firefighting efforts arrived late, with no water bucket.*
>
> *As the fire began to escape containment, a new burn boss began his shift by developing a new fire suppression strategy that involved setting backfires. This might have worked, except that winds of 50 m.p.h. came up, accelerated as they were channeled into nearby canyons, and caused the fire to explode.*
>
> *The resulting wildfire burned for 15 days and required deployment of over one thousand firefighters. It consumed 48,000 acres, burned 235 homes to the ground and*

destroyed 39 of the Los Alamos National Laboratory buildings, causing one billion dollars in damage.

This chapter coalesces the idea that a good narrative is a complex one and that complexity is best understood with a narrative. "Complexity" can be defined as non-linear relations, driven by small forces that result in the emergence of sudden changes that produce unexpected outcomes (Taylor, 2000; Morowitz, 2001). The Cerro Grande fire in New Mexico works perfectly to demonstrate complexity concepts because the outcome of an organizational plan is a surprise; in fact, the plan went awry, administrative forces overcame common sense, and timing delays exacerbated the problem far beyond what was expected. We begin this chapter with a different organizational arrangement because complexity, as it happened in this case, denies structure—at least obvious, clear, linear structure. There is so much "going on" and so many possibilities for interpretation that narratology is a natural area for considering complexity and control. This attention to consideration means that individuals are watchful and cautious under conditions of complexity, which is a gloss for how Weick and Sutcliffe interpret complexity.

Overall, this chapter suggests that complexity is best understood through narrative, that the best narratives are themselves complex, and that the period of circumspection following enmeshment in complex, consequential interactions is ideal for generating complex and interesting stories.

The Nature of Complexity

Complex relationships are non-linear. In comparison to other structures, they are scattered and unpredictable. Let us exemplify this with the image of a two-dimensional chart with one dimension, *age*, and place another dimension across or orthogonal from that the *total income spent* on prescription and over-the-counter medication. If the amount spent on medication increases predictably with age, then we have demonstrated a linear relationship. But what could change such a predictable relationship? Assume for a moment that as age increases, so does leisure time and that older people find time to exercise and thus increase their health. Or they move to climates that encourage sunshine and exercise. Or they have less stress in their lives because their career goals have been met and they can give greater attention to exercise and diet, which are important to maintaining health. The influence of these factors would mean that rather than age and medication use being linear, the relationship is non-linear; individuals are distributed across the 2x2 table—making it necessary to examine cases individually to know what is happening with these two variables (Gladwell, 2011).

Complexity operates in relation to control when at least one significant feature of the organization is beyond control or out of control (Dent, 1999). For a sales organization, it could be a changing market so the means of promoting the product to a new customer base is unknown. Professionals in marketing and sales regularly talk about the difficulty and complexity of understanding and listening to the changing interests and needs of a customer. For a production organization, the uncontrollable could be that the materials to compose the product are scarce and difficult to reliably obtain, making the time of delivery of the product to a waiting customer uncertain. Or the materials are in the hands of an arrogant supplier who knows they hold the key to another organizations' success and as a result put the purchaser through impossible trials—just to get the materials needed to proceed with the product. Complexity is the opposite of predictability.

Complexity appears as a tension, a contrast to control over people, over their performance, over the mission, over the ways work is completed, or over the technology used to complete the goals of the organization. Even if the forces within the organization did not push for control, constituencies outside the organization, such as sub-groups who have a stake in it would. Customers, or parents of children in schools are good examples of stakeholders who have an eye toward control, especially when something goes amiss. They legitimately ask the question: how are you controlling performance?

Structural and Dynamical Complexity

Two vastly different orders of complexity need to be distinguished. First is *structural* complexity, a set of conditions characterized by numerosity (e.g., the greater the number, the greater the complexity), diversity, and interdependence of system parts (Huber & Glick, 1993). When combined, these three conditions increase the amount of uncertainty that one finds or must deal with in a given system. Structural complexity, then, describes the *conditions* inherent in that system. *Dynamical* complexity, on the other hand, is the actual process of things changing nonlinearly in a structurally complex system.

To illustrate structural complexity, let's move from the example of single individuals to layers of other individuals who are part of the structure. First, consider a setting where one person is added to the structure. In stories, we are, in the most economical sense, interested in what happens when two people with different interests fatefully intersect in a single setting where some kind of interaction between them unfolds (Greimas & Ricœur, 1989). In such instances, we may see them oppose each other, learn from each other, be attracted to each other, trust or betray each other, and as a result move in and out of positive and negative relations with each other over time—whether in a span of days or months or years. Narratology places a lot of weight on the narrative development of two characters. Two-person stories, in complex conditions, are popular cultural stories. Whether it is a beautiful romance, a clash of the powerful, or an older brother and a younger sister, the dynamic between two people contains the ingredients for a complex story.

Moving into multiple hierarchies is still more complex. The control problem in complexity is not necessarily resolved by an authority structure that defines who is to lead and who is to follow. Such hierarchies are pitted with the problems of trust. Followers distrust leaders because leaders, by the very nature of their power, can be capricious; they can change their mind or not hold to the agreement even in the moment when it is most critical for the subordinate that they do so. For the leader, confidence in the subordinate's action may be jeopardized by the premise that the follower is only taking directions because of a requirement to do so and that the follower would do something different in a moment if the structure were stripped away. The subordinate worries about betrayal; the superior worries about abandonment.

Democratic, egalitarian relationships fare no better on the complexity and control dimension. An assumption about them is whether the system is equally focused on everyone's interests, and this uncertainty results in democratic system participants continuously monitoring whether the distribution of resources, whether material or symbolic, are truly democratic—are you truly getting your share in relation to others? An assumption about such efforts at fairness and democracy is that they are incredibly fragile and open to change. The conditions that established fairness and equity yesterday may not hold today or tomorrow. As a result, decisions do not "stay" made and must be continually reaccomplished to maintain their direction and bearing. And this maintenance is itself a complex activity because what works to keep the system fair in one circumstance does not reliably work in another.

Beyond the two-person story, there is the ensemble cast, where a whole host of characters, interests, organizations, expectations, personal histories, and limited time and resources are at play. The process of their decision-making is inevitably complex, and the result equally uncertain, which is to say, unpredictable.

Here is a story from a sports organization that showcases dynamical complexity. Nolan Ryan, who was then pitching for the Texas Rangers of the American League, tells it. Baseball pitchers warm up their bodies with running or a stationary bike and then do stretching before beginning to pitch. Then they warm up their arms before the game because it is necessary to produce flexibility and body heat in the arm so that they will be ready to perform at their peak at the moment they throw their first pitch in the game. These preparatory pitches are built up gradually, moving from short pitches to longer pitches and are then followed with practicing the different kinds of pitches that spin and drop in different ways to fool the batters they will face. One evening, Nolan Ryan comments to the catcher while warming up: "I don't see how anyone could hit the ball I am throwing tonight." He meant that his speed on the fastball, his break on the curve ball, and the variation on his other pitches were so deceptive, so overwhelming, that he would be overpowering on that evening—and he was. This is an example of skill and control. When high skill is performed, whether as a salesperson, an engineer, or a baseball pitcher, the payoff for high skill is control. At Nolan Ryan's high level of performance, the difference between being very good and very average is often minor. The complexity and control question arises in relation to his performance because he was surprised, if elated, by what he saw in his performance. He could not perform like this every night, and while Nolan Ryan was a Hall of Fame pitcher, because his was a human skill, he was not going to be at his best every night; in short, he was not predictable. His performance was complex because it was not completely controllable.

Structural and dynamical complexity are often compounded. Suppose, for example, 100 leaders (numerosity) from 100 sovereign nations (diversity), whose fates are connected, must reach a decision concerning the allocation of scarce resources (interdependence of system parts). The process of their decision-making is inevitably complex and the result equally uncertain, which is to say, unpredictable. While traditional Newtonian science may identify main effects and principal features of a system, complexity theorists would argue that total control of elements within that system is impossible because combined effects that are in simultaneous interplay act—and interact—in unpredictable ways, making systems dynamical (Anderson, 1999). When structural and dynamical complexity are applied to human systems, we are reminded anew that people are only occasionally logical and rational. Because they possess imperfect information, they tend to act on the basis of ideology, chance, and perceived individual payoff. Such a mix of possibilities invites the use of narrative, for narrative alone can capture the particularities of individual cases.

Narratives Can Capture Complexity

Although a rational model of using information to understand and solve a problem can work reasonably well for linear relations, such a model is overmatched by complex relationships. Complexity is of interest in organizational narratology because the intrusion of complexity into linear relationships is surprising. Linear relations have historically been essential in structures like organizations because one of the basic purposes of organizations is to produce some kind of regularity or dependability in behavior or performance; in short, to have some control over what is going on. If it is a military organization, the goal is to direct the "assets" on the "target" in a dependable way. If it is a sales organization, we want to chart and control the sales process. If it is a production organization, we want to assure some mix of reliable production and product quality. Organizations are interested in predictability. That's the reason they set goals and publicize them. That is the reason organizations have social norms or written rules to control behavior. That is the reason organizations have dress codes or uniforms with colors, patches, and other symbols of the corporate logo—to cause people to feel more membership and as a result of that feeling to want to do as the organization insists in both direct and indirect ways. All of these are ways organizations attempt to keep complexity at bay; narratives alert us to that kind of effort as well as to its—often spectacular—breakdowns.

Stories are uncertain and complex when they consist of narrated elements but also include blanks and gaps (Sternberg, 1998). Blanks are necessary; details with no relation to the plot must be excluded to avoid deviating/diverting the listener's attention. Gaps, on the other hand, are left open to the imagination of the audience. A story without gaps to be filled in or even secrets to be guessed can hardly stimulate curiosity. *A story without a secret is not a good story* (Kermode, 1981; Kubli, 2001).

The mix of missing, equivocal, and known pieces is what makes a story complex and gives it enough power to generate the listener's interest and involvement. "As far as human affairs are concerned it is above all through narrative that we make sense of the wider, more differentiated, and more complex texts and contexts of our experience" (Brockmeier & Harre, 1997, p. 264). Narratives and complexity go hand in hand because one of the best ways to get a handle on unpredictable events is to tell a story about them.

If a story has the capacity to hold our interest, the main way of achieving that is to create tension about what comes next. The "who did what to whom with what effect?" is a formula for registering and mapping uncertainty. To be a compelling story, the teller must set up a problem with an uncertain outcome or the listener's interest will fade because the resolution is already known. What is more boring than an overused outcome? An exception to the preference for novel, uncertain outcomes exists anytime someone asks for repetition with a request like, "tell the one about the time you drove all night to see your girlfriend." Such a request is made to revisit the performance of how the story is told or to reaffirm the mythical and typical interest of that original story. But such requests for retellings are an exception. We are generally more interested in a story when it is complex, when there is enough uncertainty among the dynamics being presented that the listener is conjuring: What happens next? How does this come together? Indeed "the *narrative* mode is more flexible and can more readily accommodate discontinuities, contradictions and exceptions" (Zukier, 1986, p. 476) within its structure.

Complexity and narrative theory are close kin because of what they have to offer each other. Complexity is a part of narrative because of the valueless nature of a simple, predictable story. Once the causal relations are established and unquestionable in a story, it becomes a rule structure (do this and this will happen), or merely a rule to follow.

These two assumptions—(a) variety and (b) time volatility—are essential to complexity. Narrative tends to be the form that carries this descriptive and historical scientific finding in that a story is multi-causal and surprising (Weick, 1974). Complexity theory and narrative have the common premise that "liminal" conditions exist. By liminality we mean action occurs in phases and stages—when we are not exactly sure of what comes next or what conditions will exist in the near future (Turner, 1987). Narrative and complexity theory are designed to handle changing and dynamical situations that can be characterized as "wicked" problems that defy planning and prediction (Pacanowsky, 1995)—you don't know the solution until it is before you.

One question about complexity in narrative is the question of misinformation or ignorance. Is knowledge the answer to complexity? One of the ironies of the late twentieth and beginning of the twenty-first century is that increased information has not given a sense of security. Fear is at an all-time high; even with all the technology we have, individuals have ontological insecurity—they are unsure of who they are; they have less of a story than their ancestors. One of the values of narrative, especially for complexity, is narrative's ability to encapsulate complexity by including parts that have mysterious or uncertain powers. Narrative is able to allow for vagaries and surprising happenings that a more rational form for assessment cannot handle. But since complexity is non-linear, by definition, it is not directly controllable. In the next section, we review the appropriate responses to complexity by highlighting the concepts of the main two thinkers on complexity and narrative, David Snowden and Karl Weick.

David Snowden and Karl Weick

The two most well known and comprehensively developed models using narrative analysis for responding to complexity in organizations are that of Weick and his associates, at the University of Michigan (Weick & Sutcliffe, 2001; Weick, Sutcliffe, & Obstfeld, 2005), and that of Snowden and his work with Kurtz at the Cynefin Centre for Organisational Complexity.[1] To elaborate complexity and narrative we will identify the likeness and differences in their approaches. Remarkably, these two authors virtually ignore each other's work despite the major overlap between their premises and practices. The sole written cross-reference between the two is Snowden's criticism of Weick's use of High Reliability Organizations (HROs), that is, organizations such as aircraft carriers and nuclear power plants that require acute mindfulness if they are to avoid situations in which small errors build upon one another to precipitate a catastrophic breakdown. Snowden believes that HROs are too anomalous to be useful as a comparison for mainstream organizational practice (Snowden, 2003).

These two authors also differ in that whereas Weick, a university scholar, developed his theory before focusing on its applications. Snowden, who originally developed his work within IBM, constructed applied methods including tools and practices for analyzing narrative complexity—for example, "Story Circles" and "Knowledge Disclosure Points" (KDPs)—in concert with his research program.

These authors' ideas also differ in origins. Snowden's Cynefin group anchors its program in literary and science-fiction references (Snowden, 2000), as seen in its very name, "Cynefin" (pronounced *cyn-ev-in*), a Welsh term that, as noun, roughly means "habitat" and as an adjective roughly means "acquainted" or "familiar." The term more specifically means one's environment, or place of comfort or birth (Snowden, 2003). The theme of the Cynefin model is that the ability to respond to complexity requires a *sense of place*, which enables one to advance diverse views and to imagine narratives about what happened, what could have happened, and how to act differently in the future.

Weick's theories, on the other hand, reflect his education as a social psychologist and include such topics as threat-rigidity, commitment-decommitment, doubt-self-fulfilling prophecies, and dissonance-assurance. In his recent works (1995, 2001, 2005) Weick uses these ideas to develop the concept of "sensemaking."

Weick and Snowden also differ on the grammar of the central theme of both their ideas about sensemaking. Sensemaking, as Weick fuses the term, is a neologism (invented word) meant to convey the idea that the term is so all-encompassing that it deserves being distinguished as a new usage about a new concept. Snowden, meanwhile, uses the compound term "sense-making" to represent the same family of ideas. Snowden's term, more conventional, aims to describe a whole set of processes that have brand names such as the previously mentioned Story Circles and KDPs and to use narrative theory to understand the complexity of organizational environments.

Another significant difference is the type of evidence they use for their respective programs. Snowden presents his ideas to workshop participants, and then uses an interpretation of their responses as evidence for his concepts in his articles about narrative and complexity. Weick's evidence comes from his field studies of jazz orchestras, firefighters, and the aforementioned aircraft carriers and power plants. This work is amplified, in an applied version, in his co-authored 2001 book with Katherine Sutcliffe, that was revised in 2007, on managing the unexpected in an age of complexity.

These differences between Weick and Snowden's ideas are differences in style—that is, they differ in their historical, cultural, and pedagogical approaches to complexity. Yet our reading of Weick and Snowden's treatment of complexity and narrative shows that there is considerable overlap on the substance of their thinking. The purpose of this chapter is to list and interpret these points of likeness. To set up this listing, we will review their common approach to narrative and complexity.

The Similarities Between Snowden and Weick

Weick and Snowden commonly assert that the complexity and ambiguity of the environments that individuals face are best understood when language, including the richness of metaphor and the flexibility of the story, is invoked as a sensemaking device (Weick & Browning, 1986; Snowden, 2000). For Weick, "sensemaking" defines organizational action as an ongoing accomplishment that emerges from efforts to create order and make retrospective sense of what occurs (Weick, Sutcliffe, & Obstfeld, 2005). Accordingly, organizations become interpretation systems of participants who, through the back-and-forth of their own understandings, provide meanings for each other via their everyday interactions.

The exercises Snowden uses in his consulting intervention projects emphasize contextualizing to generate collective sense-making as a consequence of discourse. These workshop discussions emphasize diversity and concreteness by using narrative methods that allow specific patterns to emerge in understanding the story of a project or event. A consistent theme of Weick's theory development from the very beginning is that complex environments must be matched with equally complex processing mechanisms. The capacity of the narrative to vary in *punctuation* (when they begin and end), *pace* (what is the speed and variation between sequences), and *participant composition* (casts can range from one person, to few, to ensembles) means the narrative is a communicative form that is frequently consistent with organizational complexity (Polster, 1987; Cunliffe, Luhman, & Boje, 2004).

Snowden's strategy for sense-making is to lay out an understanding of language depending on the specificity of the environment. Snowden, like the narratologist Walter Fisher before him (1984), worries that experts' language is so restricted and abstract that it too easily remains *about* the problem, but far *above* it. Weick and Snowden jointly emphasize the role of language in sensemaking about complexity and especially the role of the communicator to create meaningful messages that are informative, comprehensive, and not oversimplified (Snowden, 2000). Stories can complexify meanings in a way that linguistic statements cannot (Snowden, 2000). For Weick, interpersonal processes play out as actors know who they are by what they say to others and how others respond to them. He observes, "People verbalize their interpretations and the processes they use to generate them" (Weick 1995, p. 8). A distinctive feature of sensemaking, and one that also distinguishes it from interpretation, is the way action and organization collaborate to make up the structure. Weick sees communication as a type of action because generating discourse is an act of performance and production. Sensemaking is about "authoring as well as reading" (Weick 1995, p. 7).

This view of narrative as a special answer to complexity is further laid out in the writings by Snowden, Weick, and associates. In common, they propose a set of conditions, a set of useful practices, including the kinds of structures necessary to adapt to complexity successfully. We have identified eight major statements that capture these commonalities:

1. Acknowledging and accepting complexity is better than placating it with planning models. Snowden contends that the physics on which Fredrick Taylor based the rational theory of scientific management is no match for the contemporary environment. There are simply too many situations where the standard tools and techniques of policy-making and decision-making do not apply (Kurtz & Snowden, 2003). This position is consistent with Snowden's general emphasis on learning. Because most environments are turbulent, individuals experience considerable change; hence, the best thing we can do is to learn from it. Weick parallels this idea with the concept of "threat rigidity," which refers to the tightening of categories that occur when people's understandings are threatened. In their book on managing the unexpected (2001), Weick and Sutcliffe promote a mix of action and stability—a mix of structure and change—that is akin to the complexity concept of "far from equilibrium." They contend that the best response to complexity is diversity and an information consciousness that enables a person to become a mindful observer and actor, a vigilant and attentive actor, rather than one dependent on mindless control systems.

Snowden reaches much the same conclusion from a different route. He believes that the traditional organization, with its emphasis on planning, policy, procedures, and controls, leads to a *training* culture of obedience rather than a *learning* culture of understanding and action. Weick and Sutcliffe (2001) share the preference for moving away from planning recipes toward a focus on individual mindfulness and anticipation.

2. It is important to acknowledge failure and learn from instances of it. While this concept has been most extensively developed by Sitkin (1992), it exists both directly and indirectly in Weick and Snowden's work, and it appears in several different forms. In his workshops, Snowden has his participants review past projects to identify a fateful moment when their project might have failed, which enables them to see how close they came to failure and how they might avoid it in the future.

Both Snowden and Weick tie failure to learning—seeing things in a new way— such that the surprise becomes a communicable story, even if it is "near miss." Narrators are able to say, "This might have happened." Snowden sometimes asks the following question in his seminars: "What spreads fastest in your organization— stories of failure or stories of success?" He says the usual answer is "failure" because we realize that stories of failure are more valuable than success stories (Snowden, 2003). Because people tend to agree more on what is going wrong than what is going right, what are called "best practice" efforts in fact rely on the ability to identify *both* past successes and past failures (Snowden, 2003). Given Weick and Sutcliffe's (2001) premise that HROs must focus on potential catastrophic failure, such organizations constantly complete reviews and exercises that gauge their preparedness— without a fear of punishment from reporting a failure. Focusing on failure is so important because its opposite, success, is such an emotional and fulfilling rush that it leads to hubris (Weick & Sutcliffe, 2001). A major component of sensemaking for Weick and Sutcliffe is a "preoccupation with failures rather than successes" (Weick & Sutcliffe, 2001, in their executive summary).

3. Self-organization is an order that has no hierarchical designer or director. Snowden contends, "there is a fascinating kind of order in which no director or designer is in control but which emerges through the interaction of many entities" (Kurtz & Snowden, 2003, p. 464). In his approach to self-organization he reaffirms Peter Drucker's idea that "in the Knowledge Economy everyone is a volunteer" (Snowden, 2000, p. 3). A key feature of narrative is that characters are most interesting when they make, or struggle with, independent choices. Snowden says that organizing business on the Web creates a community of volunteers who operate in an open and free system. This change shifts organizations away from hierarchical forms to ones where they become networks of communities directed toward a purpose (Snowden, 2000).

For Snowden, when an environment is ambiguous, the proper scope for inter-pretation and action is at the individual rather than the hierarchical level (Snowden, 2000). This view is commensurate with Weick and Sutcliffe's fostering individually distinctive interpretations of what is going on and accepting diverse inputs in responding to complexity. They encourage managers to act with an anticipation that counteracts oversimplification and easy confirmation by structuring differences in personal background and experience into the organization. Weick and Sutcliffe also reflect the move away from hierarchy toward self-organization in this recommendation: "Create a set of operating dynamics that shifts leadership to the person who currently has the answer to the problem at hand. This means people put a premium on *expertise over authority* and decisions migrate both downward and upward as conditions warrant" (Weick & Sutcliffe, 2001, p. 49, italics added).

4. Narratives are valuable for showing role differentiation and poly-vocality. Weick's most prominent example of problem-recognition resulting from role difference appears in his story on how child abuse came to be a medical diagnosis in American medicine. The story of the development of the battered-child syndrome (BCS) in Weick's (1995) sensemaking book beautifully illustrates the features of labeling and institutional resistance. Weick's analysis also illustrates how individual reputation becomes implicated in "seeing" a problem. Before BCS became well enough known to become an institutional label, child injuries that appeared in X-rays or other parts of a medical report were treated as anomalies. The first report of BCS appeared in a radiology journal rather than a pediatric journal, which illustrates how an outsider, a distant voice, became a key participant in developing the medical diagnosis for BCS. As a result of that radiology journal's report, a mix of participants overcame the "fallacy of centrality"—which is reflected in the ego-centric argument, "If I don't know about this event, it must not be going on" (Weick, 1995, p. 2). In that story, it is the radiologists, not the pediatricians, who, from a distance and from different data, come to perceive childhood injury as something other than an accident. The delay in recognizing the battered-child syndrome is ironic; the truth was right in front of the doctors, but they did not recognize abuse because of the social and political setting of the examination.

Diverse information causes a person not only to see different information but also to see information differently. In the last quarter of the twentieth century, the complexity of the story allows for many voices, from marginal to central, to register as a response to complexity because it matches the local, fragmented, emergent story so well (Boje, 2002; Cunliffe, Luhman, & Boje, 2004). Boje's idea that a fragmented and ambiguous narrative makes any single event transient and multivocal is consistent with Snowden and Weick's positions. Snowden has a section in his most comprehensive statement on this topic called "humans are not limited to one identity" (Kurtz & Snowden, 2003). He develops exercises in his workshops that are designed to develop narrative databases without particular attention to their truthfulness. Instead, the purpose is to generate ingredients that might be raw material for story-based interventions. They suspend truth to generate provocative content. Such diversity is part of how Snowden defines complexity, which is "how patterns emerge through the interactions of many agents" (Kurtz & Snowden, 2003, p. 469). Both Snowden and Weick see a non-egoistic, diverse, probing, interacting style of communication as a response to complexity.

5. Conformity carries risks, and thus we need diverse inputs when responding to complexity. Much of Snowden's thinking about this is captured in his conception of learning, which he sees as a replacement for order and structure.

A difficulty with systems built on technology is that people are seduced by order often at the cost of usability and adaptability. Snowden's use of the term "Cynefin" is counter to the idea of conformity because it represents "the place of our multiple affiliations, the sense that we all, individually and collectively, have many roots, cultural, religious, geographic, tribal, and so forth" (Kurtz & Snowden, 2003, p. 467). He now extends that notion to larger cultural issues under the rubric "the cognitive edge."

Narratives are dominant in organizations because conformity often reflects local power and circumstances. Narrative is a democratic concept (anyone can tell a story and anyone can criticize and analyze a story) rather than a privileged one (rationality requires special technical skills). When people tell a story, they are invoking a personal "philosophy of reason, value, and action" (Weick & Browning, 1986, p. 249). Weick's emphasis is on interaction that involves both speaker and receiver to achieve understanding, and on the role of storytelling to capture the nuance and uncertainty present in a given situation (Weick, Sutcliffe, & Obstfeld, 2005). To combat conformity they urge looking for evidence that disconfirms "cherished expectations" (Weick & Sutcliffe, 2001, p. 155). Finally, Weick and Sutcliffe urge developing a mindfulness that encourages variety in people's analyses integrating the information people have that is not held in common, and to "train people to manage these differences" (Weick & Sutcliffe, 2001, p. 66).

6. Action is valuable under conditions of complexity. Weick returns to the importance of action repeatedly and identifies it as a process that is ongoing, instrumental, subtle, swift, and social: "When action is the central focus, interpretation, not choice, is the core phenomenon," which means that communication is a type of action (Weick, Sutcliffe, & Obstfeld, 2005, p. 409). One of Snowden's categories of the environment is the "un-ordered and chaotic domain" (Kurtz & Snowden, 2003, p. 469) in which there are no perceivable cause-and-effect relations. He sees the proper response to this environment as "to act, quickly and decisively, to reduce the turbulence; and then to sense immediately the reaction to that intervention so that we can respond accordingly" (Kurtz & Snowden, 2003, p. 469). Snowden's writing on action is developed, in part, in his writing on virtual communities and the value of these structures for allowing people to express understandings they might feel too radical for face-to-face communication. Individuals can act to "experiment with ideas and experience" (Kurtz & Snowden, 2003, p. 469) when they are confident that the ideas will not be attributed to them.

For Snowden, the most useful information is contextual and need-driven. Thus, there is a mismatch between mechanistic models and organic human decision-making (Snowden, 2000). His goal is to enable organizations to identify what knowledge they have in a contextual, detailed description that leads them directly to action. A good example is his thinking on anthropological observation. His general sense of action allows Snowden to contend, provocatively but accurately, that a single day of learning observational techniques is enough to make researchers successful in the field, especially when they are imbued with a deep curiosity for their subject (Snowden, 2000).

For Weick, action leads to identity because the nature of a person is "constructed out of the processes of interaction" (Weick, 1995, p. 20). Since interpersonal communication and conversation constitute the organization, those very interactions are part of the structure. As Weick says, "Actions and structures of organizations are determined in part by micro-momentary actions of their members" (Weick, 1995, p. 8). Action is also showcased in Weick's example of KLM Airlines' communication that shows when individuals communicate about concrete matters that clarify their understanding, they are acting to create meaning (Weick, 2001).

7. The focus is properly on small forces and how they affect complex systems. One of Weick's most popular concepts is his idea of "small wins," which are essentially small steps that have the potential of affecting the direction and understanding of larger systems. He defines a "small win" as "a concrete, complete, implemented outcome of moderate importance" (Weick, 2001, p. 431). In his stories of small wins, symbolism and communication are predominant. One example is the Task Force on Gay Liberation succeeding in getting the US Library of Congress to change its cataloging system by re-labeling its codes and taking the term "deviance" out of the definition of "gay." Another is the Administrator of the Environmental Protection Agency locating an obscure law on the books that allowed him to legally challenge pollution practices in several large American cities; the Administrator's strategy was to take small visible steps that drew the notice of others and thus enlist their "small" actions on a larger project (Weick, 2001, pp. 429–31).

Snowden inserts as a topic head in one of his articles the phrase "the small guy wins out" (Snowden, 1999, p. 34). The phrase refers to the tendency of experts to use too much of their deep knowledge of a task and minimize its practical requirements. Snowden relates a story of two software development groups—one expert, the other a lesser group—whose experience in programming was limited to the fairly routine requirements of payroll systems. In a competitive exercise between these two groups for learning purposes, the experts created a plan for an elegant piece of code that would take two months to develop. The payroll programmers, meanwhile, downloaded a "good enough" list from the Internet that cost five dollars (Snowden, 1999). Thus one feature for smallness for Snowden is the decisions that can be made that allow the group to move on—to accept "good enough," implement it, and then see what that action means.

In their work on HROs, Weick and Sutcliffe observe that the risk of not attending to small moments increases the possibility of escalating toward much more serious and unfavorable events. One indicator of mindfulness is the ability to perceive "clues had been accumulating for some time that small, unexpected things were happening" (Weick & Sutcliffe, 2001, p. 49).

8. It is important to understand the irony of bureaucratic control. The irony here is that the attempt to control something often produces results opposite of what was intended. Charles Perrow's *Normal Accidents* (1984) is a collection of stories chronicling what goes wrong when the fix is worse than the original problem. One irony is that organizations produce volumes of information that, instead of comforting individuals, result in insecurity and overload. When an organization *does* happen onto an organic and innovative achievement, it often swamps it with measurement and control (Snowden, 2000). A classic example is that of Jack Kilby from Texas Instruments, an electronics firm in the United States. Dr. Kilby, co-inventor of the integrated circuit and, for his effort, winner of the Nobel Prize in physics in 2000, attributes his invention of the chip to his having arrived at Texas Instruments as a new hire in the summer of 1958. Since most of his colleagues were off on vacation, he enjoyed two weeks to tinker and play in the lab completely alone, which resulted in his world-changing invention. Ironically, Texas Instruments responded to this miraculous and independent achievement by canceling all vacations for inventor employees for several summers thereafter so that they, too, might invent something brilliant (Turner Hasty interview, 1992). In organizations, the higher one sits, the more difficult it is to resist the tendency to transform the effective into the mandatory.

Snowden frames his work in this area by criticizing the influence of the Newtonian metaphor on management science's focus on linear development. As he sees it, management science aims to "develop algorithms that would predict human behavior in the same way as the movement of heavenly spheres could be predicted" (Snowden, 2000, p. 3). Snowden represents this point with the following story. A group of West Point cadets were assigned the task of managing the playtime of some kindergarteners. Given some time to plan, the cadets identified objectives and backup plans so as to order the children's play rationally. What they achieved instead was chaos. Experienced teachers, on the other hand, given the same task, allowed the children degrees of freedom from the start and tweaked their behavior by stabilizing desirable patterns and destabilizing undesirable ones (Kurtz & Snowden, 2003).

With this example, Snowden shows that efforts to reorganize and reduce authority can ironically often have the opposite effect: "A familiar example in organization life is the cyclic reorganization of authority by industry, then by function, then by industry, and so on in an endless cycle; or the fact that well-intentioned revolutionaries sometimes put into place bureaucracies even more stifling than those they overthrew" (Kurtz & Snowden, 2003, p. 476). Surprise—that of expecting one thing and being shocked by the appearance of another—is consistent with narrative theory because a "catch" or a "hook" in a narrative frequently takes the form of a surprise, and in the language of sensemaking, such an irony suggests the need to understand the story (Weick, Sutcliffe, & Obstfeld, 2005).

The diverse approaches to complexity amplify their power and increase the credibility of both ideas. Weick and Snowden's style differences are no small matter; one might do quite different things as a result of studying and knowing only one or the other of them, yet their common attention to how one diagnoses and responds to complexity advances the larger idea of complexity and narrative. Complexity, as an intellectual force, is in its "understanding phase." Its larger aim is to answer the question, "What are the managerial consequences for viewing the world as an adaptive, dissipative, and, most importantly, a non-linear system?" Narratives are useful for complexity because there are no hypotheses in complexity research; instead, there are historical, technical, and simulation analyses of processes over time that result in unexpected outcomes. With this caution about complexity, we turn to the notion of circumspection as the application of the idea.

Application: Narratives of Circumspection on Experience and Leadership

If the point we have made about numerosity holds for complexity, then having several stories in the application section exemplifies circumspection, which refers to both interpretation and message construction and delivery (Kelley, 1987). Circumspection means to be watchful and discreet; cautious.[2] From psychological studies of different kinds of love, "circumspect love" focuses on practicality and friendship as opposed to neurotic, or passionate love (Feeney, 1990). Keeping with the focus on practicality, Hewson and her colleagues (1996, p. 481) found circumspection—taking "action to minimize the possibility of missing other critical diagnoses"—to be one of nine major strategies for the treatment of primary medical care patients. Sharper knowledge of the relationship of complexity and control finds ready application in worklife narratives that look back on new experiences, especially leadership experiences. These stories often feature being thrown into challenging situations, often without what was considered adequate preparation. Actors step forward, do the best they can under the circumstances, and reflect upon what the narrated incident means for their identity as an organization member who belongs and/or as a capable leader. We refer to these as "narratives of circumspection," in that they take into consideration both what happened and what would have happened had circumstances been slightly different. They have a common theme of getting through a tight spot. They encapsulate what they took away from the incident, which is often a newfound sense of understanding and capability, but sometimes go on to suggest prudence on the narrator's part about how to approach similar situations that may arise.

Circumspection narratives about worklife experience need not be about major organizational or life decisions and actions, though this is possible, of course. Commonly, these narratives relate how people encountered novel situations, as when they were assigned tasks as interns or new employees. The narratives report what it was like to learn the ropes and what it meant to them to become accustomed to work routines and practices that, when first encountered, seemed incomprehensible. For instance, an intern related:

> *Although there is a hierarchy in place at [the OPL& R advertising agency], it is so rarely acknowledged that it feels like it does not exist. Technically, the founders are in charge and below them account managers govern their teams. However, in practice every individual on the team is given the freedom to express ideas, credit and encouragement*

when those ideas are superior. This is illustrated when the intern is allowed the same input as the Director of Account Services in a creative meeting. During the first week of my internship I was sitting in on a meeting about web advertising when someone asked for my opinion on a concept. I was a little surprised since I was new and unsure of the protocol on sharing ideas at meetings. This reminded me that "in the knowledge economy everyone is a volunteer."

The request for information is in keeping with the principle listed above that valuable information can emerge from anywhere. In the following case an intern in a university athletic recruitment unit reported on his struggles understanding the reasons for office routines he was supposed to follow:

Although I was always given explicit instructions on how to complete tasks, there was no way for me to really understand how the organization worked as a whole until I had spent a significant amount of time there and became familiar with the different systems that intertwined and worked together. The first time I realized I did not have a sense of the place was when I first learned about the recruiting mail system. As was the usual procedure, the first day I sent a mail out, I was told to print one copy of the letter for every recruit, sign it with [the coach's] signature on the signing machine, and fold it in three folds to stuff in the envelopes. What was not explained to me was why there were three different piles of envelopes that all had three sets of addresses stacked on top of each other. I kept wondering, "Why are there three copies of the exact same address?" Unfortunately I did not ask the right questions to clarify this matter. Instead, I would say things like "So do I need to make another copy of all three sets of addresses?" and I would get a "Yes" in return. I still had no idea why there were so many envelopes, and it was infuriating.

One day I thought I had it all figured out and sent the same recruit three copies of the same letter all in the same day. They all probably thought we were insane at the University. Once I was explained to that having three copies at a time was just a convenience so for every mail out we did not have to write new addresses, I felt a little more "in the know." After I had been in the office a little while longer, things became much clearer to me and I was able to look back and create a narrative for myself about what happened and why I had been so confused about the stupid envelopes.

Given the discussion on mutual causal systems in this chapter, it is not hard to imagine how the three copies of letters problem mentioned above could have disastrous consequences. What if receiving even a second letter capriciously annoys a supporter or donor? Some of the circumspection narratives contrast cultural practices and meanings one might expect, with those a newcomer actually finds on the ground. For example, in the following case an intern at a magazine publishing company learned about interpreting messages from the top:

Within my department, there are conference calls once a month to ensure that everyone is staying on track and meeting the desired and predicted goals for the magazine. In essence, [the regional office] is not bothered by [corporate headquarters] on a daily basis, letting go, but it is this constant thought hanging over them always, control. It was during a conference call that I began to understand that the more you essentially try to control something, the more that you will see the opposite of the desired outcome. During the conference call there were many attempts to try and calm everyone down about the idea that they are not bringing nearly close to the amount of ads published in last year's issues. It was said over and over, "Just keep doing what you're doing. We know you are trying your hardest." It was as if they were trying so hard to reassure everyone that things were going to be okay that it sent my boss into layoff mode. She turned to me and writes down on a piece of paper: "LAYOFFS." It was then that I realized how the poor attempt to calm people down only sends them into a wonder as to why they are being comforted.

In the story just offered, the equivocality of communication despite the claim of clarity is remarkable. Both preparation and improvisation are prominent in narratives of circumspection. However, whatever preparations were made are cast as preliminary or inadequate. Departures from what could have been expected make it necessary for actors to leap into action in unfamiliar circumstances and with some doubts about their readiness. In the following instance, a day-camp employee relates and then looks back on a day of unexpected leadership that challenged but ultimately affirmed her ability to improvise:

When the bus drove up and the Unit Leader, Kristi, stepped off, I knew she was having a bad day. We loaded all the kids on the bus by calling their names in alphabetical order and then we chatted while the campers sang "We Will Rock You." She explained to me that she had gone out the night before and had too much to drink. She was hung over, nauseous, and then proceeded to tell me that she had not planned anything for the day. Kristi boarded the bus and went to the camp with the campers while I followed in my car as usual. When we arrived at camp she told me that she was too sick to lead camp so I would have to do it. She contacted our supervisor to see if there was any Unit Leader that could cover for her but there was no one.

This is when I started to feel nauseous. It was only my fourth day of camp and I would have to fill the next 6 hours with fun activities for the campers to do. Not only was I new at this camp, but also the children would complain constantly if they were not having a good time. After being informed that I would have to run the camp on my own, I took a quick walk to gather some materials for some games. As I walked to the trailer that contained the extra materials, I repeated to myself, "I am capable. I can do this." Once in the trailer I gathered as much as I could. Balls, bandanas, ribbons, frisbees, cones, paintbrushes, paint, paper, water balloons and buckets. I figured that the more stuff I had, the easier it would be to keep the campers entertained for six hours. I gathered all my materials at the front of the trailer and made two trips from the baseball field to the trailer. While I gathered the materials, Kristi laid on the grass of the baseball field as the campers talked with the other campers.

Once I made it back with all the materials there, I began to instruct the campers in a game. The first game we played was a frisbee game. The campers formed a tight circle and flew a frisbee around. As time elapsed, the campers would take steps back and I added more frisbees to the circle. This game lasted about 10 minutes and then the campers were ready to move onto something else. With all the materials, I would make up new games as the day went on until all the campers went home. Even though the day was kind of hectic and sporadic, the kids enjoyed it because we played lots of games at a fast pace. The following day the campers asked if we could play some of the games we made up the day before.

At first I was intimidated and scared to take the leadership role for the day, but once I was playing the part somewhat successfully, I really enjoyed it. Sometimes when people are forced to take the leadership role that they would not take the initiative to play, they find that they enjoy it more than the position they desired to play. Assuming this leadership role for the day gave me confidence that I could perform as a leader when under pressure and with little preparation.

It is not unusual for the circumspect person to conclude, as in the above case, that although he or she was made to feel a sense of discomfiture by the experience, matters did not turn out as badly as expected. These tales generally do not describe wholesale failures or catastrophes, but they do seem constructed to remind their audiences that "The best laid plans … " In the following case, a Marine and Iraq veteran relates what happened the first time he led his unit in battle and what it meant to him:

My chance to show my leadership skills was given to me after my first deployment to Iraq. I was assigned as a squad leader which meant that I was now in charge of and responsible for 13 men. I was no longer the junior Marine and now had younger Marines looking at me just as I was looking at my senior Marines when I was a "boot." I would find myself in situations that even though I felt I was a good leader I was clueless in what to do. All of my observing had not prepared me to the actual situations. Many of these things were very minute in the larger scheme of things, but they still snuck up on me and I realized that trial and error were a fundamental part of leadership. One such example where I was put into that situation was when my squad was operating in the suburbs of Fallujah.

We had heard on the radio that our Forward Operating Base (FOB) had come under attack and we were the nearest element to help. Our squad was mounted at the time (in our Hum-V's) and only 2–3 miles down the road. I had no time to explain all the details that I was receiving on the radio to the rest of my squad, so I took off as the lead vehicle while the rest of my vehicles followed. There was a large dump truck that was somewhat blocking the road leading into the town. Later I realized that the dump truck was being used by the insurgents to block all the traffic coming in to the town. One of those times I wish I could go back to and put a few rounds through the wind-shield. We continued on and I was in constant contact with a very young Marine that was on the radio at the FOB who stated that the enemy had retreated north. I acknowledged and stated that I was going to chase after them.

The intelligence was bad. As we passed by the FOB one of my team leaders' Hum-V was directly hit with an RPG (Rocket Propelled Grenade) and immediately took out the driver. The vehicles were now stopped in the middle of the road so we could provide aid to my wounded Marine. The enemy rounds were flying from all directions and we were pinned down behind our vehicles. We couldn't see where exactly the enemy was shooting from. I stood up and walked over to see if it was coming from a certain alley. It was. At that moment I took a round in the right arm. I fell back and then ran over to our machine gun truck and told my driver and my machine gunner that we had a job to do.

As my squad kept security and continued aid on the injured Marine us three jumped into the Hum-V and did a sort of "kamikaze" action down this alley where the rounds were coming from. All I could see is muzzle flashes everywhere. We drove 4 blocks into the city. When we stopped, the shooting had ceased and we realized that we were now all alone. We looked around and realized that the enemy had just fled the area. There were AK-47's and RPG's littering the ground. We quickly picked up the weapons and then hurried back to the rest of the squad. Afterwards we assessed the situation and I order my squad to bound through the streets flushing out the rest of the insurgents.

Looking back, I have analyzed many of the decisions that I had that day and what I would have done differently. I also wonder what exactly I was thinking.

Complexity is increased here not only by the presence of both structural and dynamical complexity, but also by the volume and equivocality of the information about it. The leader was operating in a complex interactive system of tasks, perspectives, employees, and uncertainty in all of its formations, including too much information, too little information, varied information, equivocal information, non-digital information, and uncontrollable information (Browning & Shetler, 2000).

People throughout the hierarchies generate narratives of circumspection. They are to be distinguished from great leader myths in that they showcase the actions of "the little guy." However, these narratives also appear to be a prototype for more expansive narratives that pertain to complex circumstances involving more participants and multiple organizations. Such narratives of a wider scope might just be analytic in character, but they might also be of a prophetic nature, offering cautionary and/ or enabling visions of where matters are leading. They stem from the same foundation of prudence, but they are also extremely risky because the reputational consequences of being wrong can be so dire.

9

REPRESENTING NARRATIVE REALITIES

Introduction

Throughout this book, we have advocated a wide latitude in what counts as a story and we have aligned ourselves with a democratic theory of narratives. According to this theory, anyone can tell a story and anyone can critique one (Fisher, 1987). It seldom matters whether two stories are compatible or, if not, which of two tellings is true. The six angles for narrative appreciation we have explained are all part of what we term an "open architecture" for organizational narratology. Our intention has been to lay down some premises about narratives and how they may be interpreted and used that leaves ample room for augmentation. The angles are vantage points from which to enlarge and deepen understanding and appreciation of narratives in our work lives.

In this last chapter, we confront a complication for the democratic theory of narratives. Even though it works nearly all the time for people who utilize and work with narratives to accept a wide range of narratives and to accept that different narrators tell different versions of the truth, not all situations allow for this open, democratic, flexible, polyvocal approach. Organization members and leaders base significant and consequential decisions on narrative data, and they are often obligated to have the same understanding and interpretation of what went on in a particular set of circumstances. The significance of narrative data lies not just in their richness and near-universal availability, but in the fact that they are the same kind of data that organizational members use to plan, enact, interpret, and evaluate their own actions and those of others. As Weick argues, "Most organizational realities are based on narrative" (1995, p. 127). Thus, when we analyze narratives, we are starting with raw material that is central to the cognitive and cultural world of our subjects (Polkinghorne, 1995; Pentland, 1999). Because narratives are so overwhelmingly involved in determining what happens in organizations, members are justifiably concerned about the truthfulness—the *verisimilitude*—of narratives. Sometimes two or more narratives clash and only one of them can be approved as the best representation of what actually happened. Some authority, such as the court system, determines what is taken for the truth. Oppositional narratives, such as the stories offered by competing sides in a court case, require adjudication and a judgment about which of them is taken to be true (Bruner, 2002). In the court system, as in other narrative contexts, the point of view of the narrative is a major part of its truthfulness. The issue for this chapter is how to reconcile our open, democratic ideals about narrative with the necessity, on at least some occasions, to select from among competing narratives on the basis of their truth.

In what follows, we address the contingent and mercurial nature of narratives by analyzing their point of view and verisimilitude. We close by taking account of the implications of our approach for narrative research.

Contingent Narrative Realities

It is commonplace in narratology to note that different narrators have different points of view and that different readers bring different interpretive resources to narrative interpretation. Therefore, narrative realities are contingent and local. It is generally not a problem to recognize this, and it is frequently acceptable to allow competing narratives and interpretations to coexist. We can ordinarily accept that there may be and often are different versions of the truth. For instance, in the following story, few would think it matters very much who is right:

> *I've lived my entire life in Houston, Texas—I haven't even moved neighborhoods. My dad hates traveling anywhere that requires a plane ticket. To say the least, I have been very grounded throughout my childhood and haven't done much moving around. For me, family vacations constituted two things: driving to the beach (nearby Galveston), or road-tripping it all the way to Ohio to visit my family. That was pretty much the extent of it.*
>
> *So I've been to Galveston, Texas, many times in my life. I've been to the seawall, the strand, the restaurants—I know Galveston. This tunnel-vision vacationing thing didn't really bother me until I started getting older and my friends started going to other beaches. At this point, I realized that Galveston was a sub-par beach, and in comparison to most seafaring destinations, it hardly even counted as a beach at all. Galveston is dirty, the sand is littered with sea-puke, human trash, and all sorts of other nasty stuff. Because Galveston is a bay, the water is not exactly blue; it's more of a coffee-colored cesspool. After about two hours of laying on the beach, it gets so hot that the water doesn't even cool you off anymore. To sum it up, Galveston is not the greatest beach on Earth.*
>
> *Well, one summer my cousins from Ohio came to Texas. They were so excited about getting to go to Galveston. I didn't want to ruin their parade, but I couldn't*

understand their excitement for visiting such a crappy beach. My mom said they were excited because Ohio had no beaches, and so for them, any beach was better than no beach. This made sense to me. Honestly though, my cousins were convinced that Galveston was a white-sanded, blue clean-watered ocean paradise. To them, this was the absolute truth about Galveston. The perplexing part was that even after they had visited Galveston, they were not repulsed by it.

My cousins see the island as clean and beautiful. I see it as a vacation wasteland, dirty and overused. Perhaps my view of the island is skewed because of my dislike for my tunnel-vision vacationing, or maybe my truth of the island is how it really is, and my cousins are just painting an ugly dog in a good light. Or, maybe, we will never know. After all, beauty is in the eye of the beholder—and in this case, so is the truth.

It is relatively easy to conclude about the above story that both points of view are true. Galveston can be clean and dirty for different vacationers. If you were from Ohio and a guest at the home of your Texas cousin and you were a teenager, chances are if you were taken to Galveston you would celebrate the vacation spot you have been taken to. At least, you would not disparage it. After all, it still has the lure of the ocean and the romance of a beach. The example is comparable to international travel, where the tourists pay more and are effusive about the meals while the locals are stolid and get the real good food. But even though it doesn't matter who is right, the author of the Galveston story had some trouble reconciling the competing points of view about Galveston and found it peculiar her cousins thought Galveston was attractive even after they had seen it up close. Still, at the end of the day, her conclusion was that beauty and truth are in the eye of the beholder. She can hold this ecumenical viewpoint because there is no necessity to decide between accounts. She might simply say, "My cousins are different."

In another more serious difference, the disputes about the patenting of the Universal Product Code offer a useful contrast, since enormous monetary consequences accrue from any decision about who invented it and who would be rewarded for it, and once the issue is raised, it needs to be resolved somehow. The UPC, or barcode, is technically elegant in its extraordinary simplicity and versatility. It consists of a display of lines that, for retail purposes, can be optically scanned by a laser to determine the product and price of whatever object the bar is printed on or attached to. Beyond product price and type, the bar code (a combination of each bar's own width and length, plus the variable width of the space between bars) communicates all kinds of product types, from toothpaste to rat poison (Brown, 1997). For example, in a retail setting, a single "0" shows that it's a grocery item. A "2" is included when the item is to be sold by weight. A "5" identifies a discount coupon. Five consecutive digits identify the manufacturer. Tall bars in the center tell the computer to anticipate that additional significant information will follow. The bar code even has security codes within it that alert the computer when someone has tried to alter the code with a felt pen.

Beyond coding retail product information, the bar code runs automated factories by pulling a product from storage, putting it into a production line, and dropping it off to an assembly site at the optimal moment. The barcode is also an application for smartphones; users can point at a product in a retail store and download product details and purchase it simultaneously. Not surprisingly, the barcode technology managed to gain world-wide acceptance within just 20 years after US Patent #2,612,994 was issued to inventors Joseph Woodland and Bernard Silver on October 7, 1952.

However, there were competing claims about who originated the UPC. Woodland and Silver had to share credit for their invention with a slight, unassuming engineer and born inventor named Jerome Lemelson (1923–97), who edged himself into the mix by patenting parts of the code that the two originators hadn't bothered or thought to patent. Some opponents derisively knew Lemelson as the guy who invented patents rather than products. A prolific idea man (indeed, he obtained more than 600 patents in his lifetime, making him second only to Thomas Edison in that area) he had a fecund imagination, a genius for anticipating the development of various technologies, and the habit of quietly patenting as many different elements of them as he could think up. But, for want of resources, he failed to develop any prototypes or products. Instead, he would have to wait until someone else had developed a profitable product, such as an electronic gizmo used by the Big Three US automakers, and then reveal what his opponents liked to call a "submarine patent" on part of that technology to claim that he deserved a share of the royalties for the product now being made. A tireless fighter for the rights of independent inventors everywhere, he eventually won most of the patent fights he initiated, and, after years of struggling to make ends meet, collected hundreds of millions of dollars in both royalties and legal fees during the last five years of his life.

As the UPC development story illustrates, narrative reality can be highly contingent and must sometimes be negotiated. It is contingent upon *who* is telling the story, *whose* ears it is intended for, and at *what* particular moment in a sequence of possibilities it is told. Thus, in stories, "contingency plays as much a part as aesthetics or politics" (Czarniawska, 1998, p. 5). In research, as in theory, stories begin with an initial state of affairs, an action or event, and some consequent state of affairs (Czarniawska, 1998). In the case of what we may call "the Lemelson story," who shall be our storyteller: the aggrieved Lemelson himself or the scoffing lawyers who are defending the big companies he is suing? Whose ears shall the story be intended for: the ears of his sympathetic fellow independent inventors or the ears of skeptical appellate judges perhaps more sympathetic to corporate interests? What shall be the moment of telling: the moment when the technology finally becomes immensely popular or the moment Lemelson anticipated that triumphant moment, perhaps decades earlier? Each of these contingencies is, in effect, a prism through which the story can be both presented and understood.

Some readers could come away from "the Lemelson story" feeling sympathy for this genius who was merely seeking to get his just desserts. Others might see him as a "gotcha" specialist who was more successful in winning lawsuits than in developing a product of value. Still others could see him as a transformational figure who showed fellow inventors the need to probe and patent as many aspects of their inventions as they can imagine. It is, in fact, now common practice for inventors to follow Lemelson's strategy of combing established products for whatever slivers their inventors failed to patent. At least some of the people involved in the Lemelson story were obliged to make determinations among these various positions and render judgments based upon them. For the patent officers and judges, among others, a view that sees competing parties' claims as equally true representations would be untenable.

Point of View

Point of view is the perspective from which a narrative is presented. It is analogous to the point from which the camera sees the action in cinema. Point of view is also represented as persona, tone, voice, angle, eye, outlook, slant, standpoint, vantage, and viewpoint, but these terms mean much the same. The key importance of point of view stems from the fact that we assess the truthfulness of narratives, in part, by identifying from whose point of view a narrative is told. This observation applies both to everyday narratives and to narrative research in organizations.

Point of view not only applies to the narrator making the interpretation, it also covers point of view of the character and the listener. Therefore, in a sense, every story and every word is "multi-voiced" (Bakhtin, 1981). Point of view for these different positions can also change over night and over time. What seems like a joyous leap at one point of life looks like a gigantic risk at another, in keeping with Bakhtin's dialogical principle, which says that meaning builds on its limitless previous contexts of use (Bakhtin, 1981). This refers to a basic individual variation as a perspective for narratives.

Central to point of view are the vested interest of the teller and the closeness of the observer who does the telling (Czarniawska, 1988). Weick says the hardest thing for an observer to do is be accurate, close up (Weick, 1985). Part of the difficulty of the close observer is that when the narrator and the character are the same s/he frequently has a vested interest in how the character in the story is represented. As Bruner says, "The Self as narrator not only recounts but justifies" (1990, p. 121). It is a natural human tendency to put one's best foot forward, to manage the impression "given off," to be strategic (Goffman, 1959). The value of a point of view rises with comprehensiveness. How much information about what is going on does the narrator have and how involved is s/he in the story? For her/his role in the narrative, s/he may be a participant (directly involved in the story) or a non-participant (merely an observer), omniscient (know all about what is going on), or selectively omniscient (has partial but specific information), objective (no vested interest) or partial (is promoting a particular version), or reliable (their word is good) or unreliable (their word is questionable) (Kennedy & Gioia, 1995). Minor characters are often the source of the point of view of the story because they are credible even when the focus of the story is not about them. They retain a place in the story and have a position for seeing it unfold, but they are merely observers of a remarkable story.

With all the possible conditions for narration, we are left with the fallibility of narrative. As we have developed at other places in this book, offering one set of facts and circumstances means that others are not being told. Stories mask what happened as much as they showcase it (Lyotard, 1984). Armstrong reminds us, "Every interpretive approach reveals something only by disguising something else, which a competing method with different assumptions might disclose" (1990, p. 10). As a result, point of view is a kind of obliviousness just as it is a concentrated focus. Thus, "Every hermeneutic standpoint has its own dialectic of blindness and insight—a ratio of disguise and disclosure which stems from its presuppositions" (1990, p. 10). In this sense, the point of view that leads to assessments of verisimilitude arise from some set of values—religious, economic, social, ethnic, and so on. As such, point of view is usually based on values and premises that make the interpretation of events and actors sensible (Fisher, 1987). Even Darwin's evolutionary theory emphasized the idea of the fittest as a social structure. Evolutionary groups work as teams. What is honorable in one camp, such as spying and deceit, will be detested in another. The idea of like-minded people making up ingroups and stereotypically opposing outgroups is consistent across evolutionary theory (Schubert & Otten, 2002). Such ingroup interpretations are not only limited, they are a risk because of the costs of leaving another point of view out of the equation. "To accept a method of interpretation is to enter into a wager—to gamble, namely, that the insights made possible by its assumptions will offset the risks of blindness they entail (Armstrong, 1990, p. 10). One's point of view can be an asset because of the energy it marshals for seeing an event or a person in a particular way, and that same focus can obliterate the chance to see anything else. If commitment is associated with the number of alternatives open to consideration, then a limited or narrow point of view is a form of dedication.

Verisimilitude

Literature on the truthfulness of stories is scant because we generally accept the plausibility and relativity of a story. Nevertheless, the truthfulness of one's point of view can be crucial to stories. Verisimilitude does not address the truthfulness of a story directly; instead, the term refers to the ways in which a story is represented as truthful. For this reason, "storytelling is the creative demonstration of truth" (Schank, 1995, p. 119), which means that the storyteller is much like a persuader who brings as many resources as s/he can to create acceptance of the story. Storytelling is an active process and stands up as the "living proof of an idea, the conversion of idea to action" (Schank, 1995, p. 119). Since a story represents action, the tone and feel of the story, and even its meaning, can change radically depending on who is telling the story. Think of a young man telling a story of his graduation prom night or some other celebratory night, a coming-of-age story, complete with details. Now think of his worried mother telling the same story. Whatever her relationship with him, she might offer many of the same the details, but the meaning is likely to be very different simply because the point of view is affected so much by who is telling the story.

Verisimilitude refers to the presentation of the truth of the story—is it believable? If so, what makes it believable? Verisimilitude addresses the question of how real a text seems, how closely it matches the listener's expectations of reality. Matching narrative to reality is accomplished via realistic-seeming characters, setting, and style. Verisimilitude makes "stranger" voices interesting. Verisimilitude has a specific meaning in drama that carries over to narrative—it refers to the extent to which a drama appears to copy the offstage reality. There are many places to examine the isomorphic connection between the story and reality. Is the tone the same? Is the pace of speech and accents the same? Is the style and sophistication of sensemaking comparable?

To bring attention to the issues of verisimilitude, the following story is a retelling of Gladwell's tale (2010) of an intelligence ruse in the Second World War. As the story goes, the British dressed a dead vagrant as a courier in business clothes and planted a misleading document inside an attaché case chained to his wrist, then caused his body to be washed up on the coast of Spain. While Spain was officially neutral in the conflict, the British knew that there were Nazi sympathizers in the Spanish military and correctly predicted that the document would find its way into the right hands to be taken seriously and passed on to the German military. The British had to be careful not to do too complete a job in the ruse because doing so would only make the interpreters of the corpse and the documents he carried more suspicious. But two individuals in the chain of interpretation had a particular need for the information in the documents to be valid and they were key in affirming the materials' validity for the Germans. The first important link in affirming the value of the documents' find was Karl-Erich Kühlenthal, the single individual responsible for German intelligence in Madrid, Spain. He was so enthusiastic that he "personally flew the documents to Berlin." One of the motivations for his eagerness was his link to a set of distant Jewish ancestors from Germany. He wanted to affirm his value in Madrid so that he would not be sent back to Germany for a permanent duty station, which would have increased the possibility of his lineage being examined. The second person in the validation steps was Alexis Baron von Roenne, an intelligence officer in Berlin. From the British view, he appeared to get everything wrong, including wildly overestimating the size of the British ground forces ready for the invasion of Europe. He appeared to be a Hitler hater, and passed on all the incorrect information sent to him with a stamp of approval. Gladwell succinctly summarizes their role in affirming the documents: "Kühlenthal was an advocate of the documents because he needed them to be true; von Roenne was an advocate of the documents because he suspected them to be false. In neither case did the audiences for their assessments have an inkling about their private motivations." Stories are less plagued by truthfulness because stories are less strained by preciseness.

Narrative analysts, in practice, approach the issue of truth in different ways (Taylor & Van Every, 2000). Some assume that language represents reality: the narrative clauses recapitulate experience in the same order as the original events (Labov & Waletzky, 1997). Others, influenced by phenomenology, take the position that narrative constitutes reality: it is in the telling that we constitute real phenomena in the stream of consciousness. Still others, interested in the persuasive aspects of language, argue that narrators inscribe into their tales their ideologies and interests (Riessman, 1993, p. 22). Of course, all three approaches are plausible.

Because we know that alternative stories sometimes do clash and that important consequences are going to flow from decisions about which story to accept as the best representative of the truth, we tend to fortify stories when we write or tell them with details and context designed to make our story stand up to scrutiny. Eyewitnesses, for instance, often begin their narratives with claims about the perfectly normal and routine things they themselves were doing when they observed what happened. This claim for routine guards against the possibility that they might themselves have played a role in the incident or that their telling is self-interested. This is especially true for objective science; the method section of a research article describes the research procedures in detail sufficient to both legitimate the research decisions made and to allow replication of the study, even though replication attempts are rare. One way to circumvent efforts to take apart a story, in short, is to *overbuild* the story so that it will stand up to scrutiny if it is ever challenged. Challenges to the details of a research study are rare, but they do happen and when they do, it is taken as a serious matter (Fish, 2010).

While verisimilitude is deeply attached to the veracity of stories, it is even more important to science. If verisimilitude has to do with believability, the extent to which the way a story is presented, and the indicators used to trust the story, certainly science has this requirement of saying, here is how we got to this truth (Niiniluoto, 1998). A crisis in verisimilitude erupted after Popper's early statement demonstrated that scientific progress moves forward when cabals of like-minded people promote a way of thinking (Niiniluoto, 1998).

Understanding verisimilitude requires examining the practical effects of believing in a particular way, which is why people emphasize the positions they have taken in relation to the outcomes of the stories they have told. Fisher (1987) resolves the idea of practicality by viewing storytelling as a kind of argument, an incomplete syllogism whose missing premise is an invitation for the audience to join in the discussion by filling in the argument with information or values they have; the effect of this is to enroll participants in the argument by their participation (Weick & Browning, 1986). A story is not a complete argument, but it is seductive and inviting in that it leaves a piece to be filled in by the listener, who combines what they know with the new information.

We couple point of view and verisimilitude in this final chapter because their combination offers a concluding position on the moral assessment of the narrative. What could be more moral than what counts for the truth? Verisimilitude is a political interpretation; the most important understanding of power is its connection to knowledge—even if that knowledge only exists because of the power structure above it, blessing it. Thus, Foucault (1979) conceives that the micropolitics of the truth are acted out in relationships and groups. When power relationships are involved, an interpretative approach is only known when it offers a contrast. There must be a comparison—what else could have happened? What if key phrases had been said a day earlier?—for any single interpretation to make sense. If a point of view requires no comparison, it operates like a fact, an absolute statement, or a religious dictum. Yet, stories are always a little off and have some ambiguity; something, sometimes lots of things, are left on the cutting room floor.

Despite all the conditions for point of view and the vagaries of verisimilitude, there are in our lives settings where uncertainty cannot be left alone. In these instances, we are forced to address and ultimately select from among oppositional narratives. Moral irony contrasts the seeming good with the actual bad or vice versa. For instance, the following narrative about agricultural practices in the UK reverses a view of the idyllic, organic countryside and its upstanding farmers with a sordid view of organized crime. The introduction alone is enough to engage the audience and pull them into a world they did not know existed. The idyllic farmlands are painted as continuous crime scenes, drastically clashing with the prevailing image of peaceful tranquility:

> In Britain, there is anecdotal evidence, that isolated farmhouses are used by members of the illegal drug trade as safe houses, or as places to cultivate cannabis plants and also as factories for the production of illicit drugs. Another contemporary issue, is the exploitation of illegal immigrants by "gang masters" to service the staffing requirements of seasonal work on farms and estates, across Europe. There is anecdotal evidence that during the "foot and mouth" epidemic unscrupulous farmers charged up to £6,000 per diseased carcass to knowingly spread the disease. That there may have been takers is testament to the depressed state of farming. In many of these cases there is an underlying element of rural gangsterism at play. Often these facilitators and organizers are entrepreneurial types who are transferring their skills from one arena/sphere into another ... Nor is the practice confined to agriculture. Dishonest practices, such as the landing of black fish in the fishing industry are rumored to occur with alarming frequency. In many of these instances the actions of the entrepreneurs who profit from these activities can only be located in stories.
>
> Furthermore, in keeping with the rural idyll rarely do such studies impinge on issues of illegal enterprise that run contrary to the romanticized image of the countryside as being associated with wholesomeness. As a consequence, rural and farming rogues have been neglected as subjects of research. Yet, in the present climate of economic decline in agricultural income, extracting value from the environment can be problematic and may give rise to the practice of illegal enterprise in the countryside. The following case study is of one such illegal enterprise, namely the—illegal slaughter of sheep—for the Muslim "halal" market, known to those who participate in it as the smokies trade. This trade

was chosen as it is a contemporary problem in the countryside and also because the author had sufficient knowledge of it to write about it. Like most entrepreneurial crimes the dealings of the trade are hidden from public knowledge.

(Smith, 2003, p. 278)

This story is interesting because of the contrast surrounding it—the romantic, idyllic scene in relation to the sordid violence within it.

Oppositional Narratives

Bruner's concept of the oppositional narrative focuses on the competition between tellers of two stories. When two points of view exist and there is evidence for both stories, how is a judgment of verisimilitude resolved? The oppositional narrative is tied directly to the legal setting because legal advocates tell their stories to a third party (a judge and/or a jury) with the intent of being sufficiently convincing to win the case. Jerome Bruner focuses on the oppositional narrative in his book, *Making Stories: Law, Literature, Life* (2002). He is a narratologist venturing into an analysis of legal stories. He is credible not only from his previous writings but because of his milieu. His conceptualization of the oppositional narrative in his 2002 book is offered in consultation with his legal scholar colleagues at NYU, yet is articulated to make the idea accessible to a general narrative readership.

Legal narration, storytelling in courts of law to determine a victor, is a contrast to the ideas of narrative covered in this book because it departs from the notion of polyvocality where everyone can have a story of their own and can critique another's story (Fisher, 1987). Polyvocality emphasizes the local and personal epistemology of stories, where a person's beliefs are autonomous and sovereign. Rather than everyone having their own story, the legal system is designed to assure that everyone has their day in court and as a result of having the opportunity to speak, the participant is respectful and accepts the findings of the court. The issue is resolved by the decision reached, there is no reprisal or continued emphasis on the differences, and no grudge is expected to follow the decision.

Bruner explains why the legal system is as seamless and accepted as it is given that it is designed to resolve intractable differences. The acceptance and respect for a court's decision is aided by the ritualistic and symbolic nature of the setting. The arrangement is predictable with a special placement for proponents, opponents, judges, and juries. The judge is further set apart with a traditional robe and s/he is offered extra respect when everyone in the courtroom rises to acknowledge the judge's arrival. Beyond these symbolic representations of order and control, we accept legal narratives and place them in a position above another story because of the reliance on precedence and solemnity. Literature and law also differ on the value of novelty. When legal stories are being considered—in contrast to fictional depictions of them—there is rarely room for playfulness in the courtroom. Whereas though a literary narrative is designed to say something new, the legal narrative is constructed to tie a present set of circumstances to a historical set of circumstances as directly as possible. While there are instances of creativity in the courtroom the usual goal is to make the story as bland and predictable as possible by connecting the present story to an historical precedence that supports the advocate's position.

Bruner brings to bear the consideration of the literary narrative in his analysis because legal decisions, despite the attempt to promote Justinean law—a product of the Roman Empire—are a mix of standardization and locality. Courts follow a legal and moral standard and simultaneously make a literary and cultural interpretation of right and wrong and Bruner's shining example of this is the context for *Brown v. Board of Education* (1954). Here is his firsthand view and cultural interpretation of that decision.

Bruner develops the context of *Brown v. Board of Education* (1954) as a transformational change in race relations. He is a Senior Research Fellow at the New York University School of Law, was educated as a developmental psychologist. He observes that out of the Second World War grew the concept of the *internal self*, of a person borne out of the possibility of the end of subjugation and the right of equality of thought and action. Since the Second World War was fought for sovereignty, it had an effect on England's colonies and America's racial practices. In the Atlantic Charter prior to the Second World War, Britain agreed to release its colonies and they subsequently declared independence over the next 30 years. While the United States had no colonies to release following the war, it did have a legal system that meant unequal rights for African Americans. Then, nine years after the end of the war, the cultural interpretation of the separate but equal clause was the razor's edge that the court decision depended on. Prior to that time, *Plessy v. Ferguson* (1896), held in a comparison of separate but equal access for blacks and whites to Pullman cars, that the material equality was enough to show that separate could be equal. But Bruner's experience helped to show that separateness itself undermined equality.

Bruner was in a unique position in that he was both a narratologist interested in the interplay of legal narratives and an agent in the *Brown v. Board of Education* dispute. Bruner was an actor in this very story two years earlier. What could have been more compelling than to have been an expert witness? His credentials in child development put him in position to offer a deposition in 1952 to address what it meant for the cognitive development of the child to be told that what you had was equal while simultaneously being told that the back of the bus was fine for you. Bruner addressed how it affected the psyche of the African American to be set apart and as evidence he offers the literary representation of inequality in such authors as Langston Hughes. Although Bruner was never called to testify because the decision turned on another matter, his story demonstrates how culture is connected to legal decisions and how point of view engages with what we accept as the truth. In the following story from a university undergraduate, the narrator tells of struggling with a friend over the difference between point of view and the truth.

My friend Bobbie, she is a great friend. She is really sweet, considerate, kind and she is really fun. But sometimes she is almost too fun. She calls me almost every night asking me if I want to go out. And sometimes I am just too tired, I have too much work to do or I just don't feel like drinking. But Bobbie, she loves to drink, she does it all the time and sometimes she drinks a little bit too much. And my friends and I have had some instances in the past where she has kind of caused a problem because of her drinking. And so I kind of started noticing that this was like a repetitive thing, all her problems she was causing. So I decided to talk to her a few weeks ago. And I sat down and talked to her about it and told her you know I think this is kind of becoming an issue maybe you should look at this and fix it. And she said: "No, I don't have a drinking problem, I'm in college. I'm drinking just as much as everyone else is that we see on Bourbon Street every week. I am totally normal." So after I talked to her I was thinking okay, you know, maybe I am being a little judgmental. She is drinking a lot, but so does everyone else we see on Bourbon street every week. So I said ok you know she doesn't have a drinking problem. So last week before we went home for Thanksgiving my friends and I decided to go out downtown before we went home. So I am at the bar, 1814, and it is around 1:30 and I find my friend, Dorinne, and I go: "Dorinne have you seen Bobbie? I haven't seen her in awhile; I am kind of getting a little bit worried." And Dorinne says: "Oh no, I haven't seen her either. You know this is weird." So we are like maybe she is outside of the bar talking to someone on the street. That happens sometimes. So we go out there and we start looking around. No Bobbie. So Dorinne starts looking around the area because we kind of start getting nervous at this point. And we find Bobbie passed out in the alley behind the bar. So we go over to her, pick her up, support her, find her a cab and get home. And of course the next morning she doesn't remember anything. So we fill her in and I mean you know this is what happened. She kind of laughs it off and thinks it's just a funny story to add to her drunken stories collection that is kind of growing at this point. And now that I think about it I kind of realize that yeah she may not think she has a drinking problem, but she doesn't really see the truth in the fact that she does. She thinks it's normal for a college student to get so drunk that you just pass out in the back of an alley. That is not safe at all and I like to drink, but I would never hopefully find myself in that situation. So until she realizes the truth that maybe she does have a problem. I guess I just have to start watching out for her when she drinks.

Organizational Narrative Research

We integrate these positions on point of view and verisimilitude by offering and categorizing polar positions about narrative veracity and proposing what we should be looking for in narrative research. We follow Polkinghorne's position that narratives are valuable for their experience alone; and they are valuable when collected and sorted for their theoretical meaning. Our analysis is organized around the following five topics: first is the celebration of narratives. Second is the folly of narratives. Third is an explication of what we should look for in narratives. Fourth is narrative as the repository of human experience. Fifth is narrative as a data source for ana-lyzing narrative reality in organizations.

First is the celebration of narratives. Narrative is a new communication resource, a new item in the toolbox, for managing and affecting outcomes in organizations. As a result, research frequently represents the power of the story and the strategies for using it. You can "story around the organization" and enact a style of leader-ship where main points are captured and retold in a story; "storying," is a way leaders disseminate and reinforce values (Armstrong, 1990). People who have a narrative perform better and organization members who buy into a narrative about a specific project are more committed to it (Brown, Denning, Groh, & Prusak, 2005). Stories are exciting and can be used to represent a simple but compelling vision of the company that is represented in a metaphor (Czarniawska, 1998; Schein, 2010).

Second, is the folly of narratives. Kimmelman (2010) cites Nancy Huston, a Canadian-born novelist: "After the war French writers rejected the idea of narrative because Hitler and Stalin were storytellers, and it seemed naïve to believe in stories. So instead they turned more and more to theory, to the absurd." This position is one of caution. Narrative is not trustworthy; a fragment, critical view is more valuable than a unitary, transformational, hopeful one. A theme that threads throughout this book is that narratives traditionally carry hope and are a vehicle for learning. An ending to a story is a necessity; time has to be bracketed (Czarniawska, 1998), a conclusion has to be reached, preferably one that affirms character, has a moral, and provides a hopeful, even a happy ending (Franklin, 1986). Kimmell reports that in Europe, especially France, the master narrative (Czarniawska, 1988), the singular story about a powerful character, is the source of the twentieth cen-tury's problems, not the solution. As a result, interpretative theories in France, including Ricœur's narratology, celebrate the fragmented, the flawed and uncertain narrator (2004). Critical theory writing, thus, celebrates the styles that leave the reader confused rather than clear (Rosenau, 1992). The American narratologist, Boje, is popular in France and runs a workshop there annually. His fragmented, ante-up, "I am bidding to be a part of this," vision of narrative that ambles forward, interesting but incomplete, fits with the larger moral vision of the French. Grand theories of leadership are not trustworthy, lots of different views, less certainty, is preferable. Don't let any single person get too strong and instead embrace the Charles De Gaulle quandary, "How can anyone govern a nation that has two hundred and forty-six different kinds of cheese?"[1] Boje's (2001) conceptualization of the antenarrative celebrates such variation, and his research examples are equally ideological and provocative. He takes interview data and writes a story around it and his work reflects Polkinghorne's (1995) concept of narrative inquiry. The complementary tie between Boje and the critical theorists makes Boje's work one of the significant contributions to narrative over the last 20 years. His work is extended in both organizational communication (Barge, 2004) and managerial theory, and is the subject of a complete handbook devoted to the fragmented narrative (Boje, 2011).

Third, in response to the distinction between the story that is good and the story that is bad is an explication of what we should look for in proper narratives. Gabriel's critique contends that our excitement for narrative, including some of the enthusiasm we've displayed in this book, is too lax (Gabriel, 2004). As evidence, Gabriel offers two stories, one of which is about a person who claimed to have experienced the holocaust, and actually didn't, and another person who won the Nobel Prize for describing a brutality imposed on her family in Guatemala, and was found, through social science research, to have been exaggerating and, in some cases, just to have made it up. On the representation of truth, who gets to make the determination and when is critical. Gabriel insists on a causal structure and plot integration so that the entire story peaks in a crescendo. He cautions us against simply buying into all voices as meriting attention and instead to take on the role as researchers to vet stories for their "blind spots, illusions, and self deceptions that crucially and legitimately make them up" (Gabriel, 2004, p. 74). He warns against joining the postmodern chorus of small voices and fears that they do little to credit academic research. Instead, he encourages us to critique stories with an eye toward privileging some and silencing others. He warns us against narratives that are rhetorical, that have a "desire to please or manipulate an audience" (Gabriel, 2004, p. 74). He instead urges us to critique the "truths of undigested personal experience" (Gabriel, 2004, p. 74). Gabriel's position is a contrast to communication researchers who see all storytelling as rhetorical (Fisher, 1987; Hartelius & Browning, 2006;).

Fourth is narrative as the repository of human experience. One of Polkinghorne's (1988) themes is that narrative is valuable not because of its historical power but because it is the way individuals organize and recount their lives. People naturally tell and remember stories because that is what they do (McAdams, 2006). This is the phenomenological position that "People by nature live storied lives and tell stories of those lives" (Connelly & Clandinin, 1990, p. 2). Research on the phenomenological story takes the premise of "lived and told stories" as intact and simply surfaces the interpretations that individuals make about themselves (Pinnegar & Daynes, 2005, p. 5). The advantage of soliciting stories about people's experiences in organizations is that they tend to offer narrative interviews readily (Czarniawska, 2005). When asked to tell the story of their experience, rather than offering a rational account for what happened, interviewees tend to offer reports that expand the range of relevant details. Such information allows the narrator to build sequence and surprise in the story. Because interviewees are more willing to acknowledge the chaotic rather than the strategic experience of the workplace, they are sometimes willing to relate the story dramatically by developing characters and recounting memorable moments. Interviewees feel less compelled to "net out" the results of their actions in the first moment of the interview and are more willing to recount the day-by-day sequential report.

Fifth is narrative as a data source for analyzing narrative reality in organizations. This position on narrative methodology takes interview data and turns them into stories about a particular theoretical point in organizations. This connection can be indirect, where the stories and theories are placed alongside each other and the reader is invited to make the connections (Browning, Sætre, Stephens, & Sørnes,

2008). The analyst ties theory to data by providing the conceptual link, then presenting the story as evidence of it. Gabriel typifies this kind of analysis and his (2000) book provides several useful examples of it. For example, he has a section on leadership, including stories of uncaring leaders, the asymmetry between leaders and followers, leaders as omnipotent, loss of faith in leaders, and fantasies about leaders. For each of these concepts, Gabriel offers snippets of stories extracted from interviews that readily affirm the categories he establishes. The distinctive advantage of Gabriel's stories is that they provide a view toward leadership that offsets the managerial view; they are evidence of another angle to what leaders do and how they are viewed by followers— who have no choice but to make sense of them. The advantage of this strategy is that it does not depend on the interviewee seeing their life as story. In interviews, words become data (Pinnegar & Daynes, 2005), and snippets about disrespectful and doubtful responses to leaders allow for the construction of a theoretical category. Gabriel's examples show that followers distrust leaders and almost never understand why they act in the strange ways they do. Other instances of this become narratives of sexist interpretation, such as the technical problem with a woman whose breasts repeatedly hit the spacebar on her typewriter until a "fix it" person adjusted her chair to change her height in relation to the keyboard (Czarniawska, 2005) and became so much of a "dumb blonde" story that it took on such a mythical proportion that it actually impeded typewriter ergonomic development in Europe.

In these cases, stories are interpreted to make a theoretical point, to offer stories as evidence of a concept. The advantage of this turn is that it expands the number of researchers making narrative interpretations beyond those who are necessarily committed to the narrative paradigm. It invites the best of both worlds, the interested narratologists and organizational theorists, positivist or critical, to make narrative interpretations and thus expands the platform for open source narrative analysis.

In summary, we bring this book to a close realizing that a call for an open architecture means that rather than tapering off to a definitive conclusion, our end game is to invite still other interpretations of concepts and applications. After all, other applications are not only possible, but likely. In keeping with a narrative, our final and hopeful image of open architecture can be summarized through invoking an archetypal movie image. The setting is an elegant pool party cast with glamorous people in black tie and evening gowns. Someone at the party cannot resist the chance to do a cannonball into the pool creating a wave and a splash so huge that nearly everyone is soaked. Then, by happenstance, the woman in the beautiful dress tumbles in and the man in the tux is right behind her. Rather than being angry about their circumstance, they emerge from the water with straggling hair and soaking clothes, and are exhilarated and happy. "Come on in, the water's fine," they might say. Views of organizational life built out of surprising, exuberant, hilarious, embarrassing, poignant, play-filled, wild, conflictual stories, and appreciative readings of them, is bound to ignite the passion for organizing in ways no other strategy could hope to achieve.

We have a similar image and hope for the open architecture of narratology. "Everybody is in" by accident or intent.

NOTES

Chapter 1

1 Our search for stories was completed by a team of students led by Kerk Kee and funded by a university grant to support undergraduate research called the "Undergraduate Mentoring Program." The team combed communication and management journals for stories that match the key concepts of the chapters of this book.
2 "Ludlow Massacre," by Woody Guthrie © 1958 (renewed) by Woody Guthrie Publications, Inc. All rights reserved. Used by permission.
3 *The Liars' Club*, by Mary Karr © 1955 by Penguin Press. All rights reserved. Used by permission.

Chapter 3

1 This is a direct quote from Senator Harris.
2 "'Our Nation Is Moving Toward Two Societies, One Black, One White—Separate and Unequal': Excerpts from the Kerner Report." History Matters. http://history matters.gmu.edu/d/6545/ (accessed November 1, 2011).
3 Our colleague, François Cooren, also of the Montreal school, has noted in a recent discussion with us that our insertion of the sender–receiver model in comparison to the Greimasian terminology is, in fact, quite different from the way Greimas defines the terms sender–receiver. For a review of his interpretation of Greimas, see Cooren's (2000) book, *The Organizing Property of Communication*.

Chapter 5

1 www.swedishwire.com/science/6521-story-of-the-merchant-of-death-alfred-nobel (accessed October 6, 2011).

Chapter 8

1 An earlier version of this conceptualization appeared in Browning and Boudes (2005).
2 http://dictionary.reference.com/browse/circumspect (accessed October 6, 2011).

Chapter 9

1 www.google.com/search?aq=1&oq=degaule+cheese&sourceid=chrome&ie=UTF-8&q= de+gaulle+cheese+quote

REFERENCES

Abbot, H. P. (2008). *The Cambridge introduction to narrative*. Cambridge: Cambridge University Press.

Adam, J.-M. (1996). *Le récit, Coll.* Paris: PUF.

Almén, B. (2003). Narrative archetypes: A critique, theory, and method of narrative analysis. *Journal of Music Theory, 47* (1), 1–39.

Almén, B. (2008). *A theory of musical narrative*. Bloomington: Indiana University Press.

Anderson, P. (1999). Perspective: Complexity theory and organization science. *Organization Science, 10* (3), 216–32.

Aristotle (1981). *Poetics*. (L. Golden, Trans.). Gainesville: University of Florida Press.

Aristotle (1991). *On rhetoric*. (G. A. Kennedy, Trans.). New York: Oxford University Press.

Armstrong, P. B. (1990). *Conflicting readings: Variety and validity in interpretation*. Chapel Hill: University of North Carolina Press.

Arrow, K. J. (1974). *The limits of organization*. New York: Norton.

Austin, J. L. (1961). A plea for excuses. In J. L. Austin, *Philosophical papers*, (pp. 175–204). Ed. J. O. Urmson (http://en.wikipedia.org/wiki/J._O._Urmson) & G. J. Warnock (http://en.wikipedia.org/wiki/G._J._Warnock). Oxford: Oxford University Press.

Bakhtin, M. M. (1981). *The dialogic imagination: Four essays*. Ed. Michael Holquist. Trans. Caryl Emerson and Michael Holquist (pp. 259–422). University of Texas Press Slavic Studies 1. 1975 (Russian). Austin: University of Texas Press.

Bal, M. (1997). *Narratology: Introduction to the theory of narrative* (2nd ed.). Toronto: University of Toronto Press.

Baldwin, M. W., & Sinclair, L. (1996). Self-esteem and "if … then" contingencies of interpersonal acceptance. *Journal of Personality and Social Psychology, 71* (6), 1130–41.

Barge, J. K. (2004). Antenarrative and managerial practice. *Communication Studies, 5* 5(1), 106–27.

Barthes, R. (1996). Introduction to the structural analysis of narratives. In S. Onega & J. A. G. Landa (Eds.), *Narratology: An introduction* (pp. 45–60). New York: Longman.

Bavelas, J. B., Coates, L., & Johnson, T. (2000). Listeners as co-narrators. *Journal of Personality and Social Psychology, 79* (6), 941–52.

Bertolino, B., & O'Hanlon, B. (2002). *Collaborative, competency-based counseling and therapy*. Boston: Allyn and Bacon.

Bird, E. S. (2002). It makes sense to us: Cultural identity in local legends of place. *Journal of Contemporary Ethnography, 31* (5), 519–47.

Bittner, E. (1982) The concept of organization. In R. Turner (Ed.), *Ethnomethodology*. New York: Penguin.

Bochner, A. (1994). Perspectives on inquiry II: Theories and stories. In M. Knapp & G. R. Miller (Eds.), *Handbook of interpersonal communication* (2nd ed.), (pp. 21–41). Thousand Oaks, CA: Sage Publications.

Boje, D. M. (1991). The storytelling organization: A study of story performance in an office-supply firm. *Administrative Science Quarterly, 36* (1), 106–26.

Boje, D. M. (1998). The postmodern turn from stories-as-objects to stories-in-context methods. Academy of Management, Research Methods Forum #3. http://cbae.nmsu.eduO~dboje/measures.html (accessed October 3, 2011).

Boje, D. M. (2001). *Narrative methods of organizational and communication research*. Thousand Oaks, CA: Sage Publications.

Boje, D. M. (Ed.) (2011). *Storytelling and the future of organizations: An antenarrative handbook*. New York: Routledge.

Bormann, E. G. (1972). Fantasy and rhetorical vision: The rhetorical criticism of social reality. *The Quarterly Journal of Speech, 58*, 396–407.

Brockmeier, J., & Harre, R. (1997). Narrative: Problems and promises of an alternative paradigm. *Research on Language and Social Interaction, 30,* 263–83.

Brown, A. D., & Humphreys, M. (2006). Organizational identity and place: A discursive exploration of hegemony and resistance, *Journal of Management Studies, 43*, 231–57.

Brown, E. (1997). Does it mean "toothpaste"? Or "rat poison"? *Fortune*, February 17, 1997. http://money.cnn.com/magazines/fortune/fortune_archive/1997/02/17/222169/index.htm (accessed November 1, 2011).

Brown, J. S. Denning, S., Groh, K., & Prusak, L. (eds) (2005). *Storytelling in organizations: Why storytellling is transforming 21st century organizations and management*. Boston: Elsevier Butterworth-Heinemann.

Brown, M. H. (1982). That reminds me of a story: Speech action in organizational socialization. University of Texas at Austin, TX. Unpublished dissertation.

Browning, L. D. (1991). Organizational narratives and organizational structure. *Journal of Organizational Change Management, 4*, 59–67.

Browning, L. D. (1992). Lists and stories as organizational communication. *Communication Theory, 2*, 281–302.

Browning, L. D. (2010). Narrative and narratology. In S. W. Littlejohn & K. A. Foss (Eds.), *Encyclopedia of communication theory* (pp. 673–77). Los Angeles: Sage Publications.

Browning, L. D., & Boudes, T. (2005). The use of narrative theory to understand and respond to complexity: A comparative analysis of the Cynefin and Weickian models. *Emergence: Complexity & Organization, 7* (3&4), 32–39.

Browning, L. D., Greene, R., Sutcliffe, K., Sitkin, S., & Obstfeld, D. (2009). Constitutive complexity: Military entrepreneurs and the synthetic character of communication flows. In L. Putnam & A. Nicotera (Eds.), *Building theories of organization: The constitutive role of communication* (pp. 89–116). Mahwah, NJ: Lawrence Erlbaum.

Browning, L. D., Morris, G. H., & Kee, K. F. (2011). Positive communication in organizations. In K. Cameron & G. Spreitzer (Eds.), *Handbook of positive organizational scholarship*. New York: Oxford University Press.

Browning, L. D., Sætre, A. S., Stephens, K., & Sørnes, J. O. (2008). *Information and communication technologies in action: Linking theory and narratives of practice*. New York: Routledge.

Browning, L. D., & Shetler, J. C. (2000). *Sematech: Saving the U.S. semiconductor industry*. College Station: Texas A & M University Press.

Brummett, B. (2008). *A rhetoric of style*. Carbondale, IL: Southern Illinois University Press.

Bruner, E. M. (1986). Ethnography as narrative. In V. W. Turner & E. M. Bruner (Eds.), *The anthropology of experience* (pp. 137–55). Urbana: University of Illinois Press.

Bruner, J. (1986). *Actual minds, possible worlds*. Cambridge, MA: Harvard University Press.

Bruner, J. (1990). *Acts of meaning*. Cambridge, MA: Harvard University Press.

Bruner, J. (2002). *Making stories: Law, literature, life*. Cambridge, MA: Harvard University Press.

Bryson, M. A. (2003). Nature, narrative, and the scientist-writer: Rachel Carson's and Loren Eiseley's critique of science. *Technical Communication Quarterly 12* (4), 369–87.

Burke, K. (1945). *A grammar of motives*. Berkeley: University of California Press.

Buttny, R. (2004). *Talking problems: Studies of discursive construction*. Albany, NY: SUNY Press.

Campbell, J. (2008). *The hero with a thousand faces* (3rd ed.). Novato, CA: New World Library.

Cherrington, D. J. (1994). *Organizational behavior*. Boston, MA: Allyn and Bacon.

Clifford, J. (1988). *The predicament of culture: Twentieth century ethnography, literature and art*. Cambridge, MA: Harvard University Press.

Clifford, J. (1997). *Routes*. Cambridge, MA: Harvard University Press.

Cohen, M. D., March, J. G., & Olsen, J. P. (1972). A garbage can model of organizational choice. *Administrative Science Quarterly, 17* (1), 1–25.

Cohen, M., March, J. G. & Olsen, J. P. (1976). *Ambiguity and choice in organizations*. Bergen, Norway: Universitetsforlaget.

Colombo, J. (2009, June). Finger painting: Storefront. Cover image. *The New Yorker*. www.newyorker.com/online/blogs/tny/2009/06/finger-painting-storefront.html (accessed October 3, 2011).

Connelly, F. M., & Clandinin, D. J. (1990). Stories of experience and narrative inquiry. *Educational Researcher, 19* (5, Jun.–Jul.), pp. 2–14.

Cooper, C. L., & Locke, E. A. (2000). *Industrial and organizational psychology: Linking theory with practice*. Oxford: Blackwell Business.

Corvellec, H. (1995). *Stories of achievement, Narrative features of organizational performance*. Malmö, Sweden: Lund University Press.

Cunliffe, A. L., Luhman, J. T., & Boje, D. M. (2004). Narrative temporality: Implications for organizational research. *Organizational Studies, 25* (2), 261–86.

Czarniawska, B. (1997). *Narrating the organization: Dramas of institutional identities*. Chicago: University of Chicago Press.

Czarniawska, B. (1998). *A narrative approach in organization studies*. Thousand Oaks, CA: Sage Publications.

Czarniawska, B. (2004). *Narratives in social science research*. London: Sage Publications.

Czarniawska, B. (2007). Narrative inquiry in and about organizations. In D. J. Clandinin (Ed.), *Handbook of narrative inquiry: Mapping a methodology* (pp. 383–404). Thousand Oaks, CA: Sage Publications.

Czarniawska, B. (2010). Going back to go forward: On studying organizing in action nets. In Tor Hernes & Sally Maitlis (Eds.), *Process, sensemaking & organizing* (pp. 140–60). Oxford: Oxford University Press.

Davin, S. (2003). Healthy viewing: The reception of medical narratives. *Sociology of Health Illness, 25* (6), 662–79.

Davis, M. S. (1971). That's interesting! Towards a phenomenology of sociology and a sociology of phenomenology. *Philosophy and Social Science, 1*, 309–44.

Deleuze, G., & Guattari, F. (1988). *A thousand plateaus: Capitalism and schizophrenia*. (B. Massumi, Trans.). Minneapolis: University of Minnesota Press.

Dent, E. B. (1999). Complexity science: A worldview shift. *Emergence, 1* (4), 5–19.

Denton, D. K. (1999). *The toolbox for the mind: Finding and implementing creative solutions in the workplace*. Milwaukee, WI: ASQ Quality Press.

Dillard, C., Browning, L. D., Sitkin, S., & Sutcliffe, K. (2000). Impression management and the use of procedures at the Ritz-Carlton: Moral standards and dramaturgical discipline. *Communication Studies, 51*, 404–14.

Dimaggio, G., Salvatore, G., Azzara, C., Catania, D., Semerari, A., & Hermans, H. J. M. (2003). Dialogical relationships in impoverished narratives: From theory to clinical practice. *Psychology and Psychotherapy: Theory, Research and Practice, 76* (4), 385–409.

Douglas, M. (1992). *Risk and blame: Essays in cultural theory*. New York: Routledge.

Douglas, M., & Wildavsky, A. (1983). *Risk and culture*. Berkeley: University of California Press.

Eisenberg, E. (1990). Jamming: Transcendence through organizing. *Communication Research, 17*, 139–64.

Eisenberg, E. M. (2006). Karl Weick and the aesthetics of contingency. *Organization Studies, 27* (11) 1693–1707.

Eisenberg, E., Pynes, J., & Baglia, J. (2003). A narrative approach to identifying some underlying problems in an urban hospital's emergency room. *Public Voices, 7,* 28–38.

Ezzy, D. (1998). Theorizing narrative identity: Symbolic interactionism and hermeneutics. *Sociological Quarterly, 39* (22), 239–52.

Fairhurst, G. T. (2007). *Discursive leadership: In conversation with leadership psychology*. Thousand Oaks, CA: Sage Publications.

Fairhurst, G. T., & Putnam, L. L. (2004). Organizations as discursive constructions. *Communication Theory, 14,* 5–26.

Feeney, J. A. (1990). Attachment style as a predictor of adult romantic relationships. *Journal of Personality and Social Psychology, 58* (2), 281–91.

Fish, S. (1980). *Is there a text for this class?* Cambridge, MA: Harvard University Press.

Fish, S. (2010). Plagiarism is not a big moral deal. *The New York Times*, August 9. http://opinionator.blogs.nytimes.com/2010/08/09/plagiarism-is-not-a-big-moral-deal/?scp=1&sq=fish%20mo (accessed October 3, 2011).

Fisher, W. R. (1984). Narration as human communication paradigm: The case of public moral argument. *Communication Monographs, 51,* 1–22.

Fisher, W. R. (1985). The narrative paradigm: In the beginning. *Journal of Communication 35,* 74–89.

Fisher, W. R. (1987). *Human communication as narration: Toward a philosophy of reason, value, and action*. Columbia: University of South Carolina Press.

Foucault, M. (1979). *Discipline and punish: The birth of the prison* (A. Sheridan, trans.). New York: Pantheon.

Franklin, J. (1986). *Writing for story: Craft secrets of dramatic nonfiction by a two-time Pulitzer Prize winner*. New York: Penguin.

Franzosi, R. (1998). Narrative analysis, or why (and how) sociologists should be interested in narrative. *Annual Review Of Sociology, 24,* 517–54.

Gabriel, Y. (2000). *Storytelling in organizations: Facts, fictions and fantasies*. Oxford: Oxford University Press.

Gabriel, Y. (2004). Narratives, stories, and texts. In D. Grant, C. Hardy, C. Oswick, & L. Putnam (Eds.). *The Sage handbook of organizational discourse* (pp. 61–78). London: Sage Publications.

Galbo, J. (2004). From the lonely crowd to the cultural contradictions of capitalism and beyond: The shifting ground of liberal narratives. *Journal Of The History Of The Behavioral Sciences, 40* (1), 47–76.

Gallie, W. B. (1964). *Philosophy and the historical understanding*. New York: Schocken Books.

Gawande, A. (2009a). *The checklist manifesto: How to get things right*. New York: Metropolitan Books/Henry Holt & Company.

Gawande, A. (2009b). The cost conundrum: What a Texas town can teach us about the cost of health care. www.newyorker.com/reporting/2009/06/01/090601fa_fact_gawande (accessed October 3, 2011).

Gee, J. P. (1999). *An introduction to discourse analysis: Theory and method*. New York: Routledge.

Geertz, C. (1973). *The interpretation of cultures: Selected essays*. New York: Basic Books.

Gellerman, S. W. (1998). *How people work*. Westport, CT: Quorum Books.

Gergen, K. J., & Gergen, M. M. (1986). Narrative form and the construction of psychological science. In T. Sarbin (Ed.), *Narrative psychology, the storied nature of human conduct* (pp. 22–44). New York: Praeger.

Gladwell, M. (2010). Pandora's Briefcase. It was a dazzling feat of wartime espionage. But does it argue for or against spying? *The New Yorker*, May 10. www.newyorker.com/

arts/critics/atlarge/2010/05/10/100510crat_atlarge_gladwell#ixzz1cIBGRiPH (accessed November 1, 2011).

Gladwell, M. (2011). *Outliers: The story of success*. New York: Back Bay Books.

Goffman, E. (1959). *The presentation of self in everyday life*. New York: Doubleday.

Goffman, E. (1967). *Interaction ritual*. Garden City, NY: Doubleday.

Goodwin, C. (1984). Notes on story structure and the organization of participation. In J. M. Atkinson & J. Heritage (Eds.), *Structures of social interaction* (pp. 225–46). Cambridge: Cambridge University Press.

Green, M. C. (2006). Narratives and cancer communication. *Journal of Communication*, *56* (1), 163–83.

Green, M. C. (2009). Personal communication.

Green, M. C., & Brock, T. C. (2000). The role of transportation in the persuasiveness of public narratives. *Journal of Personality and Social Psychology*, *79*, 701–21.

Green, M. C., & Brock, T. C. (2002). In the mind's eye: Transportation-imagery model of narrative persuasion. In M. C. Green, J. J. Strange, & T. C. Brock (Eds.), *Narrative impact: Social and cognitive foundations* (pp. 315–41). Mahwah, NJ: Erlbaum.

Green, M. C., Brock, T. C., & Kaufman, G. F. (2004). Media enjoyment: The role of transportation into narrative worlds, *Communication Theory*, *14* (4) 311–27.

Greimas, A. J., & Ricoeur, P. (1989). On narrativity. (P. Perron & F. Collins, Trans.) *New Literary History*, *20* (3), 551–62.

Grice, H. P. (1975). Logic and conversation. In P. Cole & J. Morgan (Eds.), *Syntax and semantics 3: Speech acts* (pp. 41–58). New York: Academic Press.

Grossberg, L. (1988) Rock Resistance/The Resistance to Rock. Presentation made to the College of Communication Honors Program University of Texas, Austin, Texas, October.

Guthrie, W. (1958). *The Ludlow Massacre*. Los Angeles: Woody Guthrie Publications.

Halberstam, D. (1994). *October 1964*. New York: Villard Books.

Hanson, D., & O'Donohue, W. (2010). William Whyte's "The organization man": A flawed central concept but a prescient narrative. *Management Revue: The International Review of Management Studies*, *21*, 95–104.

Harré, R., & Secord, P. F. (1972). *The explanation of social behavior*. Totowa, NJ: Rowman and Littlefield.

Hartelius, E. J., & Browning, L. D. (2008). The application of rhetorical theory in managerial research: A literature review. *Management Communication Quarterly*, *22*, 13–30.

Hawes, L. C. (1973). Elements of a model for communication processes. *Quarterly Journal of Speech*, *59*, 11–21.

Hawes, L. C. (1974). Social collectivities as communication: Perspective on organizational behavior. *Quarterly Journal of Speech*, *60*, 497–502.

Heritage, J., & Watson, D. R. (1979). Formulations as conversational objects. In G. Psathas (Ed.), *Everyday language: Studies in ethnomethodology* (pp. 123–62). New York: Irvington.

Herrnstein-Smith, B. (1981). Narrative versions, narrative themes. In I. Konigsberg (Ed.), *American criticism in the poststructuralist age* (pp. 162–86). Ann Arbor: University of Michigan Press.

Hewitt, J. P., & Stokes, R. (1975). Disclaimers. *American Sociological Review*, *40*, 1–11.

Hewson, M. G, Kindy, P. J., Van Kirk, J., Gennis, V. A., & Day, R. P. (1996). Strategies for managing uncertainty and complexity. *Journal Of General Internal Medicine*, *8*, 481–85.

Hollander, E. P. (1958). Conformity, status, and idiosyncrasy credit. *Psychological Review*, *65* (2), 117–27.

Huber, G. P., & Glick, W. H. (Eds.) (1993). *Organizational change and redesign: Ideas and insights for improving performance*. New York: Oxford University Press.

Isay, D. (Ed). (2007). *Listening is an act of love: A celebration of American life from the StoryCorps Project*. New York: Penguin.

James, K. (2000). Notes on creativity. http://iedp.com/Notes_On_Creativity (accessed November 1, 2011).

Jung, C. G. (1948). *Preface to the anonymous I Ching: Collected works vol. 11*. London: Routledge.

Kao, J. (1996). *Jamming: The art and discipline of business creativity.* New York: Harper Business.

Karr, M. (1995). *The liars' club.* New York: Penguin.

Kashima, Y., Gurumurthy, A. K., Ouschan, L., Chong, T., & Mattingley, J. (2007). Connectionism and self: James, Mead, and the stream of enculturated consciousness. *Psychological Inquiry, 18* (2), 73–96.

Kearney, R. (1995). Narrative imagination: Between ethics and poetics. *Philosophy and Social Criticism, 21* (5/6), 173–90.

Kelley, D. R. (1987). Horizons of intellectual history: Retrospect, circumspect, prospect. *Journal of the History of Ideas, 48* (1), 143–69.

Kemp, M. (2005). From science in art to the art of science. *Nature, 434,* 308–9.

Kennedy, X. J., & Gioia, D. (1995). *Literature: An introduction to fiction, poetry, and drama.* New York: HarperCollins.

Kenny, R. W. (2003). Thinking about rethinking life and death: The character and rhetorical function of dramatic irony in a life ethics discourse. *Rhetoric and Public Affairs, 6* (4, Winter), 657–86.

Kermode, F. (1981). Secrets and narrative sequence. In W. J. T. Mitchell (Ed.), *On narrative* (pp. 79–97). Chicago: University of Chicago Press.

Kidder, T. (1981). *The soul of a new machine.* Boston: Little, Brown.

Kimmelman, M. (2010). Pardon My French. *The New York Times,* April 21. www.nytimes.com/2010/04/25/arts/25abroad.html?pagewanted=all (accessed November 1, 2011).

King, R. J. H. (1999). Narrative, imagination, and the search for intelligibility in environmental ethics. *Ethics and Environment, 4* (1), 23–38.

Kubli, F. (2001). Can the theory of narratives help science teachers be better storytellers? *Science and Education, 10* (6), 595–99.

Kurtz, C. F., & Snowden, D. J. (2003). The new dynamics of strategy: Sense-making in a complex and complicated world. *IBM Systems Journal, 42* (3), pp. 462–83.

Labov, W. (1972). *The internal evolution of linguistic rules: Linguistic change and generative theory.* Bloomington: Indiana University Press.

Labov, W. (2006). Narrative pre-construction. *Narrative Inquiry, 16* (1), 37–45.

Labov, W., & Waletsky, J. (1997). Narrative analysis: Oral versions of personal experience. *Journal of Narrative and Life History, 7* (1–4), pp. 3–38.

Lacey, N. (2000). *Narrative and genre. Key concepts in media studies.* New York: Macmillan.

Lainé, A. (1998). *Faire de sa vie une histoire.* Paris: Desclée de Brouwer.

Lang, C. (1980). A brief history of literary theory, III: The reader-response theory of Stanley Fish. www.xenos.org/essays/litthry1.htm (accessed October 3, 2011).

Latour, L. (1987). *Science in action.* Cambridge, MA: Harvard University Press.

Latour, L., & Woolgar, S. (1986). *Laboratory life.* Princeton, NJ: Princeton University Press.

Lazaroff, M., & Snowden, D. (2006). Anticipatory modes for counter terrorism. In R. Popp & J. Yen (Eds.), *Emergent information technologies and enabling policies for counter-terrorism* (pp. 51–73). Hoboken, NJ: IEEE Press, Wiley.

Levin, I. M. (2000). Vision revisited. Telling the story of the future. *Journal of Applied Behavioral Science, 36* (1), 91–107.

Lindbloom, C. (1977). *Politics and markets.* New York: Basic Books.

Line, M. (2005). Management musings 20: From being managed to managing: a personal odyssey. *Library Management, 26* (3), 156–58. Retrieved August 10, 2007, from Emerald database.

Lyng, S. G. (2010). Action to edgework. Unpublished manuscript, Carthage College, Kenosha, WI.

Lyotard, J. F. (1984). *The postmodern condition: A report on knowledge.* (G. Bennington & B. Massumi, Trans.). Minneapolis: University of Minnesota Press.

Lysaker, P. H., Lancaster, R. S., & Lysaker, J. T. (2003). Narrative transformation as an outcome in the psychotherapy of schizophrenia. *Psychology and Psychotherapy: Theory, Research and Practice, 76,* 285–99.

MacIntyre, A. C. (1981). *After virtue: A study in moral theory* (2nd ed.). Notre Dame, IN: University of Notre Dame Press.

Mairson, H. (1992). The stable marriage problem. *The Brandeis Review, 12* (1), 37–41.

Mandelbaum, J. (1989). Interpersonal activities in conversational storytelling. *Western Journal of Speech Communication, 53,* 114–26.

Mandelbaum, J. (2003). How to "do things" with narrative: A communication perspective on narrative skill. In J. O. Greene & B. R. Burleson (Eds.), *Handbook of communication and social interaction skills.* Mahwah, NJ: Lawrence Erlbaum.

March, J. G. (1994). How we talk and how we act: Administrative theory and administrative life. In H. Tsoukas (Ed.), *New thinking in organizational behaviour* (pp. 53–69). Oxford: Butterworth-Heinemann.

March, J. G., & Simon, H. A. (1958). *Organizations.* New York: John Wiley.

March, J. G., & Simon, H. A. (1976). *Organizations.* (3rd ed). New York: John Wiley.

Markus, H. & Nurius, P. (1986). Possible selves. *American Psychologist, 41* 954–69.

Martens, M. L., Jennings, J. E., & Jennings, P. D. (2007). Do the stories they tell get them the money they need? The role of entrepreneurial narratives in resource acquisition. *Academy of Management Journal, 50* (5), 1107–32.

Maruyama, M. (1963). The second cybernetics: Deviation-amplifying mutual casual processes. *American Scientist, 51,* 164–79.

Mauzy, J., & Harriman, R. (2003). *Creativity, Inc.: Building an inventive organization.* Boston, MA: Harvard Business School Press.

May, S. (2003). Case study: Changing change. *Management Communication Quarterly, 16,* 419–33.

McAdams, D. P. (1985). *Power, intimacy, and the life story: Personological inquiries into identity.* Homewood, IL: Dorsey Press.

McAdams, D. P. (1996). Personality, modernity, and the storied self: A contemporary framework for studying persons. *Psychological Inquiry, 7* (4), 295–321.

McAdams, D. P. (2006). *The redemptive self: Stories Americans live by.* New York: Oxford University Press.

McKee, R. (1997). *Story: Substance, structure, style, and the principles of screenwriting.* New York: HarperCollins.

Mead, George Herbert. (1959) [1929]. The nature of the past. In *Essays in honor of John Dewey.* New York: Octagon Books. *The philosophy of the present.* La Salle, IL: Open Court.

Meyrowitz, J. (2008). Power, pleasure, patterns: Intersecting narratives of media influence. *Journal of Communication, 58,* 641–63.

Milgram, S. (1963). Behavioral study of obedience. *Journal of Abnormal and Social Psychology, 67,* 371–78.

Mink, L. O. (2001). Narrative form as a cognitive instrument. In G. Roberts (Ed.) *The history and narrative reader.* London: Routledge.

Monge, P. R., & Kalman, M. (1996). Sequentiality, simultaneity, and synchronicity in human communication. In J. Watt and A. Van Lear (Eds.), *Cycles and dynamic patterns in communication processes* (pp. 71–92). New York: Ablex.

Morowitz, H. (2001). Emergence. *Complexity, 7* (1), 15–16.

Moyers, B., & Campbell, J. (1988). *The power of myth.* (B. Flowers, Ed.). New York: Doubleday.

Mumby, D. K., & Putnam, L. L. (1992). The politics of emotion: A feminist reading of bounded rationality. *Academy of Management Review, 17,* 465–86.

Nathan, M., & Mitroff, I. I. (1991). The use of negotiated order theory as a tool for the analysis and development of an interorganizational field. *Journal of Applied Behavioral Science, 27* (2), pp. 163–80.

Niiniluoto, I. (1998). Verisimilitude: The third period. *British Journal for the Philosophy of Science, 49* (1), pp. 1–30.

Nofsinger, R. E. (1991). *Everyday conversation.* Prospect Heights, IL: Waveland Press.

Nuland, S. (1994). *How we die: Reflections on life's final chapter.* New York: Alfred A. Knopf.

Nussbaum, M. C. (2003). Cultivating humanity in legal education. *University of Chicago Law Review, 70* (1), 265–80.

Pacanowsky, M. (1995). Team tools for wicked problems. *Organization Dynamics, 23* (3), 36–51.

Pentland, B. T. (1999). Building process theory with narrative: From sescription to explanation. *Academy of Management Review, 24* (4), pp. 711–24.

Pentland, B. T., & Feldman, M. S. (2007). Narrative networks: Patterns of technology and organization. *Organization Science, 18,* 781–95.

Perrow, C. (1984). *Normal accidents: Living with high-risk technologies.* New York: Basic Books.

Peters, T. J. (2003). *Reimagine! Business excellence in a disruptive age.* London: Dorling Kindersley.

Pieslak, J. (2009). *Sound targets: American soldiers and music in the Iraq war.* Bloomington: Indiana University Press.

Pinnegar, S., & Daynes, J. G (2005). Situating narrative inquiry. In D. Jean Clandinin (Ed.), *Handbook of narrative inquiry: Mapping a methodology* (pp. 1–34). London: Sage.

Polkinghorne, D. E. (1988). *Narrative knowing and the human sciences.* Albany, NY: SUNY Press.

Polkinghorne, D. E. (1995). Narrative configuration in qualitative analysis. *International Journal of Qualitative Analysis in Education, 8* (1), 5–23.

Polster, E. (1987). *Every person's life is worth a novel.* New York: W. W. Norton.

Polster, E., & Polster, M. (1974). *Gestalt therapy integrated: Contours of theory and practice.* New York: Vintage Books.

Pondy, L. R., & Mitroff, I. I. (1979). Beyond the open system models of organization. *Research in Organizational Behavior, 1,* 3–39.

Porter, J. C. (1986). *Paper medicine man: John Gregory Bourke and his American West.* Norman: University of Oklahoma Press.

Putnam, L. L., & Pacanowsky, M. E. (Eds.) (1983). *Communication and organization: An interpretive approach.* Beverly Hills, CA: Sage Publications.

Quinn, B. (2005). A Dramaturgical perspective on academic libraries. *Portal: Libraries and the Academy, 5* (3), 329–52.

Ramzy, A. (1992). The influence of American mass culture in Europe. Paper for the Netherlands Institute of Advanced Studies in the Social Sciences and Humanities. Wassenaar, Netherlands.

Rand, A. (2000). *The art of fiction. A guide for writers and readers.* New York: Plume.

Randall, W. L., & McKim, A. E. (2008). *Reading our lives: The poetics of growing old.* Oxford: Oxford University Press.

Rhodes, C., & Brown, A. D. (2006). Narrative, organizations and research. *International Journal of Management Reviews, 7* (3), 167–88.

Ricks, C. (2003). *Dylan's visions of sin.* New York: Harper Collins.

Ricœur, P. (1965). *Fallible man: Philosophy of the will.* Chicago: Henry Regnery.

Ricœur, P. (1974). *The conflict of interpretations: Essays in hermeneutics.* (D. Ihde, Ed.). Evanston, IL: Northwestern University Press.

Ricœur, P. (1984). *Time and narrative, Volume one.* (K. McLaughlin & D. Pellauer, Trans.). Chicago: University of Chicago Press.

Ricœur, P. (1985). *Time and narrative, Volume two.* (K. McLaughlin & D. Pellauer, Trans.). Chicago: University of Chicago Press.

Ricœur, P. (1991). *From text to action: Essays in hermeneutics II.* (K. Blamey & J. B. Thompson, Trans). Evanston, IL: Northwestern University Press.

Ricœur, P. (2004). *Memory, history, forgetting.* (K. Blamey & D. Pellauer, Trans.). Chicago: University of Chicago Press.

Riessman, C. K. (1993). *Narrative analysis.* Thousand Oaks, CA: Sage Publications.

Riessman, C. K. (2008). *Narrative methods for the human sciences.* Los Angeles: Sage Publications.

Riker, W. H. (1982). *Liberalism against populism: A confrontation between the theory of democracy and the theory of social choice.* San Francisco: W. H. Freeman.

Robichaud, D. (2001). Toward a narrative analysis of organizational action, Seventeenth Annual EGOS Colloquium, July, Lyon, France. (From an original piece of work by U. Eco.)

Robinson, J. A., & Hawpe, L. (1986). Narrative thinking as a heuristic process. In T. Sarbin (Ed.), *Narrative psychology: The storied nature of human conduct* (pp. 111–25). New York: Praeger.

Robinson, S. (2004). Tweaking the math to make happier medical marriages. *The New York Times*, August 24. www.stanford.edu/~niederle/RobinsonNYT04.htm (accessed November 1, 2011).

Roos, V., & Lombard, A. (2003). Interdisciplinary collaboration: An ongoing community narrative. *Journal of Community Psychology, 31* (5), 543–52.

Rose, D. (1990). *Living the ethnographic life.* Newbury Park, CA: Sage Publications.

Rosenau, P. M. (1992). *Post-modernism and the social sciences: Insights, inroads, and intrusions.* Princeton, NJ: Princeton University Press.

Roy, D. F. (1959). Banana time: Job satisfaction and informal interaction. *Human Organization, 18,* 158–68.

Russell, C., & Porter, M. (2003). Single older men in disadvantaged households: Narratives of meaning around everyday life. *Ageing International, 28* (4), 359–71.

Sager, T. (2001). Manipulative features of planning styles. *Environment and Planning, 33,* 765–81.

Salancik, G. R., & Pfeffer, J. (1977). Who gets power—and how they hold on to it: A strategic-contingency model of power. *Organizational Dynamics, 5,* 3–21.

Salvatore, G., Dimaggio, G., & Semerari, A. (2004). A model of narrative development: Implications for understanding psychopathology and guiding therapy. *Psychology and Psychotherapy: Theory, Research and Practice, 77,* 231–54.

Sarbin, T. (1986). The narrative as a root metaphor for psychology. In T. Sarbin (Ed.), *Narrative psychology, the storied nature of human conduct* (pp. 3–21). New York: Praeger.

Schank, R. C. (1995). *Tell me a story: Narrative and intelligence.* Evanston, IL: Northwestern University Press.

Scheibe, K. E. (1986). Self-narratives and adventure. In T. Sarbin, (Ed.), *Narrative psychology, the storied nature of human conduct* (pp. 129–51). New York: Praeger.

Schein, E. H. (2010). *Organizational culture and leadership* (4th. ed.). San Francisco: Jossey-Bass.

Scholes, R. (1980). Language, narrative, and anti-narrative. *Critical Inquiry, 7,* 204–12.

Schubert, T. W., & Otten, S. (2002). Overlap of self, ingroup, and outgroup: Pictorial measures of self-categorization. *Self and Identity, 1,* 353–76.

Scott, M., & Lyman, S. (1968). Accounts. *American Sociological Review, 33,* 46–62.

Scult, A. (2004). *Being Jewish / Reading Heidegger: an ontological encounter.* New York: Fordham University Press.

Seinfeld, J. (1993). *Seinlanguage.* New York: Bantam books.

Sillince, J. A. A. (2007). Organizational context and the discursive construction of organizing. *Management Communication Quarterly, 20* (4), 363–94.

Sitkin, S. (1992). Learning through failure: The strategy of small losses. *Research in Organizational Behavior, 14,* 231–66.

Skoldberg, K. (1994). Tales of change: Public administration reform and the narrative mode. *Organization Science, 5* (2), 219–38.

Smith, R. (2003). Rural rogues: A case story on the "smokies" trade. *International Journal of Entrepreneurial Behaviour & Research, 10* (4), pp. 277–94.

Snowden, D. J. (1999). Story telling: An old skill in a new context. *Business Information Review, 16* (1): 30–37.

Snowden, D. J. (2000). Cynefin, a sense of time and place: An ecological approach to sense making and learning in formal organizations. Proceedings of KMAC, knowle dgeboard.com. www.knowledgeboard.com/library/cynefin.pdf.

Snowden, D. J. (2003). Managing for serendipity or why we should lay off "best practices" in KM. *Knowledge Management, 6* (8). www.cognitive-edge.com/articledetails.php?articleid=39.

Somers, M (1994). The narrative constitution of identity. *Theory and Society, 23,* 605–49.

Starkey, K., & Crane, A (2003). Toward green narrative: Management and the evolutionary epic. *Academy Of Management Review, 28* (2), 220–37.

Sternberg, R. J. (1994). Love is a story. *General Psychologist, 30* (1), 1–11.

Sternberg, R. J. (1998). *Love is a story: A new theory of relationships.* Oxford: Oxford University Press.

Stokes, R., & Hewitt, J. P. (1976). Aligning actions. *American Sociological Review, 41,* 838–49.

Strati, A. (1992). Aesthetic understanding of organizational life. *The Academy of Management Review, 17* (3), 568–81.

Strati, A. (1999). *Organization and aesthetics.* London: Sage.

Straub, J. (Ed.) (2006). *Narration, identity, and historical consciousness.* New York: Berghahn Books.

Strickland, B. (with Vince Rause) (2007). *Making the impossible possible.* New York: Doubleday.

Szmania, S. (2004). Beginning difficult conversations: An analysis of opening statements in Victim Offender Mediation/Dialogue. Unpublished PhD dissertation, University of Texas at Austin.

Taylor, H., & Tversky, B. (1997). Indexing events in memory: Evidence for index dominance. *Memory, 5,* 509–42.

Taylor, J. R. (2000). Thinking about organization in a new way: An inquiry into the ontological foundations of organization / Reflexion sur l'organisation dans une nouvelle optique. Enquete sur le fondement ontologique de l'organisation. *The Electronic Journal of Communication/La Revue Electronique de Communication, 10* (1&2). www.cios.org/www/ejc/v10n1200.htm (accessed October 3, 2011).

Taylor, J. R., & Van Every, E. J. (2000). *The emergent organization: Communication as its site and surface.* Mahwah, NJ: Lawrence Erlbaum Associates.

Taylor, S. S., & Hansen, H. (2005). Finding form: Looking at the field of organizational aesthetics. *Journal of Management Studies 42* (6), 1211–31.

Terkel, S. (1972). *Working: People talk about what they do all day and how they feel about what they do.* New York: Pantheon Books.

Tompkins, J. P. (1980). *Reader-response criticism: From Formalism to Post-structuralism.* Baltimore, MD: John Hopkins University Press.

Tracy, K. (2002). *Everyday talk: Building and reflecting identities.* New York: Guilford Press.

Turner, V. (1987). Betwixt and between: The liminal period in rites of passage. In Louise Carus Mahdi, Steven Foster, & Meredith Little (Eds.), *Betwixt & between: patterns of masculine and feminine initiation.* Peru IL: Open Court Publishing.

van Dijk, T. A. (1975). Action, action description, and narrative. *New Literary History, 6,* 273–94.

Várady, P., Benyó, Z., & Benyó, B. (2002). An open architecture patient monitoring system using standard technologies. *IEEE Transactions on Information Technology in Biomedicine, 6,* 95–98.

Wallace, M. (1986). *Recent theories of narrative.* Ithaca, NY: Cornell University Press.

Walzer, S., & Oles, T. (2003). Accounting for divorce: Gender and uncoupling narratives. *Qualitative Sociology, 26* (3), 331–49.

Watzlawick, P., Weakland, J. H., & Fisch, R. (1974). *Change: Principles of problem formation and problem resolution.* New York: Norton.

Weick, K. E. (1969). *The social psychology of organizing.* Reading, MA: Addison-Wesley.

Weick, K. E. (1974). Middle range theories of social systems. *Behavioral Science, 19,* 357–67.

Weick, K. E. (1979). *The social psychology of organizing* (2nd ed.). Reading, MA: Addison-Wesley.

Weick, K. E. (1984). Small wins: Redefining the scale of social problems. *American Psychologist, 39,* 40–49.

Weick, K. E. (1995). *Sensemaking in organizations.* Thousand Oaks, CA: Sage Publications.

Weick, K. E. (2001). *Making sense of the organization.* Malden, MA: Blackwell Publishers.

Weick, K. E., & Browning, L. D. (1986). Argument and narration in organizational communication. *Journal of Management, 12* (2), 243–59.

Weick, K. E., & Browning, L. D. (1991). Fixing the world with our voices: A research agenda for applied communication. *Journal of Applied Communication Research, 19*, 1–19.

Weick, K. E., & Sutcliffe, K. M. (2001). *Managing the unexpected: Resilient performance in an age of uncertainty.* San Francisco: Jossey-Bass.

Weick, K. E., & Sutcliffe, K. M. (2007). *Managing the unexpected: Resilient performance in an age of uncertainty* (2nd ed.). San Francisco: Jossey-Bass.

Weick, K. E., Sutcliffe, K. M., & Obstfeld, D. (2005). Organizing and the process of sensemaking. *Organization Science, 16* (4), 409–21.

Weschler, L. (1982). *Seeing is forgetting the name of the thing one sees.* Berkeley: University of California Press.

White, D. A. (1996). "It's working beautifully!" Philosophical reflections on aesthetics and organization theory. *Organization, 3* (2), 195–208.

White, H. (1987). *The content of form: Narrative discourse and historical representation.* Baltimore, MD: Johns Hopkins University Press.

White, H. W. (1980). The value of narrativity in the representation of reality. In W. J. T. Mitchell (Ed.), *On narrative* (pp. 1–23). Chicago: University of Chicago Press.

Wildavsky, A. (1979). *Speaking truth to power: The art and craft of policy analysis.* New York: Little, Brown.

Wolfe, T. (1979). *The right stuff.* New York: Farrar, Straus and Giroux.

Workman, M. (2004). Obscured beginnings in personal narratives of sexual jealousy and trauma. *Narrative, 12* (3), 249–62.

Wright, P. K. (1995). Principles of open-architecture manufacturing. *Journal of Manufacturing Systems, 14*, 187–202.

Wysong, J. (1978). An oral history of gestalt therapy, part three: A conversation with Erving and Miriam Polster October 19, 1978 in Provincetown, Massachusetts. www.gestalt.org/postview.htm (accessed October 3, 2011).

Zechmeister, J. S., & Romero, C. (2002). Victim and offender accounts of interpersonal conflict: Autobiographical narratives of forgiveness and unforgiveness. *Journal of Personality and Social Psychology, 82* (4), 675–86.

Ziegler, J. A. (2007). The story behind an organizational list: A genealogy of Wildland Firefighters' 10 Standard Fire Orders. *Communication Monographs, 74* (4) 415–42.

Zukier, H. (1986). The paradigmatic and narrative modes in goal guided inference. In Richard M. Sorrentino & Edward Tory Higgi (Eds.), *Handbook of motivation and cognition: The interpersonal context,* Volume 3 (pp. 465–502). New York: Guilford Press.

SUBJECT INDEX

AUTHOR INDEX